Techno

THE ROUGH GUIDE

There are more than one hundred and fifty Rough Guide
travel, phrasebook, and music titles, covering destinations
from Amsterdam to Zimbabwe, languages from Czech to
Thai, and musics from Opera to House and Drum 'n' Bass

Forthcoming titles include

Hip Hop • Irish Music • Cuban Music

Rough Guides on the Internet

www.roughguides.com

Rough Guide Credits

Text editor: Peter Shapiro
Series editor: Mark Ellingham
Typesetting: Helen Ostick

Publishing Information

This first edition published April 2000 by
Rough Guides Ltd, 62–70 Shorts Gardens, London, WC2H 9AB

Distributed by the Penguin Group:

Penguin Books Ltd, 27 Wrights Lane, London W8 5TZ
Penguin Books USA Inc., 375 Hudson Street, New York 10014, USA
Penguin Books Australia Ltd, 487 Maroondah Highway,
PO Box 257, Ringwood, Victoria 3134, Australia
Penguin Books Canada Ltd, 10 Alcorn Avenue,
Toronto, Ontario, Canada M4V 1E4
Penguin Books (NZ) Ltd, 182–190 Wairau Road,
Auckland 10, New Zealand

Typeset in Bembo and Helvetica to an original design by Henry Iles.
Printed in Spain by Graphy Cems.

© Tim Barr, 2000
384pp
A catalogue record for this book is available from the British Library.
ISBN 1-85828-434-1

Techno

THE ROUGH GUIDE

by Tim Barr

Contents

Introduction

Techno made its way into the technicolour world of pop consciousness — officially, at least — in May 1988 courtesy of an article by Stuart Cosgrove in that month's issue of *The Face* and the release of a now legendary Virgin compilation, **Techno! The New Dance Sound of Detroit.** Prior to that, the few Techno records which had leaked out of the Motor City on labels with strange, vaguely sci-fi names such as Metroplex, Transmat and KMS had found themselves filed alongside the other pervasive electronic dance phenomenon of the time, House music. They sounded different, of course, but what Cosgrove provided was a seductive manifesto, recorded almost verbatim from those at the centre of the new music, to underscore that difference. Loaded with the rhetoric of the counter-culture — rebelliousness, dislocation, alienation and a dystopian futurism — it was the perfect opening shot in a musical revolution that has continued to reverberate through pop culture.

"The Detroit underground has been experimenting with technology," declared Juan Atkins, "stretching it rather than simply using it. As the price of sequencers and synthesisers has dropped, so the experimentation has become more intense. Basically, we're tired of hearing about being in love or falling out, tired of the R&B system, so a new progressive sound has emerged. We call it Techno."

"It's like George Clinton and Kraftwerk are stuck in an elevator with only a sequencer to keep them company," explained Derrick May, delivering what has become the most notorious definition of Techno.

Sounding as if it had been kidnapped from another planet, May's early Rhythim Is Rhythim classic "It Is What it Is" opened **Techno! The New Dance Sound of Detroit.** Tougher and more angular than the music which had surfaced from Chicago, it nevertheless shared obvious similarities with the raw, electronic sound of House. But May was quick to point out the difference: "It's a difference of respect. House still has its heart in '70s disco. We don't have any of that respect for the past, it's strictly future music. We have a much greater aptitude for experiment."

It's this "aptitude for experiment" which has propelled Techno along an extraordinarily rapid evolutionary path. Techno now embraces sub-genres as radically different as the bruising, super-accelerated strains of Gabber, the beatless psychedelia of Ambient, the subtle, be-bop-inflected cadences of Tech-jazz and the stripped-down, utilitarian shapes of minimalism. Within these notional divisions exist limitless subdivisions, new variants and novel hybrids, each pushing the music's boundaries, sometimes incrementally, sometimes exponentially. The genetic imperative of Techno is to develop, or, as Detroit's Drexciya once put it: "There is only one rule — innovate."

The artists and producers in this book have all played a key role in Techno's journey from there to here. In some cases, their contribution to the music's development has been limited to a single, definitive release. In other cases, contributions have spanned numerous albums, significant chart success and the kind of profile that many mainstream acts might envy. The majority, however, remain somewhere between these two extremes, participants in a work in progress which, at least in creative terms, has seen Techno outstrip every other modern dance genre and generate new musical strategies which continue to evolve, change shape and metamorphose. No one knows where this journey will end or what it will sound like, but along the way what is certain, and what has already been proven, is that astonishing music will emerge from it.

For reasons of time and space there are obvious omissions. The sub-genres of Hardcore and Gabber Techno would require another volume altogether. Similarly, the mid-'90s proliferation of a hippie-oriented Techno sound, Goa Trance, has been bypassed. Selections have been made according to a number of criteria and with reference to the other books in this series, Peter Shapiro's *Rough Guide to Drum 'n' Bass* and Sean Bidder's *Rough Guide to House*, to provide an overview of the central currents in Techno and its landmark releases. Alongside well-known names there will be some which are less familiar. In the main, these are artists whose releases may not easily be found outside specialist record shops, but who nonetheless have made important behind-the-scenes contributions to the forward momentum of the music. Recommended releases have been chosen to provide an accurate introduction to specific artists or groups, with preference given to releases which have been particularly influential or important.

Some years after Derrick May provided his definitive account of Techno, DJ and producer Jeff Mills offered an alternative explanation: "Techno music is actually something that you can't imagine. If you hear something that you'd never expect to hear, that's Techno." The aim of this book is to provide access to, and information about, music that you haven't yet imagined. If you already listen to The Prodigy or Underworld but haven't discovered Stacey Pullen or Underground Resistance, then this book is for you. Equally, if your tastes include Carl Craig and Derrick May but you haven't yet discovered the pleasures of The Connection Machine or Neil Ollivierra you'll find what you're looking for here.

Finally, you may recognise among the contributors to this book a few already familiar names. Dom Phillips is a former editor of *Mixmag* and presenter of the BBC's *Clublife 98*; Martin James is a journalist and author of *Adventures With The Voodoo Crew*, the definitive history of The Prodigy; John Burgess is editor of *Jockey Slut*; Tony Marcus is an underground writer and sometime technology editor of *i-D*; Sherman was formerly editor of *Melody Maker*'s weekly dance section, "Sherman At The Controls", and now runs his own record label and club night, Cloak & Dagger; Peter McIntyre writes for *Mixmag* and *The Wire*; Dan Sicko is a contributing editor at *URB* magazine and author of *Techno Rebels*, a superb account of the beginnings of Detroit Techno; Jonas Stone is a contributor to *Jockey Slut* and *7* magazine.

This book has been improved immeasurably by the help, patience and understanding of a number of people. Sizeable thanks go to: Jonathan Buckley, Peter Shapiro, Scot Jackson, Alex Milne, Rad Rice, Paul Mann, Martin Allen, Ruud 66, Will Thomas, Derrick Ortensio, Bridget Banks, Christa Witherspoon, Marsel van der Wielen, Jill Mingo, Graham Urquhart, Hans Veneman, Tom Wilson, Domenic Capello, Neil Ollivierra, Plug Lazonby, Alessandra Margarito, Carola at Tresor, Jennifer Dempsey, Erwin van Moll and Alan Oldham. Special thanks for their contributions to: John Burgess, Martin James, Tony Marcus, Pete McIntyre, Dom Phillips, Sherman, Dan Sicko and Jonas Stone.

Tim Barr

Adam X

One of New York's best-known hard Techno DJs, Adam X's formative years were spent in the company of some of the major forces on the East Coast's embryonic dance scene – his early production partners included both Ray Love and Jimmy Crash – while his day job as buyer for the Brooklyn Groove record store (owned by his brother, Frankie Bones, himself one of the seminal forces on the UK's emerging rave scene) provided a healthy conduit to the latest releases. His earliest, most enduring influences encompassed Sheffield "bleep" Techno, Kevin Saunderson and the harder, European strains of Frank De Wulf and CJ Bolland. By the time he became one of the residents at New York's Stormrave parties in 1992, he was already experimenting with his own distinctive, hard Acid sound.

1991's "Listen" – a sample-oriented, breakbeat affair – launched his solo production career, though the sound that emerged on subsequent releases such as "Lost in Hell" and "Into the Void" signalled a move towards the hard but funky minimalism which has become an Adam X trademark. A series of singles on labels such as Magnetic North, Drop Bass Network and Communiqué mapped an increasingly hard and rapidly accelerating production style that was perhaps best articulated by the title of X-Crash's bruising "Don't Fuck With Brooklyn".

More recent offerings, such as 1997's "Steel Giants" (on Neil Landstrumm's Scandinavia label), demonstrated a more relaxed, loping funkiness. **Audiobiography** (1998) was still a resolutely minimal affair, with tracks such as "Self Destruction" and "Road Rage" connecting to a now-established network of producers, such as Neil Landstrumm, Justin Berkovi and Chicago's DJ Rush, who were engaging with the looser formats of dancefloor experimentalism. A hybrid of the sound first mapped out by New York's Nu Groove label and the sinewave

Techno of early Sheffield, 1999's "Reverse Forward" may offer some indication of where he's headed.

⊙ **Audiobiography**   Sonic Groove, 1998

He may have mellowed in recent years, but Adam X's debut is still fierce in all the right places.

The Advent

Drawing on a shared pool of influences – early Electro, Studio One dub and the proto-Techno of Kraftwerk and Cabaret Voltaire – Colin McBean and Cisco Ferreira have shaped a successful sound, based on high-velocity minimalism and a distillate of hard, 150 bpm dancefloor grooves, Detroit and jack-era Chicago. Since their earliest releases as The Advent they've proclaimed an unwavering allegiance to underground Techno that has sustained despite their major label status and the changing patterns of club fashion.

McBean and Ferreira were first introduced to each other in 1990. Colin had been a pattern cutter for Stüssy; Cisco was on the upswing of a career which had begun in the '80s as a studio engineer working on the polished Brit-soul of Loose Ends among others. A stint as the house engineer for the legendary Jack Trax label followed, which was where he was introduced to the sound of Derrick May, Adonis and Fingers Inc., discovering a new musical vocabulary that eventually translated into solo releases for May's Fragile label and his subsequent ground-breaking work with CJ Bolland on tracks like "Nightbreed", "Mantra" and "Camargue". He also engineered hard 190 bpm industrial records for Renaat Vandepapeliere's pre-R&S Ferrari imprint, but the

first work he did with McBean was as part of the House sound system KCC, the name under which they first recorded together, making Garage records like "Groove Thing" for Azuli.

The Advent emerged gradually, through a series of self-financed, limited edition EPs, full of incandescent electro, hard metal-edged loops and the unmistakable shapes of Detroit Techno. **Elements of Life** (1995) coalesced The Advent sound perfectly. Deep in the range of sci-fi funk tracks such as "Bad Boy" and "Mad Dog", it was possible to trace influences from P-Funk to Hashim, the heavyweight thump of sound system culture and – in "It One Jah" – the low frequency stutter of dub.

New Beginning (1997) was a typically forceful follow-up. In many ways, **New Beginning** was a more focused affair than its predecessor. Loaded with incandescent grooves and the kind of bruising muscle power that has distinguished their best work, it was a more linear, straight-to-the-floor experience than **Elements of Life**. Tracks like "Nervous Energies" or "Stasis (Pt II)" sounded like a drag-race through distant galaxies while deep percussive workouts like "Armageddon" and "Testing" ran on repetition and tough, trippy riffs. The spaced-out, stop-start Electro of "Funkage" was a particular standout.

A distinctive mix album, **Kombination Phunk** (1997), spliced a series of tracks by the likes of Dopplereffekt, Planetary Assault Systems and Keith Tucker through razor edits and fast transforms. It also included two new Advent tracks – "Elektra Fix" and "C-On" – that twisted the Electro theme and shoved it deep into the kind of territory mapped out by Jeff Mills and Surgeon. Conceptually, if not commercially, it was a *tour de force*. But their relationship with London Records had run its course and, by the time of the album's release, The Advent were already mapping out a release schedule for their own Kombination Research label.

Early releases on Kombination Research – including "Distance", "Panther" and "Another Planet" – continued to explore the duo's fiery, dancefloor aesthetic. The duo also began recording for a number of other labels, including Billy Nasty's Tortured imprint, Dave Angel's Rotation (under the name Subjective) and Damon Wild's Sinewave. Towards the close of 1998, they also began a series of releases for the Berlin-based Tresor label with "The Advent Presents Soundsketches" and began plotting out a Tech-House label of their own to be called G-Flame.

⊙ **New Beginning**   London, 1997

Aimed firmly at the dancefloor, the follow-up demonstrated none of the signs of "difficult second album syndrome"; its bruising muscle power still sounds outrageously confident.

Air Liquide

ormed around the nucleus of Ingmar Koch and Cem Oral (otherwise better known as Dr Walker and Jammin' Unit), Air Liquide have been enthusiastic participants in the Cologne scene's penchant for collaborative ventures, working with numerous other producers and artists under a variety of names and sometimes on different continents. During the mid-'90s both Walker and Jammin' Unit sustained a creatively successful relationship with New York's DJ DB and the Sm:)e label among others while, elsewhere, their records have appeared on Rising High, EMI Harvest, Mille Plateaux and their own Blue label.

Walker was a teenage programming prodigy – a graduate of Cologne University's electronic music course where he was under the tutelage of Karlheinz Stockhausen. He began working as a producer for an early, Frankfurt-based House label, turning out a number of successful hits which – following the company's bankruptcy – he was never paid for. Soon afterwards, he launched Air Liquide with Jammin' Unit and vocalist/lyricist Mary Applegate (among other claims to fame, Applegate was responsible for writing the lyrics for Jennifer Rush's million-selling "Power of Love" single).

Together the trio began shaping a distinctive, mutant strain of Techno which fused Applegate's half-whispered, half-sung vocals with a backdrop that was equal parts Cologne Electro-funk, distended ambience and subtle, shape-changing experimentalism. Early albums such as **Air Liquide** (1993) and **Nephology** (1994) were light years away from the Trance sound dominating Germany at the time.

The Increased Difficulty of Concentration (1995) inaugurated a period of frenetic activity which involved a dizzying number of solo and collaborative ventures. Some of these had begun during the previous year with the recording in New York of **Rolleiflex-Weltron-Time-Square** (1994) as Global Electronic Network. Stripped of Applegate's little-girl vocals, the music seemed to drift into an altogether more hypnodelic sphere. Tracks such as "Time Square Part 1" were achingly beautiful confections, designed for hard tripping and late-night dreaming, though confusion about the group's rapidly spiralling identities (Jammin' Unit had just released an album of spiky Techno as Ultrahigh) deflected attention from what was, in all respects, an exceptional release.

As the years wore on, Air Liquide's release schedule seemed increasingly as though it had been inspired by the old cliché about London buses: you wait for ages and then three come along at once. In one astonishingly brief period in 1998, the pair were responsible for **16 Love Songs for the Spice Girls** (Dr Walker + M Flux), **Simplex** (Khan & Walker), **97 98** (Head) and **YHII Attackz** (Global Electronic Network).

Veering increasingly towards a deep experimentalism, Walker and Jammin' Unit have nevertheless retained a neatly ironic turn of humour. **16 Love Songs for the Spice Girls** featured a full-colour booklet full of '60s *Playboy*-style images. The punchline was a nude photo of Sporty Spice underneath the legend: "This album is dedicated from the depth of our hearts to the best, sexiest, blablabla music group of the world; the Spice Girls – we love you!"

Though they are undoubtedly possessed of the talent required to achieve commercial success, it's unlikely that Walker and Jammin' Unit will ever abandon the margins and backwaters where their fluid, elastic approach operates best, but if their career so far is any indication, it's perhaps best to expect the unexpected.

⊙ **Air Liquide**   Blue, 1993

Hallucinogenic soundtracks that combine prettiness and weirdness in equal measures, this still stands as an innovative and inspired record.

⊙**Nephology**   Blue, 1994

Abstract, unsettling and often brilliant, this is Techno refracted through the prism of Stockhausen, pop culture and downright eccentricity.

Alter Ego

From their base just outside Frankfurt, Jörn Elling Wuttke and Roman Flügel have been responsible for a bewildering variety of releases under an equally bewildering number of aliases. At various times, in various places, they've disguised themselves as Acid Jesus, Primitive Painter, Holy Garage, Warp 69 and Sensorama, though they're perhaps best known – and not without a little irony – as Alter Ego thanks to their mid-'90s albums for Harthouse.

Wuttke and Flügel had known each other since childhood (the story goes that they were both expelled from the same school) in the sleepy college town of Darmstadt. They first worked together on an eponymous Acid Jesus single for Ongaku, sampling Lou Reed over a backing drawn from Detroit's minimalism. That was followed quickly by **Acid Jesus** (1994) before the duo began to explore more cerebral terrain as Primitive Painter, keying in to the moods of Warp's influential **Artificial Intelligence** series for **The Primitive Painter** (1994).

The Harthouse connection provided Wuttke and Flügel with a link to the commercially successful Trance scene (as Alter Ego they provided a number of remixes for the label's expansive roster) and a platform for their third album of 1994. **Alter Ego** was an oddly unsettled outing, trying hard to reconcile the duo's interest in a more experimental, Detroit-influenced vein with commercial demands. Tracks such as

JÖRG KOPFER

"Soulfree" were uneasy marriages between vocals and techno that were reminiscent of the UK's Rising High Collective while "Sentimental Books" was a delicate, ambient Detroit outing, full of abstract riffs and warm strings.

Some of the themes which had been tentatively explored on **Alter Ego** became fully realised on **Welcome Insel** (1995), recorded as Sensorama for Hamburg's Ladomat 2000 imprint. A masterpiece of delicate, under-stated grooves and seductive brilliance, the Sensorama release located itself alongside the work of Heidelberg's David Moufang and Deep Space Network. Plangent melodies, fluttering synthetics and the kind of weightless sound which felt like it had been recorded somewhere far outside the earth's atmosphere made **Welcome Insel** an essential buy for all those interested in Techno's most spaced-out perimeters. A remix album, **Zu Gast auf der Welcome Insel** (1996), featured contributions from Moufang, Global Communication, Claude Young and Plaid, but failed to match the innovative and inspirational mood of the original.

Meanwhile, Wuttke and Flügel returned to their Alter Ego sideline with **Decoding the Hacker Myth** (1996), a more cohesive and convincing effort than its predecessor, though Harthouse's declining reputation meant that it failed to attract the attention it deserved, despite a series of remixes from Planetary Assault Systems, Matthew Herbert and Two Lone Swordsmen.

Love (1998) was the follow-up to Sensorama's **Welcome Insel** and continued its predecessor's exploration of subtle tones and moods on tracks such as "Aeroplane City" and "Sunday Morning Superstar", but Wuttke and Flügel's low-profile approach again ensured that the album failed to make the impact it richly deserved.

⊙ **Sensorama – Welcome Insel**   Ladomat 2000,1995

Still the essential Wuttke and Flügel album, full of spaced-out textures and languid grooves. A must.

Dave Angel

W hen he was eight years old, Dave Angel (Nicholas Gooden) was given a drum kit by his jazz musician father. By the age of 12, Angel had played his first session as a drummer and spent happy hours with his father jamming on jazz classics. But within a few years, the teenage funk and soul enthusiast found himself running with the wrong crowd and on the wrong side of the law. Several spells in prison followed, but while he was serving time, a sequence of life-altering events – the death of his beloved father, the birth of his son Daine and the arrival of Acid House – prompted some serious self-reflection.

Two weeks after his release, armed with a cheap Casio keyboard and a box of records, he crafted a silky, six-minute groove and spun in excerpts from "Sweet Dreams (Are Made Of This)" by Eurythmics. Looking up contacts he'd made during a stint on the pirate radio station Phase One, he gathered enough money to press up some white labels which picked up interest from major labels and Eurythmics themselves. Angel's "Nightmare Mix" eventually reached the charts and gained him a contract with Dave Dorrell's Polydor subsidiary, Love. With the advance from the deal, he paid off his debts and began buying studio equipment, turning out the highly-rated "Never Leave" and "Atmosphere" singles for the label.

Within a year, he had switched to R&S, debuting with the first in a series of **Voyage** EPs which took the trip as a theme and collided heavyweight percussive grooves with the kind of wild sonic adventurism that characterised the best of Detroit's output. Recorded in Belgium with CJ Bolland providing engineering assistance, the new material proved that Dave Angel possessed a unique and significant talent.

Angel was also carving himself out an impeccable reputation in Europe as a DJ. A headline name at some of the continent's biggest events, he honed his style, tweaking the turntables to provide a wider range of pitch control (he still carries a screwdriver to every gig) and fusing deep Detroit Techno with hard but melodic outings which invested his sets with a compelling intensity.

On the **Second Voyage** EP and the **Outrageous Angel** EP on

Outrage he fused rave-signal synths with subtle rhythmic twists to come up with a fusion that was part Belgian Hardcore and part Ornette Coleman. And there was 1992's **Family** EP which added swooning, romantic strings (as on the impeccable "Great Daine" or the gorgeous "Brother From Jazz") to the blend. These were moments which matched the astonishing imaginative leaps of second generation Detroit producers such as Carl Craig and Kenny Larkin, but Angel was still hardly a *cause célèbre* for the UK dance press.

By 1993, he had set up his own label, Rotation, which was funded entirely from the fees he received from his DJ appearances. On it, Angel released some of his most stunning records yet; gorgeous confections full of liquid jazz cadences and Detroit-inflected grooves like the **Royal Techno** EP or the seductive **Seas of Tranquility** EP. This period also produced Angel's acknowledged masterpiece, the achingly romantic, blissfully alien "Artech". He also began releasing a number of singles under the name Sound Enforcer for the Rising High label. These tracks focused on a

more straight-ahead dancefloor aesthetic but enjoyed a degree of cult status that signalled Angel's growing popularity as a producer.

A year later, Angel's profile grew and he signed with Island, releasing "Airborne" in the summer of '94. He was also approached to record a mix album for Total/BMG and the resulting **Trance Lunar Paradise** (1994) offered a perfect snapshot of a DJ at the peak of his powers. A second mix album, **Beyond the Heavens** (1995) on the Studio K7 label, reprised many of the highpoints of **Trance Lunar Paradise**.

Angel's debut album, **Tales of the Unexpected** (1995), arrived the following autumn. Laden with lush, jazz-fuelled epics and the kind of prettiness that marked the apex of Techno's romantic drift, it was one of the year's most compelling releases and, for the first time, Angel found himself the focus of adoring media attention. R&S were quick to spot the upswing in his fortunes and a few months later rushed out **Classics** (1996) which collected together the best of his releases for the label.

Relations with Island began to sour during the recording of **Globetrotting** (1997). The singles which preceded the album – "This Is Disco" and "Tokyo Stealth Fighter" – constituted Angel's least convincing material yet; a fact that was thrown into relief by the superior quality of his remixes for Ken Ishii ("Overlap"), Joey Beltram ("Time") and even Echobelly ("Here Comes The Big Rush"). A messy divorce from the label ensued and when Angel finally extricated himself it was to concentrate on activities with Rotation. In the summer of 1998, he released "Insights", an outing which had more in common with the tough dancefloor shapes of his Sound Enforcer singles than the polished tech-jazz of the previous years.

⊙ **Classics**   R&S, 1996

The best cuts from Angel's series of EPs for R&S. Inspired, innovative and awesomely good, this is the Dave Angel album everyone should own.

Aphex Twin

Aphex Twin, aka Richard James, is perhaps the most unpredictable and spiky of modern digital artists. He's also one of the most deified. Critics have compared him to Eno, Debussy, Throbbing Gristle, Mantronix, Derek Jarman, My Bloody Valentine, Arvo Part, John Cage, Marcel Duchamp, Stockhausen, Bach, The Clangers and Syd Barrett. It might seem an unlikely set of correspondences, but Aphex Twin is a capricious artist. He can make assault-oriented hardcore, lullaby-soft ambience, assume the most refined airs and slump (often entertainingly) into a brattish self-regard.

Richard James was born in 1971 and raised in Cornwall. He has mythologised his childhood as that of an electronics prodigy, promoting the fact that – long before rave and Acid House – he was recording tape after tape of strange home-made electronica. He claimed to have been taking his keyboards and synthesisers apart – rewiring and re-patching them to find new sounds. A key part of his aesthetic and influence is the idea that mass-produced machines can be re-tweaked to find personal and individual sounds. His records feature such signature elements: squelching percussives, warm basses and new keyboard sounds as weightlessly beautiful as a classic Rhodes piano.

His first release, "Analogue Bubblebath #1", came out in 1991 and featured Schizophrenia (aka Tom Middleton of Global Communication who, at this point, was widely believed to be the other half of Aphex – thus the 'Twin' part of the name – although this is the only release on which the two collaborated). Lyrical, fluid, liquid and rhythmic, it was a striking record and earned an early cult following. Aphex Twin really broke through when R&S released "Digeridoo" in 1992. A frightening and tenebrous record, "Digeridoo" ran at 160 bpm and was driven by a synthetic, growling sound shaped to resemble the aboriginal instrument. It was a global Hardcore dancefloor hit at a period when evil, dark and fierce tunes were *de rigueur*.

His "Power-Pill" release under the Pac-Man alias was a fast and dippy tune based on the computer game soundtrack. The launch of his Rephlex label (together with friend Grant Wilson-Claridge) only furthered confusion about his sonic identity. Early Rephlex releases encompassed ultra-hard, Ambient and strange Techno releases. Many Rephlex artists were Aphex aliases – his 1992 EP as Caustic Window, **Joyrex J4**, featured a sparky version of Jean Michel Jarre's "Popcorn".

R&S released his first album, **Selected Ambient Works 85–92**, in 1992. It was a record of beautiful electronic ballads, a born-again psychedelia in the image of Eno and Kraftwerk. It was hailed as an all-time classic and has gained in stature ever since. Like the first Velvet Underground LP, it's one of those albums that's spawned thousands of imitators. Interviewed around the time of its release Aphex claimed never to have listened to Eno before he made the album. Yet in retrospect, **Selected Ambient Works** seemed to update classic Eno with modern beats and the feral energy of rave and drug youth.

More diverse and upbeat than its predecessor, his first album for Warp, Polygon Window's **Surfing on Sine Waves** (1992), was predictably received as a classic. Warp also featured several of his tracks on their ground-breaking **Artificial Intelligence** compilation which was acclaimed for having cemented a new genre of home-listening, or intelligent, Techno, and Aphex was hailed by some as the movement's spiritual hero, creator and leader.

In 1993 he scored his first and only UK Top 40 single so far with "On". His third album, **Selected Ambient Works Vol. 2** (1994) made the Top 20, but was poorly received by critics. More Eno-esque than ever, it was felt to be too meandering and self-indulgent. Perhaps aware that more was expected of him, his subsequent LPs **I Care Because You Do** (1995) and **Richard D James** (1996) were more focused and beat-driven. They also introduced a manic version of drum 'n' bass. Beyond far-out Junglism, these albums showed a wide range of Aphex initiatives – trip-hop's cool beats, classical string arrangements and engaging fusions of powerful rhythms with jazz-inflected and new age leanings.

Aphex then scored high-budget adverts for Pirelli and Orange and collaborated with Philip Glass (who reworked his "ICCT Hedral" track as an orchestral piece). He was increasingly seen as a maverick and eccentric – much was made, for example, of his DJ gig at London's Disobey club in 1994 where he turned up with discs made of sandpaper instead of vinyl records. Or his 1995 single, "Ventolin", which incorporated the sounds of asthma inhalers.

His work continued to show uniquely bizarre strains. His 1996 **Girl/Boy** EP on Warp included "Milk Man" which featured James as a vocalist. In a performance not unlike the LSD-fried twitterings of Syd Barrett or Julian Cope, he endlessly intoned a bastardised child's ditty: "I wish the milkman would deliver my milk in the morning/I would like some milk from the milkman's wife's tits." His live and festival appearances were similarly outrageous. He performed from inside a child's Wendy-house while dancers in teddy-bear suits sporting Aphex Twin cut-out face-masks occupied the front of the stage. Some wondered if he wasn't just laughing at them.

By 1997 many were ready to write off Aphex Twin as a hopeless, if brilliant, eccentric. Then he released "Come To Daddy". Driven by powerful and dancefloor-effective breakbeats, it featured nightmare sonics and a fiendish vocal screaming "I want your soul". It out-nas-tied The Prodigy, rivalled Marilyn Manson for Satanic intent and showed superflash and even virtuoso digital programming. An accompanying video shot by cult promo director Chris Cunningham was also received as a pop culture classic. Set in a sink estate, it featured the birth of a demon worshipped by an army of small girls all wearing cut-out Aphex masks. Cunningham has revealed plans to film William Gibson's *Neuromancer* with Aphex creating the soundtrack. If the project is ever completed, then it's possible Aphex's critical and commercial value will shoot through the roof. It's the kind of move that could permanently cement what has often been an erratic career.

⊙ **Selected Ambient Works 85–92**   R&S, 1992

Exquisitely beautiful, strange and compelling, this was the album which launched Aphex's career.

⊙ **Classics**   R&S, 1995

"Analogue Bubblebath", a version of "Digeridoo" recorded live in Cornwall and the best of Aphex's material for the R&S label make this a worthwhile introduction for anyone who hasn't yet picked up on the weird, wired world of Richard James.

Tony Marcus

Juan Atkins

U sually, as in the case of House music or even rock 'n' roll itself, genres develop from a confluence of cultural imperatives, ideas and events which transmute into the work of a number of different artists, producers and DJs to create an embryonic format that's then pulled, stretched and refined into shape. In the case of Techno, however, the ideas, concepts and sound came from one man: Juan Atkins.

He got his first electric guitar when he was ten years old. Later that same year, he persuaded his younger brother, Aaron, to ask for a drum kit for Christmas. When the kit appeared on Christmas morning, Juan took it over. After moving to the Detroit suburb of Belleville Atkins began recording at home, dubbing between two cassette decks and laying down all the parts on his own. By the time he graduated from high school, he'd also bought his first synthesiser and spent the next few months shaping and perfecting synthetic drum sounds, basslines and approximations of what a UFO might sound like. The result was a series of tracks – enough to fill a single cassette tape – that contained, somewhere inside them, the genetic code of Techno.

NOVAMUTE

During his first semester at Washtenaw Community College, Atkins met up with a former Vietnam veteran, Rick Davis, and discovered a shared love of synthesisers and the cyber-philosophy of Alvin Toffler. Together they formed Cybotron and began recording tracks which concealed the shadows of Techno inside a framework of proto-Electro. Despite moderate success, Atkins left the group after the recording of **Enter** (1983) and returned to Detroit to map out the beginnings of a new project, Model 500, based initially on a number of tracks which had been written during his final months with Cybotron. Unable to land a record deal and remembering the success of Cybotron's first independently released single, he set up his own label, Metroplex.

The first Metroplex release, "No UFO's" (1985), still bore traces of Electro, draped as it was in the spaceship sounds which so fascinated Atkins, but its bassline, melodic structure and basic groove suggested something else entirely. That indefinable something was made explicit on the follow-up, "Night Drive (Thru Babylon)", which operated on a similarly radical bass riff and developed an abstract, angular melodic pattern that suggested Atkins had somehow reached beyond previous pop templates to create a revolutionary new sound.

Atkins' influence on Derrick May and Kevin Saunderson was also a crucial factor in the genesis of Techno. Originally schoolfriends of Aaron Atkins, the pair were originally drawn to his elder brother because of the minor celebrity he enjoyed as part of Cybotron. Atkins taught them the rudiments of production, patiently explained his concepts, helped mix their tracks (sprinkling enough fairy dust on them to earn him the epithet "Magic Juan" which stuck throughout the late '80s) and provided encouragement. Soon, May and Saunderson brought their own friends – among them James Pennington, Thomas Barnett and Art Forrest – who formed the nucleus of Techno's first wave of producers.

Atkins provided mixes for Techno's first two international hits – Inner City's "Big Fun" and "Good Life" – though similar mainstream success has eluded him. Instead he spent the rest of the '80s and much of the early '90s issuing a series of inspirational singles which continued to provide a blueprint for scores of other producers. A deal with the Belgian R&S label resulted in **Classics** (1993), a collection of his most influential singles including "No UFO's", "Ocean to Ocean" and "Off to Battle".

Regular appearances as a DJ in Europe brought Atkins into contact with a number of Berlin-based producers including Moritz von Oswald and Thomas Fehlmann. A loose collaboration between the three evolved under the name 3MB and the resulting singles for Berlin's Tresor label – including "Die Kosmischen Kuriere" and "Jazz Is the Teacher" – were key elements in Techno's forward trajectory during the mid-'90s.

As with the 3MB material, Atkins' debut album, **Deep Space** (1995), had been recorded at Basic Channel's Love Park studio in Berlin and it was a masterpiece of subtle textural shifts and carefully sculpted grooves. Atkins' releases on Tresor as Infiniti (including a sizeable underground hit in the shape of "Game One") were collected on **The Infiniti Collection** (1996). Less cerebral than the Model 500 material, it was nevertheless crammed with superb moments such as "Impulse" and "Flash Flood". Together with his collaboration with 4 Hero (on the Jacob's Optical Stairway project), the Infiniti album helped maintain Atkins' momentum even though one of his most inventive recordings of that year – a remix of Little Johnny's "It's Like That" for Mark Taylor's Greyt Records – remained unheard outside of the Motor City.

Atkins returned to his Infiniti alter ego for **Skynet** (1998), an overlooked but compelling gem which suggested itself as the logical successor to **Deep Space** when hints about a quantum leap in the Model 500 sound began leaking from Atkins' Metroplex Studios. These indications were confirmed when a single, "Be Brave", emerged towards the tail end of 1998. Constructed with an elegant arrangement and a delicately interweaving vocal structure, "Be Brave" sounded unlike anything Techno had previously attempted. **Mind and Body** (1999) proved once again that Atkins was capable of huge, imaginative leaps. Tracks such as "Psychosomatic" and "Just Maybe" were arranged to sound as if they were twisting, turning and metamorphosing in complex, shifting patterns beneath a remarkably accessible exterior. There were still audible traces of Model 500's roots – most notably on "It's Time" – but overall the album sounded like Atkins was intent on reinventing Techno... and succeeding.

⊙ **Model 500 – Classics**   R&S, 1993

Techno's original blueprints collected together for the first time in one essential package.

⊙ **Model 500 – Deep Space**   R&S, 1995

Atkins' debut is a masterpiece of breathtaking quality. From "Milky Way" to "Lightspeed" this is a sonic voyage to the stars and beyond.

Atom Heart / Uwe Schmidt

I f there was such a thing as an index of prolific producers then it's almost certain that Uwe Schmidt would be somewhere near the top. His numerous alter egos – Atom Heart, Coeur Atomique, Atomu Shinzo, Lassigue Bendthaus and others – have provided cover for a prodigious output which, between his debut in 1991 and the appearance of Lassigue Bendthaus's **Render** (1994), had amounted to no less than 86 releases.

Schmidt started his musical career in the mid-'80s as a drummer, although he quickly swapped his acoustic set for a drum machine. Inspired by Acid House, he began making tracks for the dancefloor, eventually making his debut with "Whitehouse" in 1991. Subsequent releases on labels such as Cyclotron, Pod Communications and Rising High traced the development of the embryonic Frankfurt Trance sound. 1992's "Mihon" – made with Ata and Heiko under the name Ongaku – was typical. Full of fluttering 303 sequences, off-beat syncopations and dark, liquid reverbs, "Mihon" mapped out the new sound almost perfectly. Bi-face's "Ambience 137" (1992), the result of a collaboration with Pascal F.E.O.S., delineated the brighter, poppier side of Trance – blueprinting a genre that was to become a permanent fixture in the German pop charts throughout the '90s.

But for those who cared to listen a little more carefully, Schmidt's releases always carried a concealed freight of experimentalism, in terms of both sonic texture and ambition. Even in a track as obviously commercial as "Ambience 137", Schmidt's left-of-centre instincts emerged, transforming the back half of the track into the frame for some wildly abstract synth games.

As the '90s progressed, Schmidt grew increasingly uninterested with the Trance sound and began charting ever more experimental waters. He collaborated with Pete Namlook as Millennium (on Pod Communications) and as Subsequence (for Namlook's Fax label), exploring a fascination with Ambient Techno which was to become just one of the many creative threads he has pursued since.

At the same time, Schmidt's parallel career as a producer of industrial dance under the name Lassigue Bendthaus was proving to be equally prolific. Albums such as **Matter** (1991) and **Cloned** (1992) were cerebral affairs sketched with a distinctly experimental outlook which harked back to his pre-House music compositions on the cassette label NHG Medien.

By 1995, Schmidt's restless creative spirit had prompted him to found his own label, Rather Interesting. One of the early releases on the new label was **Dots** (1995), an updated variation on Eno's **Music For Airports** theme, while **Very Synthetic Virtual Noise** (1995) was a dramatic distillation of ambience, dancefloor Techno, avant garde experimentalism and wild sampladelica.

Schmidt continued to record for a bewildering variety of labels – including Delerium, KK and Rephlex – under an equally diverse number of aliases. A collaboration with veteran producer Bill Laswell and Tetsu Inoue, **Second Nature** (1995) was well-received but despite the growing critical acclaim accorded to his work, Schmidt was growing bored and looking for a change of scenery.

Eventually, Schmidt abandoned Germany and in 1997 relocated to South America. Almost immediately, a Latin influence emerged in his work, notably on **Señor Coconut** (1997). Since then his releases have continued to proliferate, particularly in Japan where he has strong links, due in part to his long-standing collaborative project with Tetsu Inoue under the name Datacide. Much of his material has found a home on Haruomi Hosono's Daisy World label and there have also been a number of releases for Towa Tei's Akashic Records, including the second Señor Coconut album, **El Gran Baile** (1998).

1999 began with a series of radically reinvented cover versions, including songs by The Beatles, The Rolling Stones, Bowie and Prince, recorded under the Lassigue Bendthaus banner. It was just the latest indicator that Schmidt prefers to follow his own instincts rather than conventional notions of what electronic music should, and should not, be about.

⊙ **Compilation V1**   Pod/Instinct, 1993

A fine introduction to the many guises of Uwe Schmidt, including tracks from Lisa Carbon Trio and his Datacide collaboration with Tetsu Inoue.

Aubrey

Allen Saei – better known as Aubrey – is one of the UK's most consistent producers of underground Techno, yet he has rarely been accorded the kind of acclaim which has been visited on lesser talents. In part, this is the result of a three-year "lost weekend" which stretched through the early '90s, breaking the momentum built up by early releases on his own Solid Groove label and tracks such as 1990's "Voices Of Energy" and "Last Injection" (under the name Panic) for Ozone and Wax Factory. But it can also be regarded as proof that the dance scene is still far from being the meritocracy that some have claimed it is.

Aubrey – a schoolyard nickname inspired by a '70s cartoon series – began his musical career as a DJ around the Portsmouth area in 1989. He worked in Razzels, an underground House and hip-hop record shop for three years before moving to Luke Slater's now legendary Jellyjam store in the early '90s. Influenced by a diverse record collection that stretched from Johnny Hammond to Grandmaster Flash, his days working behind the counter were punctuated by nights spent behind the turntables at Sterns, the influential south coast club which helped to catalyse a number of production and DJ careers.

When the harder, more linear sound of European Techno began to sweep through the club scene towards the end of '92, he "dipped out" – as he puts it – only returning to DJ work later in the '90s when interest in the Solid Groove label led to bookings in Amsterdam, Brussels and Madrid. In 1995, two singles – "Pass the Tool Box" and "Restart", both on Solid Groove – announced Aubrey's return as a producer as did a series of collaborative releases with Schatrax's Josh Brent under the name Cheap Knob Gags. Over the next three years Aubrey continued to release perfectly crafted dancefloor records such as "Chameleon" and the **Back to the Projects** EP on Solid Groove, while continuing to expand on the partnership with Josh Brent. He also launched a subsidiary label, Textures, to provide a platform for his excursions into Deep House.

Aubrey turned out a number of 12"s for labels such as Steve O'Sullivan's Mosaic (the superb **Contact Funk** EP) and Russ Gabriel's Ferox, but it was two successful releases on the London-based Offshoot imprint ("Marathon" and "Octane") that eventually led to the arrival of Aubrey's debut album. **Liquid Funk** (1999) provided the perfect overview of the Aubrey sound – a deep, warm amalgam that drew on the spaced-out flightpaths of Detroit, the feverish disco-funk of early Chicago jack trax and the avant garde synth explorations of Isao Tomita and Klaus Schulze. On the gorgeous "Dreams Of Tomorrow", the groove shifted from House to Techno under a web of shifting melodics, sounds subtly mutating from soft and liquid to hard and brittle. It was a technique that few dance producers – accustomed to the more static, linear approach which sequencing software facilitates – had attempted to explore.

By the time **Liquid Funk** emerged, it had begun to seem as though the dance scene had finally caught up with Aubrey. Typically, however, he was already making plans to shift forward once more, this time with a new project in conjunction with Russ Gabriel.

⊙ **Liquid Funk**   Offshoot, 1999

It took Aubrey almost a decade to get around to releasing his debut album and it proved well worth waiting for. The title says it all.

Autechre

Manchester duo Sean Booth and Rob Brown first came to the public's attention in 1992, alongside such luminaries as The Black Dog and Aphex Twin on the seminal Warp Records compilation, **Artificial Intelligence** (1992). Even amidst such distinguished company, however, Autechre stood out. They may have side-stepped such traditional influences as Kraftwerk, Detroit and Eno, in favour of Mantronix, Afrika Bambaata and the Miami Bass scene, but their two tracks, "The Egg" and "Crystel", seemed to contain no external reference points whatsoever. The multi-layered sleeve of their debut album, **Incunabula** (1993), a monochrome abstraction of typography and geometry, seemed as close to a description of their music as any words. An artfully designed work, ascetic yet aesthetic, fluid yet angular, it was clearly greater than the sum of its intricately constructed parts.

Following the **Anti** EP, a response to the government's draconian Criminal Justice Bill (later Act), the end of 1994 bought the eagerly awaited release of the duo's second album. If **Incunabula** was a series of jagged edged landscapes, **Amber** (1994) was an aural bitmap every bit as contoured as the natural beauty of the beachhead that graced its cover. In fact, in its ebb and flow, its constant forming and reforming, it resembled nothing less than a gently rolling sea of sound. The calm, melodic undercurrents were countered by the bombardment of cross rhythms slightly below the surface of the mix, hinting at the ominous dangers lurking deep beneath the surface.

1995 saw the release of two EPs – three if you count **The Sound of Machines Our Parents Used**, a collection of warped Electro released on the Clear label under the artist name Gescom. Of the two official

Autechre EPs released that year, **Garbage** forsook the surface calm of **Amber** and headed for murkier depths, moving ever further into abstraction. **Anvil Vapre**, released as prelude to their third LP, saw Rob and Sean in abrasive mood, producing four tracks of dark, distorted rhythms, phase-shifting loops and drifting fragments of melody. This was Autechre at their most extreme: a singular journey into the hinterlands of brutal beauty. Autechre's third album, **Tri Repetae** (1995), was a record that completely distorted the listener's sense of perception. With its strange metallic clanks and drum loops shifting in and out of phase, it was a hall of mirrors in sound.

The **Envane** EP (1997) was as disorienting as **Anvil Vapre**, swapping flame-thrower breakbeats for a brutal rewiring of hip-hop history. Nothing within these four tracks, however, could have prepared anyone for **Chiastic Slide** (1997). Static and distortion competed on equal footing with the music; noise levels were pushed and pulled from one extreme to another, in and out of focus, seemingly at random. This was a journey into uncharted waters. "Cichli Suite", a track drawn from the LP and "mechanically reclaimed" as a five-track EP, showed a new level of harmony between man and machine. Built on programming so complex one radio presenter was heard to ask whether it had been produced using self-generating music software, it was as if Sean and Rob had finally found a way to tune their own brain waves into the zeros and ones of their computers.

LP5 (1998) was a continuation and refinement of this – the sound of two artists perfectly in tune with both themselves and their machines.

Tracks unfolded like puzzles, constantly changing shape to reveal new aspects. As Sean says of their music: "you can follow it, because it works at the same pace as your brain works. The trick is not to get it to work faster or slower, but to get it in tune with yourself."

⊙ **Chiastic**   Slide Warp, 1997

The aural equivalent of being at the bottom of the sea. Dark, claustrophobic, with a sense of pressure that threatens to split your head open, yet full of strange beauty rendered even more dazzling by the darkness surrounding it.

Peter McIntyre

Aux 88

In the mid-'80s, Tommy Hamilton and William "BJ" Smith were in a high school band called Regime playing cover versions of tracks like Cybotron's "Clear" and Kraftwerk's "Numbers". They didn't know anything about recording technology or sequencers or computer music, so they learned to play everything by hand. "Every day, we'd finish school at around three in the afternoon," remembers BJ (who traded a brand new push-bike for his first keyboard – a cheap Casio "with a clock on it!"), "and then we'd practise for hours. We wouldn't get home until 11 o'clock at night and then we'd get up and do it all over again. We did that every day for a long, long time."

The roots of Aux 88 lie in Regime, classic Electro and the raw, embryonic techno of Model 500. But it wasn't until Hamilton and his then partner Keith Tucker submitted a tape of their prototype grooves to the fledgling 430 West label that Aux 88 began to take shape.

Encouraged by Lawrence Burden, the pair began developing a firm template for their back-to-basics sound. Aptly, the group found a home on 430 West's new subsidiary, Direct Beat.

Aux 88's first album, **Bass Magnetic** (1994) was a thick adrenalin roar, packed with hard Electro stylings and bruising kick drum dynamics. Tracks like "Technology" and "Boom" careered along at full speed, lacing tough funk through odd keyboard melodies. The overall effect sounded like Kraftwerk's **Computer World** stripped down and rebuilt like a Detroit street racer. Other releases like "Aux Quadrant" and "My A.U.X. Mind" followed, with the adrenalised, muscular sound making Aux 88 one of the biggest-selling Techno acts in their home city.

With the arrival of BJ Smith, the group metamorphosed briefly into a three-piece for **88 FM** (1995) which collected a series of loosely relat-

ed releases recorded before Tucker left to pursue his DJ K-1 project. In the aftermath of Tucker's departure, Smith and Hamilton moved into a new studio and began refining the hybrid they had begun referring to as "Electro-Techno".

Is It Man or Machine? (1996) was essentially a Kraftwerk homage, a straight-forward amalgam of rapid-fire electro beats, synthetic vocals and automaton hype geared for the no-frills dancefloors of Motor City clubs like The Dancery and Legends. **Reprogramming the Machine** (1997) offered variations on three of the album tracks from "official" Aux 88 DJ Dijital, and various 430 West luminaries including Will Webb, Microknox and Octave One.

BJ Smith left the group soon after the release of **Reprogramming the Machine**. Hamilton continued alone to deliver the virtually solo **Xeogenetic** (1998).

⊙ **Bass Magnetic**   Direct Beat, 1994

Raw, hard-jacking Electro, Kraftwerk and classic Detroit techno met on this straight-forward but heavily funky debut.

B12

I t's hard to discern a link between the hard-as-nails Brooklyn Techno jock Frankie Bones and the lush music of Mike Golding and Steve Rutter, arguably the keepers of the "pure Techno" flame in the UK. Yet it was the tough Hardcore of the **Bonesbreaks** EPs that provided the initial inspiration and impetus that sent B12 on their way. Prior to this, the duo had been making music for three years, after hooking up through Golding's sister. These early efforts were, by their own accounts, less than impressive, but they learned quickly and soon the machine dreams of Detroit became the guiding influence. Indeed, when the duo began to release tracks on their eponymous label in 1991, under a number of aliases including Red Cell, C-Metric and Musicology, record buyers assumed that these stickered, shrink-wrapped 12"s were from the Motor City itself. Here was music charac-terised by gently shuffling percussives, mile-wide synth vistas and splashes of electronic colour as abstract and arresting as a Jackson Pollock canvas. Adopting a determined anti-sampling approach and constructing their music almost entirely from computer-sequenced keyboard passages, Rutter and Golding produced a sound completely at odds with the adrenalin rush of the post-rave, Happy Hardcore sound that swept through UK dance culture.

At the time, however, they seemed to exist almost in a vacuum of their own creation. Even when they found themselves placed amongst allegedly like-minded artists such as Aphex Twin, Black Dog and Autechre as part of the **Artificial Intelligence** (1992) compilation that heralded the rise of so-called "Electronic Listening Music", they seemed to stand out on their own, working within their own parame-ters with seemingly little thought for the world outside. B12's debut LP – something of a misnomer, being largely a compilation of previously released material plus four new tracks – **Electro Soma** (1993) saw them continue in the same vein. Easily the most beautiful of all the artist albums released under the AI banner, it moved from the ethereal beauty of "Drift" through the bass-led dynamics of "Obsessed" to the celestial symphonics of "Soundtrack of Space".

By the time of their second LP, **Time Tourist** (1996), they seemed to have broadened their musical horizons, echoing the Oriental influ-ences of Black Dog on "DB5" and anticipating the contemporary redis-covery of '60s English electronica in "Radiophonic Workshop". It still had that typically majestic air of spacious melancholy, but now it was as if Detroit formed part of a larger world.

The duo's most recent release, **3EP**, forged further links between Detroit and the outside world. Juan Atkins once declared that "Jazz Is the Teacher" and this EP took that dictum literally, with the three tracks titled after jazz legends Ron Carter, Dave Brubeck and Joe Morello, and based around samples from the work of each one. On first listen, it seemed the complete antithesis of their previous work, with those gorgeous synths submerged beneath intricate jungle microrhythms. Yet, inside these obsessively chopped-up breaks was a textural depth that was typically B12.

⊙ **Electro Soma**   Warp, 1993

Positive proof that electronic music can stir the heart, as well as the mind. Gently pattering rhythms, gracefully arcing synth parabolas, and melodies from those dreams you wish you'd had. And the best slice of sinewave funk since Rhythim Is Rhythim's "Wiggin" on "Obsessed".

Peter McIntyre

Bandulu

A long with a number of other UK Techno producers, Bandulu have been responsible for excavating the intersection between dub and Techno. Drawing inspiration from both Juan Atkins and King Tubby, their albums, including **Guidance** (1993) and **Cornerstone** (1996), have ploughed a distinctively underground furrow, alternately blazing new trails and sometimes slipping out of sync entirely with the volatile trends of the dancefloor.

Lucien Thompson, Jamie Bissmire and John O'Connell – part-time carpet fitters and record distributors by day and graffiti-tagging b-boy originals by night – were a gang who metamorphosed into a group. Introduced to Acid House by sometime Bandulu/Orb/System 7 collaborator DJ Lewis, they became regulars at Shoom but found themselves increasingly detached as the scene drifted towards more commercial waters. Passionate about US House and Techno, they originally began working on their own music "just to see if we could make something we would wanna hear."

Their first endeavours together – a series of heavily Detroit-influenced futurist missives – were released under the name Thunderground. When the first Bandulu album was finally released, **Guidance** (1993) hinted at a potential that wasn't quite realised by the embryonic fusion of tracks such as "Messenger", though somewhere in the dub-wise chants and fizzing Detroit strings the blueprint for Bandulu's future was there for anyone who cared to listen. One possible trajectory was suggested by Carl Craig's mix of "Better Nation", a loosely funky confection that linked '80s electro-disco, Techno and – in a brief, dubbed-out coda – Lee "Scratch" Perry.

Though released less than a year later, **Antimatters** (1994) represented a quantum leap in the group's increasingly refined synthesis. Less orchestrated than its predecessor, **Antimatters** was a more minimal, modern-sounding affair that connected more with the group's rapidly spiralling side-projects (including Koh Tao, Sons of the Subway and, most recently, Bissmire's Space DJz collaboration with Ben Long) than with any traceable influences.

A short-lived deal with Blanco Y Negro resulted in **Cornerstone** (1996). To date, it's the most perfect articulation of Bandulu's sound – an airy, though sometimes oppressive and abrasive fusion of dub and Techno – and remains the album which could well have crossed the group into the mainstream.

More underground pleasures awaited, however, and since leaving Blanco Y Negro, Thompson, Bissmire and O'Connell have focused on their own Ground label and a number of satellite projects. Though Bandulu seems to exist in a state of suspended animation these days, an excellent Space DJz album, **On Patrol** (1999), did emerge on the Glasgow-based Soma label.

⊙ **Cornerstone**   Blanco Y Negro, 1996

The definitive Bandulu album fuses underground Techno, dub and minimalism over the course of twelve unstoppable tracks.

Thomas Barnett

F ew artists have gone as unrewarded and unrecognised for their contribution to the development of a genre as Thomas Barnett. As Derrick May's original partner in Rhythim Is Rhythim, he was responsible for one of Detroit Techno's defining moments as the co-writer of the ground-breaking "Nude Photo", yet few people outside of the scene's inner circle even know his name.

Barnett came to music early: by the age of 13, he was drawing a crowd as the DJ at a local arcade, spinning a mix of Kraftwerk, Funkadelic and electronic disco hits such as Lipps Inc.'s "Funky Town". Eventually, Chez Damier introduced Barnett to May. Soon he began dropping over to May's apartment on Second Avenue and the pair would play each other snippets of tracks-in-progress or chat about ideas. This led to their embryonic Rhythim Is Rhythim partnership and, of course, "Nude Photo".

"Tom was the inspiration behind that track," remembers May. "He had this song he'd been working on, so he brought it over and we tried to work on it together for a couple of days. But it wasn't working out – to me it sounded more like New Order's "Blue Monday" – so after a while Tom went off and I worked up the finished version on my own. But he brought the concept, he has to get credit for that."

"Nude Photo" finally emerged early in 1987, sounding like it had just dropped intact from another planet. Though May now regards it as his least favourite track, it was pivotal in the schism which separated Techno from its musical antecedents. The seductively alien, wildly abstract sound that he and Barnett had conjured up represented a profound break with everything that had gone before – Motown, Kraftwerk, funk, disco, electronic pop – and suddenly Techno was launched into a developmental curve which has yet to reach its outer limits.

Barnett's partnership with May foundered soon after the single's release. As Subterfuge, Barnett released the **Liquid Poetry** EP and contributed to Infonet's influential **313 Detroit** (1992) compilation. The material from this time was still marked by the alienation which had been evident on "Nude Photo", but was somewhat less elegantly shaped and suffered from Barnett's tendency towards over-production.

A deal with the Dutch label Prime gave Barnett the chance to restake his claim with "My Nude Photo" – a remake of the original – which received little in the way of promotion. Two further releases, the **Reality** EP and "The Enchantress", followed before Barnett began work on his debut album. **Synthetic Dream** (1993) again suffered from a lack of profile, though many of its tracks found their way onto various compilations.

Barnett unveiled his own label, Visillusion, at the beginning of 1996 with the release of the **Brotherhood of Blood** EP. He returned to the Subterfuge name for "Reunited With Myself" and the **Foundation Series** EP which explored a leaner, funkier hybrid than his Prime material. Since then he's continued to work on music but, in effect, he remains the unsung hero of Techno.

○ Rhythim Is Rhythim – "Nude Photo"   Transmat, 1987

The record that altered the direction of Techno forever. Shockingly abstract, beautifully strange and probably the most influential record ever made in a bedroom studio.

○ Subterfuge – Synthetic Dream   Prime, 1993

Barnett's debut album is worth tracking down for rarity value alone, but there are plenty of other reasons to recommend it too. An undeservedly overlooked release.

Richard Bartz

B est known during the mid-'90s for his uncompromising releases as Acid Scout, Richard Bartz has since carved himself a reputation as one of Germany's most consistent underground Techno producers. In a studio near the legendary Ultraschall club, he crafts a sound that is hard and brooding, sometimes pushing velocities towards Techno's upper limits, at others suggesting the more restrained pace of early Chicago classics such as "No Way Back" or "I've Lost Control".

In 1992 Bartz approached Disko B with a tape. The label were keen to release the material, but an accident with the master tape (someone left it on top of a speaker, thereby erasing some of the recording) meant that Bartz didn't make it onto vinyl until the following year. In 1993, recording as Richie, he provided remixes of Robert Görl's "Psycho" for Disko B and also contributed (with DJ Hell and Indigo) to the label's **Ultraworld** EP.

Bartz and Hell continued to work together on the "Buttersäure" single for Kickin' and "3° Kelvin" for Dave Clarke's Magnetic North label. Bartz also contributed to the DJ Hell album, **Geteert & Gefedert** (1994), but it was "4 Degree" – his first single as Acid Scout – which blueprinted the distinctively urgent and edgy sound that Bartz is best known for. "Balance" – a significant hit on harder dancefloors during the latter half of 1994 – typified Bartz's Acid Scout output, layering high-speed sequences against a punishing sub-tone kick drum.

Safari (1995) was an equally powerful debut, though many of the tracks seemed purpose-built for emphasising the delirium inherent in the MDMA experience rather than the more sedate confines of home listening. A more measured gauge of Bartz's talents came in the form of **Sci-Fi** (1995) which was released under his own name some months later. Broader in scope than the Acid Scout album, **Sci-Fi** was still a remarkably assured release from a producer who, at that time, had still only just turned 19.

Escape (1996) provided a useful overview of Bartz's uncollected 12" releases though, predictably perhaps, it was the second Acid Scout album, **Musik für Millionen** (1996), which attracted most of the attention from the reviewers. By this time, Bartz was exploring a deeper, more atmospheric territory, but traces of the raw power of old were still present. Since **Musik für Millionen**, Bartz's output has been remarkably sparse – just a handful of singles on his own Kurbel label (including a DJ Hell versus Richard Bartz 12") and the "Subway" single for Kanzleramt – though he is currently working on a new album for release on Kurbel.

⊙ **Richard Bartz – Sci-Fi**   Disko B, 1995

Bartz's most rounded LP to date, it offers an excellent introduction to his sometimes bruising, sometimes beautiful sound.

Basic Channel

S ome of the most influential records to emerge in the course of Techno's progress through the '90s leaked out of Berlin by way of a small mastering plant in Wayne, Michigan. Those are the facts. In the case of Basic Channel, everything else is just pure conjecture. Their operation is shrouded in mystery – they don't do interviews, their records are rarely credited and few people outside of Techno's inner circle are even aware of their existence. But their music has inspired countless DJs and producers and, in no small way, altered the forward trajectory of Techno.

It began in April, 1993 with the release of Basic Channel 001 – ostensibly a record called "Enforcement" by an artist named Cyrus – which coupled a muscular, loping groove with a sonic palette that seemed to draw as much from the unique vinyl mastering it utilised as it did from tones produced in the studio. This was followed by the seminal "Phylyps Trak" which confirmed what the first single had suggested: this was an innovative new sound based on hypnotic rhythmic patterns and a warm grittiness that was in some ways reminiscent of Detroit, but in others completely unique.

As more releases emerged, Basic Channel began to acquire an almost mythical reputation, but hard facts were as sparse as the minimal track listings on the records. Fragments of information – involving Berlin's Hard Wax record shop, an early '80s experimental indie outfit called Palais Schaumburg and 3MB's Moritz Von Oswald – were pieced together, but neither confirmed nor denied.

Palais Schaumburg were Germany's answer to the left-of-centre indie experimentalism of Manchester's Factory. The group boasted a fluid line-up which included Von Oswald, Holger Hiller and Thomas Fehlmann. Another one-time Schaumburg recruit, Mark Ernestus, was rumoured to be part of the Basic Channel set-up alongside Von Oswald, but the records offered no credits and with so little to go on it was hard to pin down any information. Quadrant – another Basic Channel alias (Quadrant's "Q1.1" was one of the label's early classics) – turned up on Carl Craig's Planet E label with the "Infinition" single, but if Craig knew any details he wasn't telling.

And so it went on throughout the mid-'90s until – after just nine releases – Basic Channel suddenly metamorphosed into Chain Reaction. As a parting shot, a retrospective collection, **BC CD** (1995), emerged in a typically minimal and uninformative cardboard sleeve (later versions appeared in a more robust metal tin). Since then, releases on Chain Reaction and related labels such as Burial Mix, M, Rhythm & Sound and Imbalance have continued to explore the vein of deep, dub-textured Techno that Basic Channel's brief but compelling career etched onto the dancefloor.

⊙ **BC CD**   Basic Channel, 1995

A cunningly plotted trajectory through Basic Channel's brief but influential career, including the sublime "E2E4 Basic Reshape" – their mix of Paperclip People's Manuel Göttsching tribute, "Remake Uno".

Blake Baxter

Blake Baxter played an important supporting role in the beginnings of Detroit Techno. A one-time street poet turned DJ who was adored by many of the city's female club-kids thanks to his pretty-boy looks and a relatively carnal demeanour loosely inspired by Prince, he was one of the small group – also including James Pennington, Eddie Fowlkes, Art Forrest and Santonio Echols – who helped proliferate Techno beyond the nucleus of the so-called Belleville Three (Juan Atkins, Derrick May and Kevin Saunderson). But unravelling the tangled impulses of his music and DJ sets since the mid-'80s reveals an ambivalent relationship with Techno – Baxter has oscillated between House and more identifiably straight-forward variants of the Motor City sound throughout his career.

Baxter's early releases emerged on Chicago's legendary DJ International label, but it was 1987's "When We Used to Play" on Saunderson's KMS label which provided his first major underground hit. He was also a significant player on the seminal **Techno! The New Dance Sound of**

Detroit (1988) compilation put together by Neil Rushton. Baxter contributed three tracks to the album – the Jamie Principle-styled "Forever and a Day", a collaboration with Kevin Saunderson and Mia Hesterley on "Spark" and the erotomaniac Techno of "Ride 'Em Boy".

When the scene's main protagonists found themselves in demand in Europe, Baxter elected to stay in Detroit. As the '80s bled into the '90s, however, he hooked up with the embryonic Underground Resistance, releasing the seminal **Prince of Techno** EP for the label, and eventually accompanied them to Germany where he met up with Tresor's Dimitri Hegemann who played a pivotal role in Baxter's career (Baxter released his first LP, **Dreamsequence** (1992), for the label and later became resident DJ at Hegemann's Tresor club). **The Project**, a collaborative EP on Tresor with Eddie Fowlkes, saw Baxter connecting with a number of important producers on the Berlin scene including Moritz Von Oswald, Thomas Fehlmann and Max Loderbauer. The result was one of Baxter's most intriguing releases.

Despite the critical acclaim accorded to **Prince of Techno** and **The Project** and the formation of his own labels, Mix Records and Phat Joint, Baxter continued to focus mainly on his activities as a DJ, releasing singles only occasionally. A short-lived deal with Logic Records produced "One More Time", "Brothers Gonna Work It Out" (later sampled by the Chemical Brothers on "Leave Home") and the typically lewd "Sexual Deviant", but they weren't among Baxter's best releases. **Endless Reflection** (1995), however, proved that his unique fusion of Techno, House and whispered vocals was capable of delivering a provocative and seductive long-player.

Less fully realised than **Endless Reflection**, **The Vault** (1995) nevertheless contained gems such as "I'm Given" and "Touch Me", though the throw-away vocal sample and garage groove formula elsewhere on the album was less convincing. On a European DJ tour in the wake of the album's release, Baxter dramatically declared his retirement from Techno, confiding that he felt more interesting things were happening on the House scene.

H-Factor (1997) was a definitively House-oriented affair. On tracks such as "N-Sync" his fixation with vocals was also still much in evidence. An ongoing series of 12" collaborations with the UK's Trevor Rockcliffe failed to provide any outstanding moments, though **Globus Mix Vol. 2 – A Decade Underground** (1998) offered the opportunity for Baxter to document his versatile abilities behind the decks. Currently working on new material, it remains to be seen whether Baxter can deliver the truly ground-breaking work of which he is undoubtedly capable or whether he will settle – as he has consistently done in the past – for second-best.

⊙ **Dream Sequence featuring Blake Baxter**
Endless Reflection   Tresor, 1995

Tracks such as "Drum Major" and "Kiss It" hinted that Baxter was at last on the verge of something supremely innovative on this, his most intriguing release to date.

Dan Bell

I n 1994, DBX's "Losing Control" seemed almost inescapable. If you were in a club where deep, underground Techno was being played, it was a certainty that the track's raw, stripped-down groove and claustrophobic atmosphere would leak out of the speakers and fill the dancefloor. While the track seemed to reconnect with the darkest and most narcotic moments of Chicago's output, there was another influ-

ence at work. The sparse, eerily atmospheric moods and perfectly timed pace of Dan Bell's records had more to do with the influence of Alfred Hitchcock films than with other records or musical styles.

Bell's production career initially began in hip-hop, taking time off from studying film and editing at Niagara College to work with rappers and DJs in various locations between Buffalo and Toronto. After spending some time in Detroit, he met Richie Hawtin and John Acquaviva which led to their collaboration on the first Cybersonik release, "Technarchy", and Bell's subsequent "Cabaret Seven" single (also under the name Cybersonik, although Hawtin and Acquaviva didn't feature) on Plus 8.

After graduating from film school in 1991, Bell moved to Detroit to continue making music. His unique production style, he says, developed from his training as a film editor, juggling countless hours of celluloid to create a finished movie, but the influence of his hip-hop background is also traceable in the grooves and textures of his music.

In 1992, along with Claude Young, he launched the short-lived Seventh City label (the name was borrowed from Alan Oldham's *Gambit & Associates* comic book) with a double-headed 12" featuring "Planet Earth" by Young under his Brother From Another Planet alias and Bell's "Trance Missions" under his new project name, DBX. Despite the success of this release, the label quickly folded and Bell set up his own Accelerate imprint as a platform for DBX material such as 1992's "Blip" and 1993's "Electric Shock".

After two years spent expanding the distribution arm of Detroit's Record Time, Bell inaugurated his own Seventh City distribution company in 1994 as a way of helping develop the proliferation of new labels and artists in the Midwest. The company revived the Seventh City label and provided an outlet for Bell's own Accelerate and Elevate imprints, but the pressure of running the operation effectively halted his production career just as "Losing Control" was breaking through on an international scale. Over the next few years, only his "Science Fiction" track for Tresor (1995) and the "Lost Tracks" release for Klang (1997) punctuated the silence.

In March 1998, Bell decided to wind down his distribution activities and resume recording, although he still runs the labels Seventh City, Accelerate and Elevate. His return to production was announced by a series of limited edition releases under the Elevated Special Projects banner.

⊙ **Blip**   Accelerate, 1999

A solid compilation of Dan Bell's early DBX releases that provides the perfect introduction to his distinctive style.

Joey Beltram

I n 1991, the broodingly intense, amphetamine rush of Joey Beltram's "Energy Flash" almost single-handedly remapped Techno's trajectory towards a harder, more brutal sound. Based around a throbbing sub-bass riff, a single resonant filter hook line and a handful of queasy, horror-flick string sounds, "Energy Flash" commandeered the dancefloor until it seemed you wouldn't ever find yourself on a Techno dancefloor without hearing its trademark "ecstasy, ecstasy" chant. Almost a decade on, it's still one of the most influential moments in Techno – responsible for a scattershot of different directions from European Hardcore to the dark, tenebrous minimalism of the mid-'90s and beyond.

To some, it seemed like "Energy Flash" made Beltram an underground Techno star almost overnight, but by then he'd already served a considerable apprenticeship. Growing up in Queens, he began spinning Electro for the street crowd. Early in the summer of 1986, Beltram tuned in to Tony Humphries' late-night radio show. "He was playing crazy shit from Chicago. It was so different from anything I was into. It sounded like it had all been recorded in someone's bedroom – that brought it down to my level, the level of a normal kid in Queens. To me it felt like a totally new form of instrumental music. The seeds were sown then. That music totally inspired me. The records that defined that summer – Fingers Inc.'s "Can You Feel It" and "No Way Back" by Adonis – are still among my all-time favourites."

Beltram began making his own records in 1988, just as New York's vocal-oriented Garage sound was in the ascendant. "I had a lot of doors slammed in my face," he later recalled. But Nu Groove's Frank Mendez decided to take a chance. The records that followed, such as

Code 6's "Forgotten Moments", Lost Entity's "Bring That Back" (with Mike Munoz), "The Start it Up" (on Chicago's revered Trax label) and "Secret Code" (on Nu Groove under the name Jazz Documents), articulated a sound, based on the wilder tropes of Chicago House, that was instinctively finding its way towards Techno. "I never considered myself Techno," remembers Beltram, "because I got all my influences from the early House scene. I considered myself a direct descendant of that stuff. I didn't discover Techno until I met Derrick May in Europe."

"Energy Flash" had originally been intended for Nu Groove, but Beltram held onto the track for a time "because," he explained later, "it was so different". After Belgium's R&S label licensed "Let It Ride" from

MARTYN GALLINA-JONES

Nu Groove, Beltram was approached by R&S boss Renaat Vandepapeliere who subsequently signed a number of exclusive tracks from the producer – including "Energy Flash", "Subsonic Trance" and the aptly titled "Psychobase" – which became the ground-breaking **Beltram Volume 1** EP.

As "Energy Flash" swamped European dancefloors, Beltram traded relative obscurity in New York (where he'd been DJing at roller-skating rinks and discos) for high-profile gigs in Belgium, Holland, Germany and the UK. He became a fixture on the emerging Hardcore rave circuit where subsequent singles such as the queasily snaking "Mentasm" became anthems. In the US, Trax released two albums to capitalise on his new-found fame, **Joey Beltram Presents Dance Generator** (1991) and **The Beltram Re-Releases 1989–1991** (1991).

A document of his DJ sets at this time was provided by **Mixmag Live! Joey Beltram** which was eventually given a full release in 1996. It captured Beltram connecting with breakbeat, spinning "Energy Flash" and "My Sound" into tracks by Goldie, DJ Crystl and Wax Doctor. Beltram was attracted to the raw power and edgy feel of the new sound, though he was distilling his own radically different and distinctive brand of heavyweight minimalism in the studio.

1993's "Caliber" single for Warp and the surprising ambient outing **Aonox** (1994) on Visible indicated the beginning of a creative renaissance for Beltram, but he found a more suitable home on Berlin's Tresor label. "Game Form", his first single for the label, rapidly established itself an underground classic. Impossibly hard and driven by a sharp, metallic riff, "Game Form" signalled the perfectly sculpted, but still rambunctious, minimalism he was now exploring. The outstanding **Places** (1995) proved that Beltram was surfing a creative peak. Tracks such as "Instant" or the warping, psychedelic roughhouse of "Floaters" easily matched his best so far – hard, bruisingly intense workouts that might have threatened to bludgeon the dancefloor into submission if they hadn't been shaped with a rare subtlety.

Close Grind (1996) was the next step. The result of a new deal with NovaMute – hence Beltram metamorphosing into JB3 for contractual purposes (the new moniker stemmed from the fact that Beltram's father and grandfather were also Joey Beltram, thus making him Joey Beltram III) – it was a harder and less forgiving affair than **Places**. Shot through with hypnotic, biting funk and twisted atmospherics, the new album found Beltram sewing together an exquisitely tough disco cut-up ("Curb") amongst the stripped-down, abrasive grooves which edged **Close Grind** towards pure Techno perfection.

Almost simultaneously, R&S released **Classics** (1996), the definitive guide to Beltram's early releases on R&S, Easy Street and Atmosphere. "Joey's Riot", "Mind to Mind", "Energy Flash" and "Mentasm" were all on board, though it was evident that Beltram was now moving fast to eclipse the legacy of his past. **Live Mix** (1997) was released by the heavyweight partnership of Logic/BMG, but failed to provide more than a brief glimpse of Beltram's skill behind the decks. Mixing his own material with tracks from Chicago's Mike Dunn, K Alexi Shelby and Abacus, it served to underline the links between Beltram's steroid-enhanced sound and the House music which first inspired him. Since then, Beltram has continued to focus on the muscular sound suggested by singles for Tresor such as "Metro" and "Ball Park", refining and reinforcing the sound first delineated by **Places**.

⊙ **Places**   Tresor, 1995

Stripped-down, hard-as-nails and perfectly sculpted dancefloor Techno that signalled Beltram's return as a major creative force.

⊙ **Classics**   R&S, 1996

The album that no Techno fan should be without; contains all Beltram's seminal classics and a few more besides.

John Beltran

J ohn Beltran first emerged on the Techno scene back in 1991 with the "Aquatic" single on Carl Craig and Damon Booker's RetroActive label. He'd been a one-time regular at Detroit's legendary Music Institute and had spent time clubbing in Chicago too, but the tones and shapes of "Aquatic" suggested an individual take on modern electronics as shades of jazz, classical and Latin whispered through the mix.

For a time, he stopped writing music altogether and took a job with a consumer organisation promoting energy conservation. But the lure of music proved too strong and he gradually returned to it, first by composing solo pieces for the piano and eventually by crafting the elegaic moods and new age tones that made **Earth & Nightfall** (1995) such a distinctive, and introspective, treasure. Perhaps its closest links were with the Tech-jazz of tracks such as Carl Craig's "At Les" or Kenny Larkin's "Tedra", but Beltran added a few unique twists of his own. On "Vienna" he sampled a loop from Bach's *Orchestral Suite #2*, whilst "Sub-Surface" benefited from Dennis Bach's mellifluous acoustic guitar solo. Elsewhere, Beltran used elements of world music, salsa and pristine ambience to mould his sound. The result was an album full of wistful moments, considered moods and rare beauty.

Ten Days of Blue (1996) built on the successes of its predecessor with sharp rhythms and pure digital sounds flooding through dreamy sequences and subtle chord shapes. If anything, the sense of melancholy drifting through Beltran's music was even stronger on this outing, a fact he ascribed to the painful romantic break-ups both he and his cousin had suffered during the making of the album. The title track and the plaintive "Soft Summer" sounded like Tangerine Dream injected with jazz bass or Kraftwerk mainlining on heartbreak. He seemed to have perfected the art of painting tones and rhythms across canvases that were almost unbearably delicate and pretty.

Instead of a follow-up, Beltran reverted to the Placid Angles moniker that he had used on the "Aquatic" single. **The Cry** (1997) was a more deliberately electronic take on his sound that ranged from the quiet ambience of "Everything Under the Sun" to the glittering Techno of "Now and Always". But, compared to his previous albums, it was a less than satisfactory outing with Beltran himself later dismissing many of the album's cuts as merely "emotional scribbles."

Moving Through Here (1997) placed the emphasis on a more ensemble-based approach with vocalist Meggan Lyon joining long-time Beltran collaborators Dennis Bach and Mark Wilson to flesh out the sound. But Beltran retained his distinctively individual approach on tracks such as "Paris Is Burning", which featured a recitation of French poetry by Julia Mahoney, and "The Antidote" which employed saxophone courtesy of Amel Eiland. Beltran's latest project is an album under the name Indio for Derrick May's Transmat label.

⊙ **Earth & Nightfall**   R&S, 1995

Swooping from pastoral electronics to deep Techno, Beltran's debut was a masterpiece of delicate textures and heart-stopping romance.

Justin Berkovi

After a childhood and adolescence spent listening to Human League, Roxanne Shanté and Mantronix, Justin Berkovi turned to the emergent rave culture, switched on by the weird seductiveness of records like LFO's "LFO", Nightmares On Wax's "Aftermath" and

Shut Up & Dance's "£20 to Get In". As the scene shifted towards Belgian Hardcore, Berkovi followed but eventually developed a taste for what he describes as "purer Techno", name-checking Djax, Transmat and Plus 8 as the labels which changed his course and reserving particular admiration for the Terrace output of Holland's Stefan Robbers and the dark, febrile Techno of Suburban Knight.

Prompted by his interest in electronic music, Berkovi had taken a music technology course at school, fitting in sessions with the school synths and drum machines around revising for his A-Levels. After a series of labels showed no interest in his tapes, Berkovi began a college course in Brighton – where he spent time as a DJ on the local student radio station – but after finishing his degree decided to indulge his production ambitions just once more and sent a tape to Cristian Vogel.

Vogel spotted his talent immediately and Berkovi's first release, the **Crouton** EP, was soon released on the former's Mosquito label. A slew of impressive 12"s followed, such as the "01273 Predicaments" outing for Force Inc., the **Gravel Heart** EP for Edinburgh's Sativae label and the beautifully titled **So Many Blurry Ceilings** EP for Solid.

Berkovi's compelling debut, **Charm Hostel** (1998), was a radical but intriguing take on the influences which had shaped his musical outlook. Experimenting with textures and rhythms, it was an at times discomfiting album, but could never be accused of being less than inspired. The potential it demonstrated did not escape the attention of Djax and, late in '98, Berkovi achieved a long-held ambition by signing to the label for the release of the "Jeopardy Part One" single.

⊙ **Charm Hostel**   Force Inc., 1998

Stretching the skeleton of Techno through fractured ambience, kick drum symphonics and a healthy dose of avant garde experimentalism, Berkovi's debut is a must for anyone interested in the forward momentum of the genre.

Biosphere

B iosphere's Geir Jenssen has been a significant player in the Ambient Techno scene since the early '90s. Although these days he admits "I don't really feel part of Techno anymore", his albums, including **Microgravity** (1991) and **Patashnik** (1994), articulated a deeply chilled, but compelling fusion of spoken-word samples, spaced-out atmospheres and brooding trippiness that played a key role in Techno's evolution away from the dancefloor.

During the '80s, Jenssen was a founder member of the Norwegian group Bel Canto, recording two albums with them – **White-Out Conditions** (1987) and **Birds of Passage** (1990) – before a combination of boredom with the band's new surroundings (they'd relocated to Brussels) and homesickness prompted him to return to his hometown, Tromsø, to embark on a solo career.

Jenssen originally began recording as Bleep, producing a classic debut, **The North Pole By Submarine** (1991), before reinventing himself again as Biosphere to avoid confusion with the distinctive sinewave sound emerging from Sheffield which critics had taken to describing as "bleep Techno".

The first Biosphere album, **Microgravity**, was an astonishing *tour de force* of liquid grooves and glacial moods, inspired by the extreme climate of Tromsø, which lies 800 kilometres inside the Arctic circle. Originally released on the small Norwegian label Origo Sound, the album was subsquently licensed to R&S. Jenssen signed to R&S on the same day as Aphex Twin. The story goes that the pair met up in the company's Ghent offices and, amidst the small talk, Aphex famously confided that he listened to **The North Pole By Submarine** almost every day – an anecdote that serves to illustrate the huge influence Jenssen's music has wielded on the more experimental currents of European Techno.

Jenssen's reputation as an explorer of Techno's more remote, penumbral regions was reflected in his hobbies outside music. An expedition to the Himalayas following the release of **Patashnik** exposed him to the strange, atonal cadences of Tibetan music which eventually found their way into elements of **Substrata** (1997), his most abstract and extreme release to date which owed more to the classical ambience of Eno and Harold Budd than to Detroit.

Jenssen has also been relatively successful in making music for film, beginning with the soundtrack for the Norwegian film *Eternal Stars* in 1992. Together with Per Martinsen of Mental Overdrive, he provided a new score for *Man With a Movie Camera* for its showing at the 1996 Norwegian Film Festival and followed up by composing the music for Erik Skjoldbjaerg's *Insomnia* (the soundtrack was later released on Origo Sound in 1997). Perhaps his best-known work, however, remains "Novelty Waves" which Levis used for their 1995 "drugstore" advertising campaign.

Biosystems – The Biosphere Remixes (1999) collated Jenssen's remixes for Frontline Assembly, Nicolette and Alania amongst others, though a more significant indicator of where he may be headed was provided by his reworkings of Norwegian new age artist Arne Nordheim which featured on the **Nordheim Transformed** (1998) album.

⊙ **Microgravity**   Origo Sound/R&S, 1991

For a number of years, Jenssen hosted a radio show on Studentradioen in Tromsø, spinning a mix of Ambient and Techno. In between tracks, he delivered what he describes as "small astronomy lectures", talking about quasars, pulsars and imploding galaxies. The show was called *Bleep Culture* and it pretty much sums where this LP was coming from.

⊙ **Patashnik**   Origo Sound/R&S, 1994

Weird, trippy and seductive, the second Biosphere album was a major landmark in European Techno. It still sounds like it was made tomorrow.

The Black Dog

T he story of The Black Dog is the story of how three into one won't go. It began in 1989, when Ken Downie, ex-Naval radio operator and friend of The KLF's Jimmy Cauty placed an ad in

Music Technology magazine for like-minded individuals to make House music. Ed Handley, a hip-hop fanatic, made contact; the two started working together, then a month or two later, he brought a friend, Andy Turner, with him. Two became three and The Black Dog was born.

Determined to communicate on their own terms, they started their own label, Black Dog Productions, and released three limited edition EPs – **Virtual**, **Age of Slack** and **The Black Dog**. By some quirk of fate, however, they found themselves part of an emerging electronic hierarchy that included B12, Kirk Degiorgio's ART label (for whom they recorded "Nort Route", still one of the most beautiful electronic tracks ever) and Rephlex. By now they had signed to GPR Records and between 1991 and 1992 released three more sublime EPs – **Parallel Squelch**, **Vir^{2}l** and **Vantool**.

But the first cracks were beginning to show. Music released under The Black Dog banner had always been largely individual efforts, recorded under different pseudonyms – Balil (Ed), Atypic (Andy) and IAO (Ken) – then subjected to the collective critical process. As long as it was three individuals, it remained an equal partnership. Plaid, however, was Andy and Ed, a collective unit in its own right. They wanted their music to stand alone, and, just as the trio signed to GPR, they released an album, **Mbuki Mvuki** (1991) on Black Dog Productions.

On the surface, however, they went from strength to strength, appearing on Warp's seminal LP **Artificial Intelligence** (1992), and becoming leaders of the so-called "Intelligent Techno" movement. Featuring appearances from all their aliases, **Bytes** (1993) was a bewildering journey through mercurial jazz, avant funk, deep-space electronics and cyber-tribal rhythms. Even more extraordinary was the GPR LP of the same year, **Temple of Transparent Balls** (1993). Their first collection of all-new material, it filtered everything on its predecessor further through dub and hip-hop machinery, creating something wilfully experimental, yet somehow almost painfully beautiful.

With two further EPs on Rising High in 1993 and 1994, The Black Dog had gone from self-imposed obscurity to high visibility. Behind the scenes, however, it was all falling apart. The Warp follow-up, **Spanners** (1995), found its way into the Top 30 and many best-of lists for that year. But in truth, it was a disappointing, regressive, episodic affair, stumbling between genres rather than gliding. Never before had a Black Dog record sounded so obviously like three individuals simply sharing studio space. With hindsight, their decision to split in June 1995 should have surprised no one.

While Ed and Andy carried on as Plaid, Ken continued as The Black Dog, and in 1996, released **Music for Adverts (And Short Films)**: 26 fleeting electronic mood sculptures, it was more like a sketchbook than a finished canvas. Parting company with Warp shortly after, he was next heard on Warners subsidiary ESP, remixing the *Bullitt* theme in 1998 on the back of the Ford Puma TV ad – an ironic move for someone who claimed to loathe marketing. **Babylon** (1999), a collaboration with vocalist Ofra Haza, proved to be little more than a couple of original electronica/Middle Eastern pastiches, remixed by a brace of artists to no great effect. It seems, sadly, that the man who was so determined to go it alone can't function without the assistance of others.

⊙ Temple of Transparent Balls   GPR, 1993

From the opening digital skank of "Cost I" to the closing circuit board tears of "The Crete That Crete Made", this is an album that took every single strand of modern music, mixed it all up and produced something that sounded like nothing else on the planet.

Peter McIntyre

55

Bochum Welt

G ianluigi Di Costanzo started out playing classical piano, began
collecting rare analogue synths at the age of 14, confesses to a
love of Shakespeare and Oscar Wilde and is currently studying science
at the University of Milan. He has worked with Thomas Dolby's Headspace Interactive Technology as a composer and has also created the
soundtrack for his very own version of Pac-Man. He also makes Techno that's as much inspired by the synth-pop of Depeche Mode as it is
by the dancefloor.

Though his earliest releases, "JX1" and "Telestatt", appeared on
TRC/Warner Chappell, 1995's "Scharlach Eingang", his first single for
Aphex Twin's Rephlex label, was so accomplished that *NME* ran an
article claiming that Bochum Welt was just another of Aphex's myriad
alter egos. Perhaps it was the strangeness of the moniker that confused them, but in fact it's a combination of the German word for
"world" ("welt") and the name of a high-powered astral telescope.

"Scharlach Eingang" was followed by "Phial" on Axodya and "Les
Dances D'Etè" on his own Kromode label, but **Module 2** (1996), his
first album for Rephlex, offered a broader introduction to his talents.
Sleeved in deliciously retro computer game graphics, tracks such as
"Asteroids Over Berlin" and "Mechanique" updated Yellow Magic
Orchestra's "Computer Games" with arcade bleeps and crashes alter-
nately sheathed in gentle pop melodies and digital noise.

Desktop Robotics (1997) was a brilliantly rendered homage to the
proto-Techno of The Human League and Depeche Mode which wove
huge bass synth patterns through bubbling, weightless melodies,
although tracks such as "Leafs Brought By Wind" flirted with pretty
ambience too. The **Feelings on a Screen** EP which surfaced towards

the end of '97 was again an exuberant rewrite of Techno seen from the perspective of UK and Japanese synth-pop. Both "Greenwich" and "Fortune Green" were absurdly catchy, impossibly beautiful pop moments that sounded as if OMD had written "Electricity" in downtown Detroit instead of Liverpool. The title track, with its mournful Walter Carlos synth vocals and Depeche Mode stylings, sounded like Techno born out of a parallel universe.

Di Costanzo moved to the Elypsia label for the release of 1999's **Program 11** EP. Now dividing his musical career between composing Techno, opera and pieces for solo piano (jazz pianist Bill Evans is a big influence), Di Costanzo continues to swim against the currents of convention.

⊙ **Module 2**   Rephlex, 1996

Imagine if Kraftwerk's place in Techno's pre-history had been taken by Yellow Magic Orchestra and Depeche Mode and you'll have a perfect thumbnail sketch of Bochum Welt's compelling debut.

CJ Bolland

There's a story about CJ Bolland and his new sports car hurtling along the autostrade between his home in Antwerp and the airport in Brussels. As the needle on the speedometer crept towards 180 kilometres per hour, he turned to the white-knuckled journalist beside him. "We should be going a lot faster," he explained, disappointedly, "only I broke the turbo a few weeks ago."

Those familiar with Bolland's early records – under names like Sonic Solution, The Project, Ravesignal and Space Opera – won't be surprised by this thirst for speed. Bolland is, after all, known as the producer who accelerated the velocity of European techno to dizzying altitudes. Throughout the early '90s, Bolland was most associated with the R&S label and the amalgam of Belgian New Beat, industrial-strength Techno and embryonic Hardcore that informed his releases. Bolland's music had its closest antecedents in classic Joey Beltram records such as "Energy Flash" and Mundo Muzique's "Acid Pandemonium", though his own debut – The Project's "Do That Dance" – laid down the essential blueprint of his sound as early as 1990.

The arrival of the **Ravesignal III** EP in 1992 delivered Bolland's first bona fide classic in the shape of "Horsepower". A muscle-bound Techno update on the theme of Kraftwerk's "Trans-Europe Express", "Horsepower" was based around a memorable bass riff processed through a flanger to emulate the feel of the high-speed TGV train. R&S immediately commissioned an album and Bolland set to work with Cisco Ferreira (later of The Advent), but the record proved to have a difficult gestation.

Despite the problems, **The Fourth Sign** (1992) was a landmark release. Containing tracks such as "Spring Yard" which R&S initially considered too weird for release and the classic freak-out of "Nightbreed" (one of the LP's stand-outs together with its alter ego, the lush, elegiac "Camargue" – both tracks were developed from the same fundamental groove), **The Fourth Sign** was a reminder that – in the gap between Detroit's first and second generation – Europe was more than capable of evolving Techno's developmental trajectory.

Bolland continued to record records under his other aliases – notably Sonic Solution – but despite the success of **The Fourth Sign,** a schism between the producer and R&S developed. Eventually, "Electronic Highway", his first single from a new deal with Internal Records, emerged. The process of extricating himself from R&S seemed to have taken its toll on

Bolland's innovative talent. In place of the heavily narcotic atmospheres that threaded through his best work was an overwrought, almost baroque, emphasis on multiple layers of sound, melody and counterpoint. A fascination with the rhythms of Jungle was apparent, but hardly executed satisfactorily, while the flipside's "Starship Universe" easily laid claim to the dubious status of Bolland's worst track ever.

When it finally arrived, the follow-up to Bolland's ground-breaking first album confirmed the worst fears about the producer's new status outside R&S. **The Analogue Theatre** (1996) was hugely successful in commercial terms, but creatively it followed the same route as "Electronic Highway", masking dangerously flimsy ideas with a confusion of melodic parts and half-realised grooves.

⊙ **The Fourth Sign**   R&S, 1992

Bolland's ground-breaking debut has rarely been matched for its combination of pulsating dancefloor moods and weird, almost claustrophobic, atmospheres.

Max Brennan

I magine if Techno had been the product of an illicit liaison between Kraftwerk and Weather Report rather than Kraftwerk and George Clinton (as Derrick May so famously suggested) and you'll have a fair idea of where Max Brennan's music is coming from. One of a loosely connected group of UK producers – including Russ Gabriel, Ian O'Brien, Steve O'Sullivan and Kirk Degiorgio – whose interests lie in exploring the potential of a more organic Techno, Brennan is an idiosyncratic but innovative producer who has built a substantial cult fol-

lowing thanks to his releases as Fretless AZM, Universal Being, Maxwell House and, more recently, under his own name.

Brennan embarked on his musical career as a member of various local groups on the Isle of Wight, playing keyboards, bass or whatever instrumental vacancy was there to be filled. A restless eagerness for pushing the boundaries quickly led to solo experiments with live instruments and electronics. By 1994, he had alchemised much of what later became Fretless AZM's debut LP for Holistic and began sending out tapes that testified to his almost supernatural ability to craft weird, innovative soundscapes from a combination of machine-driven Techno and his own loose-limbed live playing.

Fretless AZM's **Ultimate Maxploitation** (1995) was an intriguing, highly idiosyncratic debut that sounded light years ahead of its time. The even more assured follow-up, **From Marz With Love** (1996), refined the ambitious, wildly eclectic template that Brennan had limned on its predecessor. Other directions beckoned on **Maxwell House** (1996), an album that sounded like Model 500 recreating Herbie Hancock's **Headhunters** somewhere in outer space, while Brennan also embarked on an ongoing collaboration with Rupert Brown (a former session drummer who'd played with, amongst others, Roy Ayers) as Universal Being.

Astral Cinema (1997) was a less boisterous, more reflective, affair laced with languid jazz breaks and basslines. Tracks such as "Framed In Funk" or the blissful "Rhythm In Bass" were tauter and more focused than previous efforts, but Brennan was still clearly on a radically different trip. A fact more than confirmed by the far-out **Oceans of Light** (1998), again on Holistic.

A subsequent deal with Tokyo's Sublime label resulted in the lustrous Tech-jazz of **Alien to Whom?** (1998) – Brennan's masterpiece. His ability to conjure dreams from machines has never sounded better than on tracks such as "1300 Milliseconds of Brass" or "Narita Express", while elsewhere his ambition to craft the perfect hybrid of synthetics and live playing came close to realisation. The album was his most significant critical success to date.

Brennan continues to patrol the outer perimeters of modern music, most recently on Universal Being's trippily jazzed and superb **Elephant Fusion** (1999).

⊙ **Alien to Whom?**   Sublime, 1998

"Keep pushing the boundaries," directed Brennan in the sleevenotes of this brilliantly realised Tech-jazz masterpiece. It was clear he was following his own advice.

Jörg Burger

With the exception of Mike Ink, his one-time collaborator, Jörg Burger is perhaps the best representative of the Cologne sound. The city's trippy mix of 303 Acid and syncopated funk (often forged without the use of MIDI or computers) was hugely popular on the international Techno scene throughout the first half of the '90s. Less linear and often quirkier than its closest cousin, Frankfurt Trance, the sound of Cologne still bore obvious traces of the original Detroit blueprint and, perhaps because of its proximity to Düsseldorf, Kraftwerk. After discovering Acid House in 1988, Burger recorded his first tracks within a year, two of which found their way onto Thomas Fehlmann's **Teutonic Beats** (1989) compilation.

In 1991, Burger found himself in Belgium. With Mike Ink, he set up the Trance Atlantic and Monochrome labels, releasing numerous 12"s by himself, his partner and the duo's collaborative ventures in various permutations, including the Science Wonder project. His first significant success arrived with the first Burger Industries release, "Vol. 1", but other tracks as Stardiver, Biosphere #1 and B. Movement recruited a solid underground following.

Burger relocated (with Ink) to Frankfurt in 1992, in order to work with Air Liquide's Jammin' Unit and Dr Walker. This resulted in a 12" as Structure, a self-titled LP as M.F.A. and two new labels, Structure and Blue. The most important development of his move to Frankfurt, though, was the arrival of a new alter ego, The Bionaut, which became his best-known guise in the years to follow. The name was introduced with **Everybody's Kissing Everyone** (1992), a psychedelic, electronic excursion that still contains some of his most fascinating work to date.

By 1993, Burger was back in Cologne, setting up his own record shop – Delirium – and yet another label, Eat Raw, which provided the platform for a second Bionaut LP, **Frugivore**. His passion for dance culture also resulted in a magazine – *House Attack* – which Burger ran for the next four years. With Mike Ink, he recorded **Ethik I** (1993) in addition to a cluster of 12"s on Structure and his self-titled Burger Industries album, mining the same seam of funky, 303-driven Techno which had come to define the Cologne sound by this time. Within the space of the next twelve months, he also completed the **Ethik II** album (this time collaborating with Cristian Vogel, Thomas Heckmann, Air Liquide and others), along with another handful of 12"s such as "Virtual Elvis" (as Burger Industries) and "Spartacus" (as The Sculpture).

With the promotional muscle of EMI behind it, Bionaut's **Lush Life Electronica** (1995) was a substantial commercial success. The album is still considered a classic by many, including Kraftwerk's Wolfgang Flür who rated it as one of his all-time favourite electronic records and subsequently recruited Burger to provide mixes for his post-Kraftwerk project, Yamo.

Burger/Ink's **Las Vegas** (1996) signalled fresh horizons, even though it was Burger's only full-length project for that year. Outside the studio, he was beginning to extricate himself from both the record shop and *House Attack* and plotting another new venture – this time a graphics and artwork agency called Granit. One of Granit's first commissions was for the pop-art sleeves for Burger's new project, The Modernist. The polished production, trippy atmospheres and resonant imagery (singles with titles such as "Dali Bop Horizon" and "Orange Coloured Sky", Rauschenberg-meets-minimalism graphics and weird, queasy syncopations) that distinguished the new material from previous outings provided Burger with his most refined outing so far in

Opportunity Knox (1997). Tracks such as "Hellbent to Paradise" and "Data Girl" were strange and accessible at the same time, merging synth-pop melodies, jazz chords and druggy, Techno grooves into a delirious, technicolour confection.

By 1999, Burger had parted company with EMI and moved to Sony who provided an umbrella for his own Popular Organisation which comprised three new labels: Popular Tools (for dancefloor-oriented material), Popular Music (for pop) and Popular Sound (for more experimental listening music). The first release from this new deal was another Modernist single, "Architainment", which emerged on Popular Tools.

⊙ **The Bionaut – Lush Life Electronica**   EMI/Harvest, 1995

Instinctively quirky, beautifully crafted and summed up perfectly by its title, this album is the sound of Burger surfing on inspiration.

⊙ **The Modernist – Opportunity Knox**   EMI/Harvest, 1997

Burger's witty, irreverent and arty project fused funk, electronic jazz and Cologne in equal measures to create a brilliantly produced, narcotic and magical LP.

Lisa Carbon

Towards the end of 1992, "Latin jazz queen" Lisa Carbon was living in Costa Rica, where a chance meeting with Atom Heart's Uwe Schmidt led to an ongoing collaboration as The Lisa Carbon Trio. Around the nucleus of Carbon and Schmidt (though there are unconfirmed rumours that ambient guru Pete Namlook has also contributed), releases as The Lisa Carbon Trio, Lisa Carbon & Friends and simply as Lisa Carbon have punctuated the '90s with a sound that more accurately defines the term "acid jazz" than anything that's emerged since the days when Miles Davis hung out with Jimi Hendrix.

The first Lisa Carbon Trio 12", 1992's "Opto Freestyle Swing" on Pod Communications, was a breathtaking rewrite of the Techno/jazz intersection that fused raw be-bop with electronics to imagine what Techno would have sounded like had it been born on 52nd Street around the time of The Three Deuces. **Stereococktail** (1993), by Lisa Carbon & Friends, emerged on Instinct Records, but ironically proved to be too far ahead of a musical climate dominated by the linear sequences of Frankfurt Trance and was overlooked despite its obvious quality.

There was a two-year hiatus before the arrival of The Lisa Carbon Trio's **Polyester** (1995) on the Rephlex label. Tracks such as "Paraphonic" or the superb "Jazz Device" were full of wild, soaring jazz leads and dizzily syncopated drum patterns while quieter moments, like the exquisite "Jambient", explored a less frenetic path through related territory. The album gained a cult following but, again, proved too progressive for mainstream acceptance.

A third LP, **Trio de Janeiro** (1997), appeared on Atom Heart's Rather Interesting label, refining the Jazz/techno amalgam with a suitably Latinate feel. The low-key nature of the release belied the fact that the dance scene had at last caught up with the inspired fusion of jazz and Techno, but it remains to be seen whether or not The Lisa Carbon Trio will ever be accorded the kind of acclaim that they deserve.

⊙ **Polyester**   Rephlex, 1995

Strange, inspired and often too good for words, this is an avant garde Techno classic which anticipated future developments in the genre by almost two years.

David Caron

Although he has released just a handful of tracks in the course of his career, Holland's David Caron is one of a select number of Techno producers whose reputation far outweighs their limited output. When the first Detroit Techno records filtered into Holland, Caron was still a student at the Utrecht School of Arts. His course of study there – which included music software design, algorithmic composition, music theory and sound design – seemed almost purpose-built for any aspiring Techno producer, but for someone of Caron's obvious talent it provided the creative apparatus to make the kind of records that have been labelled "works of genius" by a number of music journalists.

Though it didn't emerge until 1994, Caron's debut was one of the releases which helped confirm Eevo Lute's impeccable credentials on the European underground scene. The **Dawn** EP was a quietly astonishing record, full of achingly pristine surfaces and gently ethereal grooves that nestled somewhere between Brian Eno and Rhythim Is Rhythim. One of the tracks on the EP, "Fantasy on a Fantasy on a…", was immediately licensed by James Lavelle for Mo' Wax's 'Excursions' series and subsequently became an essential addition to any would-be hipster's record collection.

It took three years for another Caron release to emerge. "Any Day" seemed like the perfect title for Caron's *laissez faire* approach to a musical career that couldn't be described as anything other than intermittent, but tracks such as "Easy Afternoon" or "Dream Shower" proved that he hadn't lost his inspired touch.

Along with his brother Sandor (who has contributed to much of Caron's own output) and DJ Aardvärck, an occasional project, Relaxo Abstracto, has occupied most of the time Caron has since devoted to music. He has also worked with video artist Rachel de Boer on a series of multimedia improvisations besides establishing a day-time career designing and building web database publishing systems. His reputation as a producer of exquisitely crafted Techno gems seems to concern Caron only fitfully. "Latest Fantasy", his late 1998 release on the newly revamped Eevo Lute label, offered just four new tracks – including an ill-advised stab at drum 'n' bass – but was of sufficient quality to kindle even more expectation for a debut album which, given the evidence so far, will only arrive sometime in the next decade.

⊙ **Various Artists – Agenda 22**   Eevo Lute/New Electronica, 1994

Caron contributed two tracks from his first EP to this essential collection which documented the highpoint of Dutch Techno's creative surge.

Dave Clarke

D ave Clarke is a Techno evangelist. For some reason, however, his passion for Techno, or more particularly for the pioneering work of the genre's innovators, has resulted in a reputation for being "difficult" and "outspoken" during a time when DJs were more celebrated for their drug consumption than their abilities behind the decks. Things have steadily shifted in Clarke's favour though, in part due to the creative and commercial success of the series of singles which began with "Red 1" and a number of ground-breaking remixes – particularly for Felix Da Housecat's Aphrohead project.

But it wasn't always this way. Back in the days when Clarke and his partner, Laura Jane, were running their Magnetic North label, providing a platform for emerging producers such as Russ Gabriel, Cristian

Vogel and Adam X, "Techno" was a word that was steadily being excised from the music journalist's lexicon. Dave Clarke kicked back. His own productions on Magnetic North, under names such as Directional Force, Graphite and Ortanique were fierce, unapologetic missives that touched base with the original vibe of Atkins, May and Saunderson or, in the case of Ortanique, the serene Techno romanticism of Carl Craig and Kenny Larkin. He wrote reviews for magazines like *Generator* and *Mixmag Update*, sifting through piles of vinyl for releases that chose to innovate rather than replicate and his DJ sets

cut fire with an incendiary rush of forward-thinking grooves and hard-as-nails acceleration.

In 1994, Clarke released "Red 1" and "Red 2" on Eric Powell's Bush imprint. Drawing primary influences from the tougher perimeters of Kevin Saunderson's output, both singles swept across underground dancefloors and threatened to cross over into the mainstream. Their impact on the dance scene was immense and Clarke suddenly found himself being described as "the UK's foremost Techno producer".

It came as a surprise to many when he signed to Deconstruction – then home of pop/dance crossover acts such as M People and a number of Italo House one-hit wonders along the lines of Usura. Close observers recognised that for Clarke it was just the latest step in a long-term strategy designed to take Techno to a wider audience. The release of "Red 3" and the subsequent album, **Archive One** (1996), confirmed this logic, but the marriage with Deconstruction was destined to be less than happy and cracks began to appear in his relationship with the label.

Undeterred, Clarke refocused on his work as a globe-trotting DJ. Two mix albums, **Muzik Masters** (1996) and **X:Mix – Electro Boogie** (1996), provided snapshots of Clarke's powers behind the decks. But these were just a prelude to a lengthy hiatus which was notable only for a hectic DJing schedule and the release of another mix album, **X:Mix – Electro Boogie 2** (1998). A handful of remixes for Underworld, DJ Rush, Moby and even U2 proved, however, that Clarke's production career wasn't quite forgotten.

⊙ **Archive One**   Deconstruction, 1996

Singles like "Southside" and "No-One's Driving" were present and correct, even an abbreviated version of "Red 1", but this was a more considered debut than simply Clarke's greatest hits to date.

Co-Fusion

W hen one-time guitar-player Shuji Wada agreed to fill in for a sickly DJ friend one evening in the early '80s, it was the beginning of a love affair with dance music which has produced some of Japan's most unusual and eclectic Techno. Around the same time, Heigo Tani was making a similar name for himself behind the decks and, following their first meeting at a club they were both playing, the pair swiftly became friends.

As Techno began to gain in popularity in Japan, the duo moved into production, eventually releasing their first single – the self-financed "Jungler Grey" – to a positive and expanding audience. As Dark Eyed Kid, they recorded **Angelic House** (1993), an overlooked but worthwhile album that combined elements of House and Techno, while 1994 saw the release of "Atom" on the in-vogue Tribal America imprint. "Atom" became one of the year's most requested Deep House 12"s, but by then Wada and Tani had already moved on.

Their first single for the Sublime subsidiary Reel Musiq was "Frontier", a tougher, more self-consciously experimental offering than any of their previous outings, but it was the Electro-tinged "Diretta" which established the ambitious and eclectic sound which was to evolve on their debut album. **Co-Fu** (1998) was the perfect expression of the duo's philosophy. "Co-Fusion actually stands for Community Fusion," they explained to journalist Sarah Champion. "By that we mean we try to bring in different elements, different styles."

Alchemising breakbeat, jazz and funk with Techno, the album was an interesting, if not entirely successful, attempt to expand the genre's sonic possibilities. While "Jungler Gray" cross-fertilised swooping synthetic textures with the gently melancholic guitar of Vini Reilly's Durutti

Column, other tracks – such as the under-par "Early Summer Daze" or the chaotic breakbeat techno of "Cycle" – were less convincing hybrids. Nevertheless, Co-Fusion remain an interesting proposition and their best work makes it clear that, if they can resist the temptation to indulge their wackier instincts, they have the potential to deliver something truly ground-breaking.

⊙ **Co-Fu**   Sublime, 1998

Cutting Techno with shapes drawn from jazz (the gorgeous "Five Forty"), drum 'n' bass and the synth-pop of Yellow Magic Orchestra, Co-Fusion's hyperactive debut captures their madcap fusion principle perfectly.

The Connection Machine

Although their recorded output amounts to just a handful of singles, one remix and an album that has never been released, The Connection Machine are one of Dutch Techno's most enigmatic partnerships. Outside of Holland, their reputation is slight – pinned solely on a remarkable 1994 release for Carl Craig's Planet E label and the few rare import copies of the **Black Hole** EP on U-Trax which filtered out the following year – but they retain a curious fascination for Technophiles, partly because of the mystery which surrounds them and partly because the quality of their sparse catalogue hints at a genuinely revolutionary talent.

Jeroen Brandjes and Natasja Hagemeier first met in a Utrecht club in 1991, just as Dutch Techno was succumbing to the full-blown hormonal menace of Gabba. At first sight, they seemed an unlikely pairing – Brandjes was a veteran of several industrial punk bands, Hagemeier played classical piano, spinet and clavichord in venues more used to recitals than gigs – but they shared a passion for computers, electronics and dance music.

Inspired by classic Detroit Techno, they turned out a series of tracks for Drome Tapes under names such as Syndrome and Bitch & Bites. Late in 1992, their first recording as The Connection Machine, "Echoes From Tau Ceti", emerged, sandwiched between two Bitch & Bites offerings – "Recognised Pain" and the suitably spaced-out "Techdrea In Andromeda". **The Dreamtec Album** (1993) combined tracks from each of their different aliases including The Connection Machine's "X-Manray" which provided glimpses of the innovative and startlingly imaginative take on Techno that would surface the following year. The release helped to create a following for the duo in their native Holland, but it was a chance meeting with Carl Craig which led to wider cult status.

Combining the unruly magic of "Molly Is Autowarping" with the exquisitely crafted electronic subtleties of "Bitflower", **The Connection Machine** EP (1994) on Craig's Planet E label was a *tour de force* which provided convincing evidence of a major talent. 1995's **Black Hole** EP delineated an even more abstract and carefully shaped sound, but it was to be the last full Connection Machine release. A remix for Morgan Geist and a harder-edged release as Cray Emoticon followed soon afterwards, but the exceptional album they completed for Planet E never surfaced. Brandjes became increasingly involved in his career as a web designer, while Hagemeier has followed a high-profile path through computer journalism. The pair continue to record, however, and are planning a comeback to coincide with the millennium.

◉ The Connection Machine EP   Planet E, 1994

One of 1994's most alluring releases, the combination of Hagemeier's classical approach and the rough electronic funk supplied by Brandjes created an idiosyncratic rewrite of the Techno blueprint.

Cosmic Baby

I n 1987 Harald Bluechel entered the Berlin Art Academy, a move which brought him into contact with the city's emerging dance scene. He met up with many key players including Tanith, Westbam and Kid Paul, though, initially at least, he concentrated on composing soundtracks for radio plays.

With Moony Jonzon, a well-known DJ on the Berlin scene, Bluechel began recording as Futurhythm (and later as Veinmelter), a collaborative project that was to continue throughout the early '90s. Another collaboration, this time with Kid Paul as Energy 52 (though Bluechel often remained uncredited on releases), began with "Take Me Higher" in 1991, eventually resulting in the commercially successful "Café Del Mar" single two years later.

In 1992, Bluechel – under the name Cosmic Baby – signed to MFS Records and began preparing his first LP, a 74-minute concept album that suggested Berlin's club scene hadn't quite managed to eradicate the progressive influence of Tangerine Dream. **Stellar Supreme** (1992) was hailed by some as a masterpiece and provided a solid foundation for Cosmic Baby's reputation as one of German Techno's most intriguing auteurs.

Work with Paul van Dyk as Visions Of Shiva proved to be equally well-received. Their first single, "Perfect Day", was acknowledged as a seminal moment in the forward trajectory of the dance scene, though

CARL COX · TECHNO

after a second release, "How Much Can You Take?", the partnership dissolved in bitter circumstances. The break-up of Visions Of Shiva encouraged Cosmic Baby to look for another label, and in the autumn of 1993 he left MFS to sign with Snap's Logic imprint. This resulted in a commercially successful single, "Loops Of Infinity", and a subsequent album, **Thinking About Myself** (1994). A second, often overlooked, Logic album, **Futura** (1995), emerged, comprising a soundtrack that had been composed for a performance by the Pyro Space Ballet.

Fourteen Pieces – Selected Works 1995 (1995) was the first major release on Cosmic Baby's own Time Out Of Mind label. The title was a reminder of both Bluechel's classical beginnings and his desire to cement his reputation as an auteur along the lines of Aphex Twin, whose **Selected Ambient Works 85–92** provided an obvious conceptual, if not sonic, reference point. The album marked the high point of Cosmic Baby's solo career as the dance scene increasingly shifted the focus of its attentions elsewhere. A subsequent release on Intercord, **Heaven**(1998), was largely ignored.

⊙ **Fourteen Pieces – Selected Works 1995**   Time Out Of Mind, 1995

The majority of Cosmic Baby's releases haven't dated well, but this LP delivers a worthwhile guide to the racing sequences, linear rhythms and strident melodies which, at one time, made him a major player on the European scene.

Carl Cox

P laying his first major professional engagement (at Embassy's in London's Piccadilly, spinning Luther Vandross and Kashif) in

1981, Carl Cox has since become one of the UK's most consistently bankable Techno DJs. His **F.A.C.T** mix albums have sold a dizzying number of units, he runs a successful label (World Wide Ultimatum) and, along with his wife Rachel, an equally successful DJ agency (Ultimate Music Management).

Back when House music was first infiltrating the UK club scene, Cox was living in Brighton, running a sound system and playing warehouse parties. Danny Rampling asked him up to London to play Shoom (he played the first two, before he was quietly edged aside) and as Acid House swept towards rave, Cox found himself in the centre of it all. Before long he was the biggest draw on the rave scene – using three decks to mesmerise crowds with a wall of sound and energy that, even today, many still remember with awe.

In 1990, Cox embarked on his first studio endeavour. He claims to have made his debut single, "Success & Effect", in just five minutes but those who are close enough to him to spot his perfectionist nature maintain that this is just part of the extensive mythology that surrounds Cox. Within a year, Cox had signed a five-

ULTIMATUM / PHUTURE TRAX

album deal with Perfecto – as the Carl Cox Experience – and was playing PA's of his "I Want You Forever" single on the Radio One Roadshow.

The Perfecto deal stalled soon after and, as the scene grew harder and faster, Cox found himself playing sets that hovered around the 160–200 bpm mark. He was still a major draw, but as the intensity of hardcore rave entered an ever-upward spiral, Cox found himself playing alongside trance DJs like Sven Vath and decided enough was enough. He returned to the clubs, began playing House sets and plotting a new trajectory. It seems hard to imagine, at this distance, that Cox was ever an outsider. But in the weird mix of rave's fade-out, nosebleed hardcore and progressive house which dominated the UK's dance scene towards the end of 1993 and 1994, Cox struggled to fit in. The way forward was a return to his original raw amalgam of House and Techno and the label which he set up soon after.

The pressure of having one of the world's busiest DJ schedules has taken its toll on Cox's production career, though a highly successful mix album, **F.A.C.T** (1995), provided an opportunity for him to redefine his legendary turntable skills. **At the End of the Cliché** (1996), his official debut after more than a decade at the sharp end of dance music, was a fusion of sturdy, sometimes House-inflected grooves and laid-back Techno that had been recorded in the converted garden shed which functioned as his studio.

A second **F.A.C.T** album in 1997 threatened to eclipse even the runaway success of its predecessor, though **The Sound of Ultimate B.A.S.E.** (1998), a document of Cox's club night, was equally worthwhile. "Phuture 2000" emerged in April 1999, preceding the release of an album by the same name a few months later.

⊙ **F.A.C.T**   React, 1995

Cox in the mix, live and dangerous: skull-crunching beats, hard motorik funk and, naturally, lots of three-deck trickery.

Carl Craig

Carl Craig is the most influential of Detroit's so-called "second generation" of producers. A protégé of Derrick May, he has been a significant force – some might say the significant force – in dance music since the late '80s, when he was inducted into Rhythim Is Rhythim for a European tour and a number of subsequent recordings. Since then – under a variety of different pseudonyms and aliases including 69, Psyche, Innerzone Orchestra and Paperclip People – he has been a prime influence not only on Techno but also on House, drum 'n' bass and a number of electronic music's most compelling hybrids.

As a student at Detroit's Henry Ford College, Craig enrolled in an electronic music class after hearing early Techno classics such as Rhythim Is Rhythim's "Nude Photo" and Suburban Knight's "The Groove". Borrowing some equipment, he set to work in his bedroom, compiling weird and (since he didn't have a drum machine) beatless versions of Detroit's new dance sound.

After he was approached by a 17-year-old Craig with a tape of his tracks, Derrick May was flipped out by an emotional opus called "Neurotic Behaviour" which floated lush string chords over a nervously modulating synth sequence. He booked Craig into Metroplex Studios and the pair re-recorded the track with what was later coyly described as "D. May's customized drum programming". It was the beginning of a close association.

Craig's simultaneous debut releases – "Crackdown" as Psyche on Transmat and "Galaxy" as BFC on Fragile – materialised late in 1989. Both were warped, twisted and brilliantly inventive takes on the Techno blueprint. The releases that followed on Craig's own RetroActive label

– "Wrap Me In Its Arms", "As Time Goes By" and BFC's "The Climax" (which resurfaced in 1995 as the third Paperclip People single) – con-

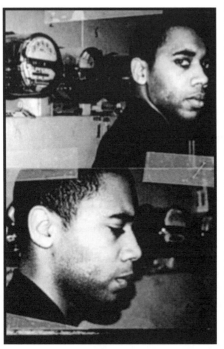

firmed that his talent was both unique and startlingly original. Financing the label with a job in a copy shop, he pushed the music in a starburst of different directions, drawing vivid new shapes with deceptively tricky beats and deep, sub-oceanic synthetics. When a fall-out with Damon Booker, his partner in RetroActive, led to the dissolution of the label, Craig simply moved on, swiftly setting up a new imprint as a platform for his own vivid articulation of electronic music.

When the new label, Planet E, announced itself on November 15, 1991 with the release of 69's revolutionary **Four Jazz Funk Classics**, Carl Craig was already establishing an unparalleled reputation on the underground dance scene as "the boy genius of Techno". But what was to come would be even more significant. It could be argued that the records which Carl Craig released up to, and including, his ground-breaking debut album, **Landcruising** (1995), almost single-handedly redefined the course of modern dance music. Junglists point to "Bug In the Bassbin" or "Please Stand By" as inspirational milestones in the evolution of drum 'n' bass, while House producers credit "Oscillator" and "Throw" as pivotal moments in the artistic resurgence of their music. And, without doubt, alongside Basic Channel and Underground Resistance, Carl Craig has been the most influential and consistently on-target artist working in experimental dancefloor Techno. He has produced breathtakingly romantic tone poems like "Dreamland" or "Microlovr"; been responsible for raw, blistering epics like "Nitwit" or "My Machines"; and stretched the art of the remix to its limits for artists as diverse as Tori Amos, Dan Bell and Incognito.

69's **The Sound of Music** (1995) and Psyche/BFC's **Elements 1989–1990** (1996) provided an essential round-up of Craig's early years. Both were radical albums but explored wildly differing directions, underlining the impressive breadth of Craig's abilities. As if to prove the point, Craig released another album (his fourth in two years), this time as Paperclip People. **The Secret Tapes of Dr. Eich** (1996) built on the phenomenal impact of singles such as "Oscillator" and "Throw" which had amalgamated structures from both House and Techno to reunite the splintered and increasingly specialised club culture of the mid-'90s.

More Songs About Food and Revolutionary Art (1997) was, in fact, the debut album Craig had envisioned before **Landcruising**. That plan had been swiftly altered when it became apparent that Warner Brothers (to whom Craig had signed late in 1994) would end up as the technical owners of some of his most influential and ground-breaking material. Rather than sign tracks such as "Dreamland", "Suspiria" and

"At Les" over to Warners, Craig had decided to complete another album for the label, which became **Landcruising**. The album he had been plotting in his head since the release of his first singles was therefore postponed until Craig had escaped his ties with Warner Brothers and was free to release it on his own terms.

The grandiose title hinted at the scale of Craig's ambitions, but was more than backed up by the music itself. The centrepiece of the album was "At Les" which still remains one of Techno's most compelling landmarks. Originally released on the seminal **Virtual Sex** (1993) compilation, "At Les" combined wildly syncopated rhythms and a backdrop of evanescent, pastel-shaded textures to create an extra-terrestrial be-bop symphony that was part heart-aching melancholy, part unfettered euphoria. Along with Kenny Larkin's "Tedra", it marked the apotheosis of Techno's romantic drift, proving not only that Techno was capable of conveying subtle emotive nuances but also that it had validity and meaning away from the dancefloor. Elsewhere, "Frustration", a collaboration with Derrick May, was a languid confection of dissolving distortion, atonal melodics and cadences wrapped in haloes of lo-fi retro-tech, while "Food and Art (In the Spirit of Revolution)" connected with the frenzied, gritty sequences of 69's "My Machines".

At a performance at Tribal Gathering in 1997 Craig recruited jazz musicians Rodney Whitaker and Francisco Mora (who'd played alongside jazz greats such as Max Roach and Sun Ra) and set about dismantling his sound and rebuilding it with live drums and double bass. The result was a fractured, mercurial fusion of searing be-bop and mutant Techno. The album which evolved from this performance touched on jazz, rap, soul and Techno. Innerzone Orchestra's **Programmed** (1999) was Craig's most fully rounded and ambitious project yet, with the producer conducting and directing a loose collective of musicians including Francisco Mora, jazz pianist Craig Taborn and Richie Hawtin. Tracks such as "Basic Math" or the eloquently jazzed versions of "Galaxy" and "At Les" stretched far beyond Techno's furthest outposts, striking a new base camp in precincts previously essayed by Herbie Hancock, Sun Ra and Miles Davis.

⊙ **Psyche/BFC – Elements 1989–1990**   Planet E, 1996

A round-up of early classics with extensive sleevenotes supplying anecdotes, recording details and a career autobiography.

⊙ **More Songs About Food and**
    Revolutionary Art   Planet E/SSR, 1997

From the fizzing opening bars of "ES30" to the sheer electronic bliss of "At Les", this is another essential Techno landmark. "Everything on this record, I just love to death," Craig once confided. "This is my ultimate album…"

⊙ **Innerzone Orchestra – Programmed**   Talkin' Loud, 1999

An ambitious fusion of jazz, Techno, soul and rap that sounds like the future just landed early. Lucid, inspired and deeply brilliant.

Dan Curtin

I t was during the early stages of a degree course at Kent State University that Dan Curtin took his first steps as a professional musician, playing keyboards in a punk band called Germ Free Adolescents. But when hip-hop broke out of the Bronx and began filtering across the Midwest, Curtin started messing around with turntables, chasing Electro and rap and hanging out with breaking crews. House music, initially at least, passed him by but a few years later, hearing the strange, alien cadences of Detroit Techno Curtin at last discovered a musical passion that was equal to his interest in astronomy and sci-fi.

Curtin's early releases such as "3rd From the Sun" and "Tales From the Second Moon" were remarkably assured, lacing an angular dance-floor groove borrowed from the original Motor City blueprint with a melodic sensibility that was drenched in the kind of yearning melan-choly that suggested either the pain of a heartbroken lover or the brittle dislocation of someone who longed to be transported to a distant galaxy. In 1992, Curtin set up his own Metamorphic imprint. Curtin invested early Metamorphic releases such as the **Planetary** EP and the **Space** EP with a unique quality that perfectly reflected his extra-terres-trial reveries.

Despite the promise of these EPs, few were prepared for the ambi-tious magic of **The Silicon Dawn** when it finally arrived in 1994. Tracks such as "Parallel" or "Population 2" kissed the same patch of sky as Black Dog or "Icon"-era Derrick May, but Curtin's ability to shape cool curves and liquid arcs with his music proved to be a compelling inno-vation. Years later, the album still stands up as one of the finest releas-es of a period which proved to be remarkably fruitful for Techno.

In the summer of 1994, Curtin teamed up with partners Stephen Cinch and Tatsuro Hayashi to open Deep Records, Cleveland's first specialist dance record shop. With Hayashi, he also began working on a side-project, The Purveyors of Fine Funk, releasing "Heights Trax", a stripped-down and more straight-forward dance amalgam than any-thing to be found in his solo repertoire. That partnership continued on "Heights Trax Vol. 2" before Hayashi dropped out to be replaced by Mike Filly and a more House-oriented sound for two subsequent releases before Curtin's eventual relocation to Switzerland at the beginning of 1998.

A compilation of Metamorphic tracks, **The Web of Life** (1995), cap-italised on the success of The Silicon Dawn and offered a good opportunity for Curtin's rapidly growing fan base to fill in the gaps. Inhabiting a space somewhere between the icy grandeur of his debut and the smokey warmth of his Strictly Rhythm material, **Art & Science** (1996) proved that Curtin was coming back to earth, albeit on a fascinating trajectory. Unfortunately, **Deception** (1996) proved to be less satisfactory. A collection of older releases, alternate mixes and remixes (by Kelli Hand and Ken Ishii), it plotted a less inspired course towards the dancefloor.

Over the next few years, Curtin focused on DJing and remixing, providing a series of stunning makeovers for artists such as Wayne Gardiner, Orlando Voorn and Ian Pooley. His return to the US early in 1999 coincided with the release of an exceptional new album, **Pregenesis**,

ROLAND GOY / FOTOSTUDIO LICHTBLICK

that saw Curtin pulling together the strands of his previous work – glacial, dislocated Techno, syncopated jazz percussives and languid late-night funk – in tracks such as "Bring It Back" and the brittle "Queen Street" which easily located themselves among his best work.

◎ The Silicon Dawn   Peacefrog, 1994

A spaced-out masterpiece full of sharp, digital cadences and crisp motorik grooves. An album that all would-be astronauts should own.

◎ Art & Science   Peacefrog, 1996

Twisting syncopated snares, wild modulating synthetics and fat bass into a dreamy, druggy cocktail where jazz, funk and Techno fuse, Curtin's second album is equally essential.

Cybotron

Cybotron occupy a unique place in the pre-history of Techno, responsible not only for providing the genre with a name (through their track "Techno City") but also for providing the first glimpses of the music that would eventually materialise fully formed in the mid-'80s.

When Juan Atkins arrived for his first semester at Washtenaw community college, he had at least part of this future mapped out on a cassette tape – the result of a summer spent recording demos on a rudimentary set-up. Another student, Vietnam veteran Rick Davis, was already a step further on. Davis had a collection of synthesisers and sequencers, and had been exploring his own version of Tangerine Dream's lush synthetic soundtracks. One of his tracks, "The Methane Sea", had even been used by The Electrifying Mojo to introduce his radio show. Sensing a shared interest, Atkins took his own synthesiser around to his new partner's studio and the pair began collaborating.

Central to their emerging world view was Alvin Toffler's recently published cybernetic philosophy treatise, *The Third Wave*. Toffler's theories were to emerge again and again in Cybotron's work, eventually leaking into the group consciousness of Techno itself. "The techno rebels are, whether they recognise it or not, agents of the Third Wave," intoned Toffler. "They will not vanish but multiply in the years ahead. For they are as much a part of the advance to a new stage of civilisation as our missions to Venus, our amazing computers, our biological discoveries, or our explorations of the oceanic depths." The impact of Toffler's thinking on Davis and Atkins had significant consequences for the new music they were edging towards.

When Cybotron's first single, "Alleys of Your Mind" on the self-financed Deep Space label, was released in 1981, black electronic music didn't yet have a name. A raw, experimental fusion of European electronica and Atkins' Parliament/Funkadelic fixation, the single reached the top of the local radio charts, securing Cybotron a major label deal with the California-based Fantasy Records.

Enter (1983) yielded a hit single in the shape of the seminal Electro cut "Clear", a more fully realised version of Cybotron's synthesis of Europe (the track owes a fair debt to Kraftwerk's "Hall of Mirrors" and to their 1981 **Computer World** album) and black American funk, but other tracks, such as "Cosmic Cars" and "Cosmic Raindance", clearly revealed moments of pure Techno.

A rift between Atkins and Davis had arisen even before the recording of **Enter** when Davis had insisted on recruiting a local music shop assistant, Jon Howesley, to play guitar. "I thought it was a retrograde step," Atkins noted drily. There were problems too when a follow-up single to "Clear" had to be chosen. Ironically, Atkins dismissed "Techno City" as a suitable choice. After being overruled, he decided to leave, taking with him some of the tracks he'd written for Cybotron – including "Night Drive (Time, Space, Transmat)" – to pursue a solo career which more definitively articulated his vision.

Davis continued to record as Cybotron, developing the portentous, less appealing aspects of the group's sound which had been apparent on **Enter**. By the time of 1993's **Empathy** and the subsequent **Cyber Ghetto** (1995) he was pursuing an R&B-flavoured direction that marked a full reversal of the group's original precepts. Atkins, on the other hand, went on to change the world.

⊙ **Clear**   Fantasy, 1990

The **Enter** album was renamed for this reissue to capitalise on Cybotron's biggest hit, though the addition of a later bonus cut, "R-9" released after Atkins' departure, adds little.

Daft Punk

I n 1987 Thomas Bangalter and Guy-Manuel de Homem Christo were just beginning high school. For Bangalter at least, a career in music was perhaps predetermined – he is the son of Daniel Vangarde, France's most celebrated disco composer and writer of Ottawan's 1980 worldwide hit "D.I.S.C.O". The pair quickly found themselves immersed in various school bands, eventually leading to their first semi-professional outfit, Darlin.

In 1992, Darlin were signed to Stereolab's Duophonic label and played some gigs in London, one of which *Melody Maker* reviewed, famously reporting that their music sounded like "daft punk". The epithet stuck and when Bangalter and de Homem Christo returned to Paris, they took the phrase with them. And that might have been that if Glasgow's Soma Records hadn't stepped in. After hearing some of the Daft Punk tracks in 1993, Soma offered the pair a deal early in 1994.

When **The New Wave** appeared in April 1994, the EP's standout cut, "Alive – The New Wave Finale", was such an accomplished fusion of Basic Channel's grinding sonics and the twisted Wild Pitch strategies of DJ Pierre that Soma's story about the record being the first release from "French teen Techno sensations" seemed pretty unpersuasive. With its warped 303 line, the second Daft Punk single, "Da Funk" (1995), led directly to a major label deal with Virgin. While negotiations with Virgin were taking place, Bangalter set up his own label, Roulé, and delivered a solo debut in the shape of "Trax on da Rocks". There was also another single on Soma – this time under the name Indo Silver Club – which emerged early in 1996. While preparing an album, Bangalter and de Homem Christo continued to focus on side projects. Bangalter supplied the "Spinal Scratch" single on Roulé, while de Homem Christo (working with Eric Chedeville as Crydamoure et Le Knight Club) recorded "Santa Claus" and the anti-summer hit "Holiday on Ice".

Homework (1997) combined the best moments from their brief but stellar career on Soma ("Da Funk", "Alive", "Rollin & Scratchin" and the Indo Silver Club release) with "Musique" (their contribution to the influential **Sourcelab 2** compilation) and a clutch of new tracks. It was an instant success, proving that the difference between independent and major labels lies not in the music, but in the heavyweight muscle to promote it. Daft Punk's singles – including "Around The World" and a re-release of "Da Funk" – proved to be equally popular, propelling the duo onto magazine covers, radio shows and television all over Europe. The promotional whirlwind helped to make **Homework** one of the most commercially successful Techno albums of recent years.

Bangalter and de Homem Christo's achievements as Daft Punk threatened, however, to be eclipsed by a track that Bangalter unveiled at the Miami Dance Conference early in 1998. When it was finally released in August on the Roulé label, Stardust's "Music Sounds Better With You" had all the hallmarks of a major hit. A collaboration between Bangalter and Roulé artist Alan Brax, the single was swiftly licensed to a major label, becoming a fixture both on the dancefloor and in the pop charts across Europe.

⊙ **Homework**   Soma/Virgin, 1997

Combining the best moments from their early releases with new tracks, this is the perfect introduction to their sound.

Sean Deason

Sean Deason began his career in Techno as a graphic artist, designing the label artwork for Carl Craig and Damon Booker's RetroActive label, Transmat subsidiary Fragile and A Guy Called Gerald's still-born Protection imprint. But after a visit to Derrick May's studio he soon switched from graphics to sonics. Deason began hanging out with Dan Bell and Kenny Larkin, sometimes working on tracks with them, sometimes just watching them work and learning as much as he could about the recording process. Richie Hawtin was another early supporter.

It was Kelli Hand, however, who eventually offered Deason a platform for his own music. As Code 3, he recorded the **Cyclops** EP for her Acacia label. A collaboration with Alan Oldham and Pen "Level A"

Jackson followed under the name X-313 (the superb **World Sonik Domination** EP) before Deason began mapping out plans for a label of his own. Deason's Matrix label began originally as a sub-label of Acacia. Hand provided the advice and the technical know-how, while Deason plotted a trajectory which was, so far, unlike any other Detroit label. Under a number of different aliases – Freq, S.I.N (it stands for "Sounds Intangible Nature") and Psykofuk – he swept unexpectedly from straight dance-floor Techno into more experimental moods and even a kind of Ambient hip-hop hybrid with assured ease.

Razorback (1996) offered both moments of rare beauty such as "New School" and the jagged phase-funk stylings of "Endomorphine".

However, it proved perhaps too expansive a debut to provide listeners with a clear-cut notion of Deason's sound. A second LP, **Heaven** (1997), this time under his Freq alias, was equally ambitious. It all came together on **Allegory & Metaphor** (1999), an exquisite mix of fragile ambience, slow motion funk and beautifully sculpted Techno. Though Claude Young made a guest appearance on "Zig", it was apparent that Deason had at last articulated the kind of creative instincts that had impressed Derrick May nearly ten years earlier.

⊙ **Allegory & Metaphor**   Matrix, 1999

The sound of an artist surfing a creative peak. Tracks such as "My World" and "2030 AD" rank amongst Deason's best work to date.

Lenny Dee

Bumping into Lenny Dee in the backstage area of the Hardcore raves at which he was a fixture during the '90s, you might be forgiven for thinking he'd wandered into the wrong event by mistake. The stocky frame, black leather jacket and shoulder-length black hair seemed to have more in common with a Black Sabbath gig than a Techno night. Dee chilled out by listening to Nirvana or Soundgarden and was fond of pointing out that he made no distinction between Techno and other forms of music. "To me it's all rock 'n' roll," he told journalist Mandi James in 1995. If Techno has an equivalent of heavy metal – a testosterone-fuelled, slightly barmy and less-than-subtle skeleton in its closet – then Lenny Dee is its figurehead.

He started out as a DJ playing disco in the early '80s. Connections with Electro and early House music followed – he recorded a number of House projects under names like Fallout and Looney Tunes – but he found himself increasingly drawn to European industrial outfits and, eventually, Hardcore Techno. The sound he began shaping dispensed with the searching abstraction of Detroit Techno and focused exclusively on exaggerating the music's fundamental groove to a peak of absurd simplicity, fusing speaker-threatening 4/4 kick drums with dizzyingly high velocities and cartoonish, often ear-splitting, riffs. The effect was as if Techno had been force-fed steroids and undergone a frontal lobotomy.

In the, as yet unsegregated, Techno scene of the early '90s – before the precise nuances which distinguished the diverse strands of the genre had been catalogued and defined – Lenny Dee played gigs alongside Jeff Mills and Derrick May but, as the decade wore on, found himself increasingly inhabiting the milieu of Dutch Gabba and European Hardcore.

Despite his growing dislocation from the hipper currents of Techno and a more-or-less universal media embargo, Dee's Industrial Strength label was hugely successful in commercial terms. Dutch Hardcore acts such as Disciples Of Annihilation, DJ Paul and Darien Kelly became mainstays of his "harder-faster-dumber" strategy though, as the '90s wore on, the label began to experience diminishing returns as the European rave scene collapsed entirely and Gabba contracted to a few isolated pockets of interest.

⊙ **Industrial Fucking Strength**   Industrial Strength, 1995

This collection might these days be described as "horrorcore" though – for a time – this was the sound that defined Techno in the '90s.

Deep Space Network

When David Moufang and Jonas Grossmann decided they needed a name for their embryonic recording project, the moniker they adopted was both a statement of intent and an apposite representation of their music. Together Moufang and Grossmann have charted territories so far unexplored by any other Techno artist, yet they remain largely unknown outside a select circle of journalists and enthusiasts. This is, in part, due to the limitations of Moufang's small, self-financed Source record label which has provided a home for most of the group's output, although some fans claim it is merely because Deep Space Network are too far ahead of current musical developments to achieve mainstream appeal.

There may well be some truth in the claim. Working from a nexus of influences that includes Juan Atkins, Miles Davis, Derrick May and John Coltrane, Deep Space Network have taken the original principles of Techno and extrapolated them far into the future, making the kind of bold imaginative leaps that characterised their prime sources. Tracks such as "Morphic Fields" or "Soylent Green" from **Earth to Infinity** (1992) sounded less like May's famous definition of Techno as "George Clinton and Kraftwerk stuck in an elevator with only a sequencer for company" and more like Techno and jazz imprisoned on a strange planet with only a six-month supply of DMT to keep them occupied. The results are both astonishingly beautiful and staggeringly brilliant. "Zenn La", the opening track from Deep Space Network's second album, **Big Rooms** (1993), used ambient bird song, spoken words, fluttering jazz drums and electronics to calm, seduce and hypnotise.

Deep Space Network's origins stretched back to Moufang and Grossmann's school days, when they were both pupils at the same school. In the wake of Acid House, Moufang and Grossmann met again in a local restaurant. "Jonas was the bartender," recalls Moufang. "He hated electronics, he only liked jazz. I played stuff to him and we ended up making a track together, which became an album. We didn't have the patience to send it off to record companies and so we put it out ourselves." So began Moufang's Source Records and the quiet, understated but definitive genius of Deep Space Network.

A live performance at 1995's Love Parade in Berlin was recorded and eventually released as **Traffic** (1996). Falling midway between the calm, instrospective Tech-jazz of Moufang's solo work as Move D and Deep Space Network's breathtaking creative surges, the new tracks suggested a gentler, more reflective style of innovation than had been heard on **Big Rooms**. This development was confirmed later that year with the release of **Deep Space Network Meets Higher Intelligence Agency**.

A new Deep Space Network album has been slowly evolving since the summer of 1997. Early reports suggest that it is a further development of the Deep Space Sound with Moufang playing live drums alongside the intricate tangle of coolly jazzed electronics which has become the group's trademark.

⊙ **Earth to Infinity**   Source Records, 1992

The title sums up the trajectory of this music. Tracks like "Clavius" and "Memphis to Mars" mark the furthest outposts of Techno's innovative orbit.

Kirk Degiorgio

S ince his first release in 1992 with the ground-breaking **Dance Intellect** EP, Kirk Degiorgio has been one of the UK's most con-

sistently on-target Techno producers. His records, under names like As One, Future/Past and Esoterik, have stretched electronic dance music both backwards (towards his original loves of jazz fusion, soul and Electro) and forwards (into a warm, embrasive, romantic future). He has masterminded two of the world's most respected underground labels, A.R.T. (it stands for Applied Rhythmic Technology) and its subsidiary Op-Art, releasing seminal tracks by Black Dog, Carl Craig, Steve Paton and Photek in the process.

Growing up in Ipswich, hanging out with Andy Turner and Ed Hanley (who later formed Black Dog with Ken Downie) and checking fusionists like Pacific Jam, Fiesta Fiesta and Ryo Kawasaki, Degiorgio began picking up spots as a DJ at local breakdance contests in the wake of the Electro boom, eventually setting up his own club, Sweat. He headed to London in the late '80s and found himself immersed in the House and Techno scene. After a 1991 record-buying trip to Chicago and Detroit, where he met Juan Atkins, Kevin Saunderson and Neuropolitique's Matt Cogger, Degiorgio sold off his record collection and began buying his own studio equipment. In the subsequent months, he recorded the **Dance Intel-**

lect EP for B12 and Future/Past's inspired "Clinically Inclined" single for Carl Craig's Planet E, but the most significant indicator of his talents was a track composed for his girlfriend. "Amalia" featured on the first A.R.T release, a joint venture between Degiorgio's As One and Future/Past projects and Black Dog's Balil and Atypic alter egos. A lovelorn confection of sighing strings and syncopated percussives, "Amalia" was closest in feel to the most romantic moments of Carl Craig's output, presaging the imminent arrival of the UK's so-called "Intelligent Techno" movement.

The label's already enviable reputation progressed even further with the release of **The Philosophy of Sound and Machine** (1992). Featuring artists such as Black Dog, B12, Aphex Twin and Mike Dred alongside Degiorgio, the album quickly achieved classic status and proved a key factor in developing a Detroit-oriented, highly experimental shift away from the dancefloor among a number of emerging UK producers.

David Toop described the music on Degiorgio's debut album, **Reflections** (1994), as "a cool world of warm sound". Drawing inspiration from Detroit techno, his travels in Israel and a musical heritage that spanned from Juan Atkins to Flora Purim and the Mizell Brothers, Degiorgio crafted beautiful, elegiac soundscapes with taut rhythms and lush strings. Exceptional tracks like "Shambala" and "Majik Jar" testified to a depth of vision and talent which belied the fact that he'd only been making music since 1991.

As One's **Reflections** was quickly followed by **Reflections on Reflections** (1995) on which a number of like-minded producers provided their own versions of Degiorgio's originals. The subsequent **Celestial Soul** (1995) was, however, relatively overlooked despite signalling a considerable creative step forward. **The Art of Prophecy** (1996), released on the French label Shield, was a *tour de force*. An exquisite mix of jazz rhythms and digitally spiked Techno, this was Degiorgio's finest long-player to date and marked the culmination of his search to find a suitable synthesis between the two genres. It was followed, a year later, by the outstanding **In With Their Arps and Moogs and Jazz and Things** (the title was borrowed from a poem on the back of Johnny Hammond's **Gambler's Life** album) which pushed even further away from 4/4 structures towards expertly programmed jazz loops and breaks.

The release of **Check One** (1996) — a superb mix album which combined tracks from Photek, Carl Craig and Stasis along with classic moments from jazz fusionists such as Weather Report, Joe Henderson and Julian Priester — offered a persuasive argument for Degiorgio's frequently stated belief in the parallels between Techno and jazz attitudes. So close were the musical strategies articulated on the album that it was often hard to tell where the Techno stopped and the jazz began. A second mix album, **Synthesis** (1998), was essentially a continuation of the agenda on **Check One** , combining tracks by Degiorgio, Herbie Hancock and Sun Ra.

Planetary Folklore (1997), Degiorgio's first album for Mo' Wax, marked a shift away from purely electronic experimentalism towards a fusion with acoustic instruments. Ian O'Brien was drafted in to play guitar on "Another Modal Morning", while elsewhere Carl Craig, cor anglais player Sarah Prosser and saxophonist Pete Lucas made guest appearances. It was another astonishing release and confirmed, if there had been any doubt, that Degiorgio was surfing an impressive creative peak which looks set to continue with his latest venture, As One presents The Offworld Ensemble.

⊙ **As One – In With Their Arps and
   Moogs and Jazz and Things**   Clear, 1997

Degiorgio alchemises with funk, jazz, Techno and Electro to create one of Techno's all-time masterpieces.

⊙ **Kirk Degiorgio – Check One**   Xtreme, 1997

Once described as "the best mix album ever made", this is an essential buy for anyone looking to explore the intersection of jazz and Techno.

Jay Denham

Jay Denham has had two distinct careers in Techno. During the late '80s in Detroit, as a protege of Derrick May, Denham recorded for Fragile, KMS and 430 West crafting classics such as "In-Sync" (under the name Fade II Black) and "Survival Instinct" (under the name Vice). A widely publicised fall-out with May led to Denham's subsequent departure from the Detroit scene and a lengthy hiatus until the launch of his own Black Nation label with the **Birth of a Nation** EP late in 1993.

Denham grew up in the small college town of Kalamazoo, midway between the twin centres of Chicago and Detroit. Originally a hip-hop DJ, his frequent visits to Imports Etc (the influential Chicago record store) brought him into contact with the raw, electronic sound of the early DJ International catalogue. His first studio experiments were attempts at reproducing the frenetic, beat-heavy, jack sound which was sweeping through Chicago, but he quickly gravitated towards Techno after hearing Rhythim Is Rhythim's "Nude Photo".

Denham met Anthony "Shake" Shakir at a party and the pair decided to pool their musical equipment in order to work on tracks. It was Shakir who passed Derrick May a tape of Denham's early material, leading to a move to Detroit and – under May's auspices – his eventual recording debut on Virgin's follow-up to the ground-breaking **Techno! – The New Dance Sound of Detroit** compilation. Denham's sound developed quickly into a mix of heavy, jack-style drums and Detroit Techno bass and synth-lines that reflected the twin influences on his hometown. His first release for the Transmat subsidiary Fragile, Fade II Black's "In-Sync", was instantly hailed a classic.

After a fall-out with Transmat and recordings for both KMS and 430 West, Denham returned to Kalamazoo and spent his wilderness years bringing up his three sons and holding down a job at the Coca Cola plant. His return to recording was relatively low-key – just a few hundred pressings on the self-financed Black Nation label – but marked the beginning of a journey back towards the centre of the Techno scene. The overtly political radicalism of Black Nation releases – titles included "White Flight", "Race Riot", "A Day of Atonement", "Player Hater" (a condemnation of gangsta rap) and "Blackazhell" (an update of James Brown's "Say It Loud I'm Black and I'm Proud" riff) – was only matched by their sonic radicalism and the label soon gained a cult following.

Behind the decks, his uncompromising style – somewhere between Mills, Atkins and DJ-T1000 – soon developed a solid reputation. In Europe, particularly, Denham swiftly became a more-than-reliable guest, which resulted, first, in an ill-fated deal with Belgian label Elypsia (only the **Dilemma** EP was ever released) and then in a more enduring relationship with the Munich label Disko B. **Escape to the Black Planet** (1998), his debut album for the label, was the perfect expression of Denham's hybrid sound – fierce, chunky drums allied with angular, abstract minimalism – though it was a relatively low-key release. Denham has now relocated to Munich, partly due to his hectic DJ schedule across Europe, and is currently preparing a new album.

⊙ **Escape To The Black Planet**   Disko B, 1998

Tracks like "The Battle" and "Ground Zero" are vintage Denham, a topography of minimal fusions which blends both Chicago and Detroit into a compulsive mix.

Desert Storm

Much has been made of Techno's supposedly apolitical stance. The truth is, however, that Detroit Techno was born out of an anti-establishment, positive mood that has since fuelled a number of vibrant strands in dance culture, from Spiral Tribe's free party ethos to the anti-CJB singles of Autechre and others. In the UK, Techno's outsider status manifested itself most spectacularly at Castlemorton. But other free party organisations had already coalesced in cities all over

GLYN ROBERTS

the country. Throughout the early '90s Glasgow's Desert Storm were responsible for a series of legendary after-hours parties and warehouse get-togethers that articulated the same anti-establishment feelings which had characterised the emergent Techno culture in Detroit.

Better described as a sound system than a band, Desert Storm didn't set out with the intention of making records. In fact, they started out just jamming sets together during parties. But then the notion of free parties captured their imagination. As spokesman Keith Robertson explained: "What we are trying to do is give people a good time outside of the normal, profit-oriented club scene. We want to change the idea of clubs so that people become actively involved in helping to create their own entertainment."

Early in 1994, members of the Desert Storm collective were charged with "the reckless and culpable promotion of a rave or similar social gathering." The consequences ranged from six months' imprisonment to a £2500 fine. With no money to pay the potential fines or replace the equipment which had been confiscated at the time of their arrest, they decided to make a record – as a means of both publicising their plight and garnering some much-needed income. "Desert Storm/Scoraig '93" developed from live jams with a 303 in between their DJ sets. It was part self-defining anthem, part tribute to a free party they'd played the previous year, but the bass-heavy Trance Techno was familiar to most who'd attended other Desert Storm parties in impromptu venues which, by this point, had included aircraft hangars, warehouses and barns.

The release had the desired effect, but it also helped to raise the profile of the UK's draconian legal assault on aspects of club culture which had, as yet, to infiltrate mainstream conciousness. When, later in 1994, Desert Storm began a series of missions to Sarajevo which were to continue over the next eighteen months, it became impossible for the authorities to view their actions in anything other than the spirit in which they were intended. Desert Storm's free parties, it seemed, had provided an important lesson in free speech.

◉ **"Desert Storm/Scoraig '93"**   Soma, 1994

Tough, Trance-ish shapes and bangin' drum patterns that anticipated the free party scene's eventual conversion to Goa.

Dopplereffekt

I n the early 1980s, Detroit's volatile youth culture experienced an extraordinary transformation that was unparalleled anywhere else in America. Taking their cue from upmarket, aspirational magazines such as *L'Uomo Vogue* and *GQ*, movies such as Paul Schrader's sumptuously shot *American Gigolo* and a series of European records (centred on Kraftwerk but also including Italian groups Alexander Robotnick and Kano, Belgium's Telex and Les Liasons Dangereuses and the obligatory Cerrone and Moroder cuts), lifestyle-conscious teenagers began formulating their own, unique scene. The mood was defiantly Europhile, the music – which came to be described as "progressive" – a dizzying mix of synthetic hooks, heavily accented vocals and machine rhythms interwoven (as Dan Sicko points out in his essential guide to Detroit Techno's prehistory, *Techno Rebels*) with the hard Midwestern funk of George Clinton, Zapp and the Ohio Players.

The progressive scene was Techno's immediate precursor – in fact, by 1981, progressive DJs already had access to two of the records which would become crucial to Techno's trajectory, Cybotron's "Alleys of Your Mind" and "Sharevari" by A Number of Names – although most traces of its existence had become obscured by the time Metroplex,

Transmat and KMS releases began finding their way into Europe during the late '80s. A few surviving elements, however, can still be traced, most notably in the case of Dopplereffekt, the group formed by Rudolf Klorzeiger, Kim Karli and William Scott.

Apart from the evidence of a handful of releases, details about Dopplereffekt are sketchy. They don't do interviews, the location of their studio is veiled in secrecy and even other artists in Detroit have rarely seen all three of the group's members together at the same time. The few grainy photographs which exist, depict a trio kitted out in identical uniforms of black tie, white shirt and black trousers maintaining the kind of stone-faced *hauteur* that will be familiar to anyone with more than a passing acquaintance with the late '70s/early '80s album sleeves of a certain electronic group from Düsseldorf.

Unsurprisingly, Dopplereffekt's music also reflects the prime influence of European synth pop from a time before the legend "Extended Dance Mix" began appearing on record sleeves. Most of their tracks (even the 12" singles) barely scrape the four-minute mark, some – like the classic "Porno Actress" – last for only two. Draped in vocals thick with a pseudo-German accent, their brand of mutant, militant Electro (collected on two vinyl-only albums, **Infophysix** (1997) and **Fascist State** (1998)) is sometimes little more than an astonishingly raw rewrite of various Kraftwerk hits ("Numbers", "Home Computer", "Pocket Calculator"), but the best Dopplereffekt releases can be vividly compelling, fusing their trademark motorik groove with inspired combinations of melody, syncopation and fiery intensity.

⊙ Infophysix   Dataphysix, 1997

Anyone who's been in the presence of a decent DJ during the late '90s Electro revival should be familiar with tracks such as "Speak & Spell", "Porno Actress" and "Voice Activated". If not, then **Infophysix** constitutes the perfect Dopplereffekt primer.

Tony Drake

While Detroit's prime musical export over the last ten years has been principally aimed at the dancefloor, there have been a few notable exceptions. Tony Drake is one of them. As the '80s segued into the '90s, Drake left Detroit to live on a communal farm in Virginia. Though he'd known Derrick May in the days before Transmat had even set up for business and had close ties with the Techno scene's inner circle, his background in visual arts (he's an accomplished painter) and his increasing fascination for the more acoustic territory of new age ambience separated him from the group of producers who were responsible for the music's initial thrust into the world. Drake made his own highly distinctive music, though, even releasing a self-financed cassette album in 1992. For a time, he returned to Detroit, but after the sleepy environs of Virginia he found life there "just too hectic" and settled on the town of Mount Pleasant in central Michigan. Once there he found a part-time job in a record store to finance both his painting and his music.

That's where the story might have finished if it hadn't been for a chance encounter with Neil Ollivierra, a mutual friend of both Drake and May from the days when Detroit Techno was still a phenomenon waiting to happen. Ollivierra knew that May was looking for new material for the Transmat label and remembered that Drake also made music. He asked for a tape and Ollivierra was astonished by what he heard. Against a backdrop of sweetly pastoral electronics laced with Drake's bass-playing (eerily reminiscent of one-time Eno sideman and fretless pioneer Percy Jones), the music predicated an alternate vision of Techno – one filled with a seductive romance. **Texture** (1996) was an astonishing release. Tracks such as "These Lips of Gold" or "In the

Hearts of Angels" merged chilled pianos and hypnotic rhythms with an almost orchestral grandeur, delivering an irresistible combination of ambience, funk, classicism and Techno. Unsurprisingly, the critics fell in love with it instantly.

TRANSMAT RECORDS

Despite the acclaim, little has been heard of Drake since. Rumours of a new album – tentatively entitled **Music for a Blue Room** – have circulated and Drake contributed two tracks, "To Touch You" and "Reflection", to the Transmat compilation **Time:Space** (1999). Whatever happens next, this quietly compelling and accomplished artist deserves further attention.

⊙ **Texture**   Transmat/
    New Electronica, 1996

Laced with delicately hypnotic rhythms and extra-terrestrial harmonics, Drake's remarkable debut feels like Detroit Techno stripped of its all-pervasive beat and shot through with the soft, evanescent melodies of Claude Debussy or Erik Satie.

Mike Dred

nce described as "the Jimi Hendrix of the TB-303", Mike Dred has the unique distinction of being the first artist signed to Richard James and Grant Wilson Claridge's fledgling Rephlex label. In fact, his early recordings – as Kosmik Kommando, Universal Indicator and Chimera – were so impressive that R&S set up the Diatomyc label as an exclusive platform for his productions. Despite this, he remains a distinctly underground phenomenon in the UK, though his frequent live performances and DJ gigs in Europe and, more recently, the USA have contributed to a passionate cult following.

He got the DJ bug early, running mobile discos with his brother while still at school and he describes his route into Acid House as "the usual one – disco, punk, electronic pop, hip-hop and, after that, House and Techno". His first solo release, "Rock the People", was an anonymous white label that leaked out in 1991. Within a year he'd signed to Rephlex and was working on tracks for the **Clear** EP and recording live gigs around the Lowestoft area for eventual inclusion on the double Kosmik Kommando set, **Freaquenseize** (1993).

Back then, the Kosmik Kommando sound was a trippy mix of syncopated 808 rhythms and twisting tangles of counterpointed Acid. These days, Dred reckons **Freaquenseize** "sounds quite rough because it was all done live", but listening back to tracks such as the achingly pretty "Lost Horizon" or the superbly funky "Peace and Love" it's not hard to imagine Dred suspended, in a state of heightened consciousness, somewhere between Chicago and Cologne.

A series of singles for Diatomyc – including "Sensory Deception" (as Machine Codes) and "Mindpatching" (as DJ Judge Dred) – followed, but it was his Kosmik Kommando contribution to ART's ground-breaking 1993 compilation, **The Philosophy of Sound and Machine** (also featuring Black Dog, Kirk Degiorgio, Aphex Twin and B12), which located Dred perfectly. "Remember the Feeling" was a weirdly beautiful outing, full of drifting funk and an unsettled spaced-out vibe which anticipated the expansive brilliance of the **Macrocosm** EP released by R&S in 1994.

Dred set up his own Machine Codes label towards the end of '93 to provide an outlet for his more experimental material. Opening with the **Fu Chin Ra** EP, Machine Codes has so far delivered only eight releases, though it did provide Dred's introduction to Peter Green, with whom he recorded **Ming's Kitchen** (1996) and the subsequent Rephlex album, **Virtual Farmer** (1998).

First Machine Codes 93–97 (1997) offered a worthwhile overview of Dred's output up to, and including, his collaborative ventures with Green, although the second, more abstract, half of this exhaustive five-LP set could have been replaced by his long-lost Rephlex album as Chimera, **Valley of the Spirits** (1994). Still working with Peter Green on an "acoustic Techno" fusion and preparing an eclectic album of Electro, hip-hop and Techno, Dred remains one of Techno's most intriguing talents.

⊙ **Freaquenseize**   Rephlex, 1993

Imagine if Larry Heard had grown up in Cologne instead of Detroit and Chicago and you'll be almost on target. Full-on acid genius.

Drexciya

One of the most revered and mysterious of Detroit's underground outfits, Drexciya steered a militant and uncompromising course through Techno's uncharted waters, amassing a significant cult follow-ing despite a relatively small number of releases and the veil of almost impenetrable secrecy which shrouded their activities. Between their inception in the mid-'80s and their final release, **The Quest** (1997), they agreed to be interviewed only a handful of times – though even on those occasions the duo refused to reveal their identities, preferring to operate under cover of anonymity.

Though they didn't release a record until 1991, the pair had been together since the mid-'80s, spending the years between the demise of Detroit's progressive scene and the eventual appearance of their debut single, "Deep Sea Dweller", experimenting and perfecting their sound. "There was a long thought process behind this group, a lot of different concepts and principles," they reported. "Before we even started putting stuff together we used to spend night after night talking about all kinds of deep concepts. That's where the energy comes from."

Drawing on a nexus of influences that stretched from George Clin-ton's P-Funk to Jimi Hendrix, Drexciya's sound was based on a single fundamental principle: experiment at all costs. Following the hardcore electronic futurism of "Deep Sea Dweller" their renegade transmissions adopted an increasing sonic urgency. The speaker-shredding grooves of "Bubble Metropolis" or the **Molecular Enhancement** EP, for exam-ple, employed street-level, low frequency Techno to deliver a fast rollercoaster ride through the dancefloor's final frontiers. Instead of the spaced-out Afronaut metaphors employed by other Detroit Techno producers, however, Drexciya's shorthand for the realm of the imagi-nation was a post-Atlantis underwater world peopled by different races. References to Drexciyans, Lardossens and Darthouven Fish Men flooded their brief catalogue. It's in these undiscovered precincts that Drexciya – in a logical parallel to Underground Resistance's "space is the place" codes – located their counter-culture images of a wide open dream-terrain, free from the prejudice, preconceptions and pre-programming of modern America.

Despite huge success in Europe, Drexciya remained consistently faithful to the sound of inner city Detroit. Their records combined the hard rush of 4am Techno with deep, sub-oceanic bass and tough, speed-thrill funk. But tracks like "Aquabahn" (from the **Unknown Aquazone** EP) or "The Countdown Has Begun" (from the **Aquatic Invasion** EP) also flirted with the quirky, crowd-pleasing shifts of classic Electro. Like Underground Resistance and Aux 88, their allegiance lay with the wild fusion of these elements which provided the Motor City's main soundtrack since the days when Electrifying Mojo and The Wizard ruled the airwaves.

Periodically disappearing from view as a way of excluding the outside world and focusing on new ideas and concepts – "we don't want to pick up anybody else's vibe so we cut off all communications" – Drexciya's career was punctuated by the kind of lengthy hiatus which, in the accelerated timeframes of dance music, has proven fatal for many artists. Yet, despite having released only a handful of heavily influential 12"s, they seemed to resurface after every self-imposed isolation re-energised and recharged. In 1996, they returned triumphantly from one such break with "The Return of Drexciya", a masterpiece of twisting, bumping grooves and brooding, kinetic energy before disconnecting once more.

In the summer of 1997, however, they announced it was all over. Their swansong was **The Quest**, a 28-track double album which included previously unreleased cuts alongside some of their most classic moments.

⊙ **The Quest**   Submerge, 1997

In the six years between their first and last releases, Drexciya consistently explored the outer reaches of Techno, fusing fierce conceptuals with hard, street-level grooves. **The Quest** is an essential reminder of why the rushing sequences and jitterbug rhythms of their music stretched out around the world.

808 State

I f Derrick May had released an album in the wake of seminal Techno classics such as "Nude Photo" and "It Is What it Is", chances are it would have sounded a lot like 808 State's **Newbuild** (1988). The album captured the Manchester trio of Graham Massey, Gerald Simpson and Martin Price mainlining on May's wild angular abstractions. On tracks like "Narcossa" or the deeply hallucinogenic "Flow Coma" they were surfing a wave of pure Detroit Techno that was all the more astonishing since no one else outside of the Motor City had yet captured the dark, hypnodelic nuances of the sound with quite such forceful precision.

On the face of it, 808 State were an unlikely proposition. Massey was a member of Mancunian avant-rock outfit Biting Tongues who'd garnered a small cult following in the early '80s; Price had run a record stall before opening Manchester's pioneering dance specialist shop, Eastern Bloc; and Simpson was a teenage gearhead who'd been making his own music for years in his mum's attic with a variety of cheap synths and home-made speakers. What brought them together was a shared love of the new music flooding in from across the Atlantic and finding its way onto the turntables at the Haçienda, Manchester's premier club. Soon the trio were putting on live jams under the name The Hit Squad, sometimes aided and abetted by a duo calling themselves The Spinmasters.

The Haçienda became a significant presence on **Newbuild**. The album had its roots in backing tapes the trio had put together for their gigs at the club and many of the tracks were recorded early in the morning after a night spent on the dancefloor, leaving the wired traces of MDMA deeply imprinted on the album's genetic code. **Newbuild** fed on the Haçienda's forward-looking soundtrack – while most clubs in London were still fixated on Acid House's lighter, less menacing precincts, the Haç's DJs were spinning a deeper fusion that centred on Detroit Techno and the harder, freakier end of Chicago House.

A second album, **Quadrastate** (1989), embraced a fuller, prettier sound (reflecting the period's influx of European House and Techno records with their more aspirational production values). Growing tensions during recording led to Simpson's departure to further his solo career as A Guy Called Gerald. The album yielded a chart hit in the shape of "Pacific State" largely thanks to Radio One DJ Gary Davies who had heard the track during a holiday in Ibiza and subsequently championed it tirelessly on his daytime show.

Following Simpson's untimely exit from the group (he had been largely responsible for writing "Pacific State"), Massey and Price recruited The Spinmasters duo of Andrew Barker and Darren Partington to work on the first album of their new deal with Trevor Horn's ZTT label. The resulting album, **Ninety** (1989), proved to be a transitional one as the two halves of the group attempted to reconcile their interests.

A collaboration with MC Tunes on "The Only Rhyme That Bites" and "Tunes Splits the Atom" provided 808 State with two more significant chart hits in 1990, though it was a resuscitation of a track from an earlier EP, **The Extended Pleasure of Dance**, that provided them with their most significant and influential hit. Re-released as a single in its own right towards the end of October 1990, "Cubik" was little more than a blistering riff and a thick, hyper-steroid groove, but it captured the altered state of rave perfectly. On its way to the upper reaches of the pop charts, it inspired a deluge of carbon copies and sent shock waves across the dancefloor that were still being felt years later.

EX:EL (1991) was, despite the inclusion of both "Cubik" and the subsequent Top Ten hit "In Yer Face", 808 State's glossiest production to date, prefiguring much of what was to come throughout the '90s. It featured collaborations with Björk (on "Qmart" and "Ooops") and New Order's Bernard Sumner (providing vocals on "Spanish Heart"), but the result was a fractured, unsatisfactory affair that seemed to be pulling in too many different directions all at once. After finishing **EX:EL**, Price decided he'd had enough and left to begin a new project under the name Switzerland.

With Price's departure the problems only intensified. Guest stars including Echo & the Bunnymen's Ian McCulloch failed to enliven the lacklustre **Gorgeous** (1993) and the inclusion of 1992's lumpen 808 State vs UB40 hit "One In Ten" seemed a clear indication that the group were in search of a new, more mainstream audience.

State to State (1994), a limited edition, fan-club-only release served only to highlight the parlous state of the group by oscillating between innovation and indulgence in almost equal measure. When **Don Solaris** (1997) finally emerged after a prolonged recording process – boasting a stellar array of guest vocalists including Manic Street Preachers' James Dean Bradfield – the album was remarkably short on ideas, over-produced and marked the creative nadir of a group who once numbered among dance music's most compelling prospects.

⊙ **Newbuild**   Rephlex, 1988

A firm favourite of Aphex Twin (hence this reissue on his Rephlex label) this is still 808 State's finest hour – jitterbugging synths, warped grooves and narco-hypnosis condensed into seven tracks of perfect Techno.

Electrifying Mojo

In the evolution of Detroit Techno, radio legend The Electrifying Mojo introduced an important survivalist gene — a kind of powerful anonymity and enigma that's been passed on to groups like Underground Resistance, Basic Channel and dozens of others. But before Mojo energised Detroit radio and the minds of young listeners, there was Charles Johnson, a young DJ who came to study law in Ann Arbor, Michigan by way of Little Rock, Arkansas.

After becoming disillusioned with the traditional approach to radio programming at WAAM, an AM rock station in Ann Arbor, The Electrifying Mojo began gathering up different music from around the station, especially the production room where Kraftwerk and Tangerine Dream records were being used as the bedding tracks for commercials and network bumpers. He added these hidden gems to an eclectic blend of new wave, funk, rock and soul — anything that fitted his mood.

Of course, being the nonconformist didn't always sit well with radio executives, and they often sent him packing. In fact, The Electrifying Mojo radio show (or "The Midnight Funk Association") has been on no less than six Detroit-area stations: WGPR, WJLB, WHYT, WTWR, WMXD and WCHB. During one dry spell, he even offered up content on the phone via 1-976-MOJO.

To this day, Mojo is still careful not to let his image or too much background information leak out and detract from his music and his message. He has even managed an entire career without ever being photographed. This is why most listeners only know him by his unmistakable deep voice and the elaborate theatrics that fill out his late-night shows. The Electrifying Mojo also made the traditionally "black" sounds of P-Funk, The Gap Band and Cameo popular among white audiences, gave white groups like B-52s and The J. Geils Band unprecedented African-American followings and single-handedly broke Prince's music in Detroit.

Most of all, The Electrifying Mojo is the unsung hero of electronic music, the DJ whose radio shows and far-reaching musical tastes created the climate for, and subsequently propagated the seeds of, Techno. When, eventually, his influence was rivalled on the airwaves by another anonymous DJ, The Wizard (who, in turn, drew himself on Mojo's eclectic, forward-thinking style), the dizzyingly intense pace of the music's forward trajectory was assured.

These days, Mojo presides over a lengthy Sunday night audience on WCHB (105.9 FM), and has been sitting behind the word processor almost as often as the microphone. His 539-page opus, *The Mental Machine*, a collection of essays, poems and thoughts, was published in 1995. Mojo is also currently working on a biography of former Detroit mayor Coleman A. Young.

Dan Sicko

Alec Empire

As you'd guess from his name, mythology is one of Alec Empire's specialities. His story is stuffed with narratives borrowed from terrorism, punk rock, corporate sabotage and the squatter's demi-monde. Sonically he's just as dramatic. His best-known material, recorded as part of the band Atari Teenage Riot, excels in the art of the maelstrom – core ingredients are usually superfast breakbeats, druggy vocals, protest lyrics, shouting, distorted guitar and furious digital programming.

In one version of his story, Empire reruns Malcolm McLaren's Sex Pistols scam. Atari Teenage Riot, he explained, purposely got themselves signed and dropped from major label Phonogram to get operating cash. Empire's personal biography is even more like classic rock/pop mythology. "At the age of eight," he writes, "I started playing the guitar, at ten I was one of the city's [Berlin] best breakdancers, and at 11, I witnessed rap, the first music I ever really liked, being commercialised like crazy… I hated everything and became a punk… I formed my first band, Die Kinder… At 16 we split up, disillusioned, because we found that punk was dead. That was 1988…"

What a tale – the *wunderkind* looking for a way to reach the world just as everything was about to change. In recent times only Marilyn Manson has told a better story. Empire recalls listening to Debussy, Schoenberg, Bartok and discovering Germany's underground Acid Techno scene. He played live at these parties and suggests they possessed the spirit of Germany's long-running squat-hacker-anarchy culture.

His use of language is fascinating – didactic, polemical, political – Empire can quote from members of the RAF (Red Army Faction) and revealed that his grandfather died in a Nazi concentration camp. "My whole life must be resistance," he has stated. His angry words became flesh and sound and image in 1992 when he formed Atari Teenage Riot together with Hanin Elias and Carl Crack. "We were formed because we could no longer identify with Techno as a band and did not want to be another DJ project which lasted for two 12"s and then that's it. Not music that is subordinate to the rules of the dance floor. Digital Hardcore – that is to say guitar samples, distorted breakbeats, 909, manga samples and shouting, very noisy. Riot sounds produce riots!"

Empire felt the German dance scene was racially exclusive – and noted neo-Nazi newspapers were celebrating Trance and Techno as positive youth movements. He responded with records like ATR's

"Hetzjagd auf Nazis" ("Hunt Down The Nazis") on Germany's Force Inc. label. Empire's relationship to the DJ-dance-drug culture is tenuous or at least unique – ATR, for example, owe much to the early '90s feminist-punk riot grrl movement and Empire sometimes DJs with dubplates he's cut using samples from riot grrl band Huggy Bear.

A confirmed maverick – he was one of the few German producers to use breakbeats – his records parallel the UK scene's journey from 'Ardkore to Jungle. A track like "The Peak" (from 1996's **Destroyer** LP) is full of fury, yet also has all the skill and breakbeat science that informs the work of artists like Photek or 4 Hero. Empire claims to be drug-free – he often sounds like one of America's straight-edge punks. One ATR record, "SuEcide", presented an apocalyptic vision of Ecstasy, Techno and capitalism locked into a nihilistic routine.

Empire's radicalism seems to be paying off – the Beastie Boys signed ATR to their Grand Royal label, he has remixed Björk and Cibo Matto, toured the US with Beck and Wu Tang. He runs his own label, Digital Hardcore, which is now accepted as a genre in its own right – the term referring to Empire's music and DHR signings like EC8OR and Shizuo. Empire produced more relaxed, almost trip-hop, tracks under the banner of Hypermodern Jazz, but still insists on a hardcore tag: "Hardcore in general is anything that's extreme. But I also call my slower stuff hardcore because even though it doesn't run at those speeds it still deals with extreme emotions." A hardcore producer, theorist and self-mythologiser – it's a winning combination.

⊙ **The Geist Of Alec Empire**   Geist, 1997

A three-album compilation of Empire's most absorbing moments on the Mille Plateaux label (though released on his own Geist imprint), including cuts from **Low on Ice**, **Generation Star Wars** and **Limited Editions 90–94**.

Tony Marcus

Envoy

While Hope Grant admits, like House pioneers Marshall Jefferson and Mr. Fingers, to an early penchant for Led Zeppelin and Rush, he's quick to point out the impact that Dave Angel has had on his music. The pair originally met soon after Angel's remix of the Eurythmics' "Sweet Dreams (Are Made of This)" and discovered a common interest in the mechanics of music-making, lending each other equipment and hanging out in each other's home studios. When Angel signed to R&S for the series of brilliantly inspired **Voyage** EPs, Grant sat in on the sessions.

After collaborating with Angel on a track for the **Royal Techno** EP,

Grant signed to Peacefrog Records under the name St. Vitus Dance, releasing the **Come of Age** EP in mid-'94 which attracted attention from Glasgow's Soma Records. The result was 1995's well-received **Solitary Mission** EP, this time as Envoy. His debut for Soma was followed a few months later by the exceptional **Heart of the Soul** EP which featured the lachrymose and impossibly lush "Machines Need Love Too".

Two further EPs, 1996's **Coalition** and 1997's **Emotional**, emerged before the arrival of **Where There's Life...** (1998). Filled with warm, floating strings, Detroit-inflected grooves and — on "Icarus Wings" — jazz scat, it was an impressive and deservedly acclaimed debut. The Envoy sound was best defined on tracks such as "Good Company" or "Leave This World Behind", emotive extrapolations of Detroit romanticism, the abstract weirdness of early Chicago classics by Adonis, Sleazy D and Virgo and the overwhelming summer morning optimism of rave's Second Summer of Love. There were darker currents too, a legacy of Grant's passion for Jeff Mills, Jay Denham's Black Nation output and Planetary Assault Systems.

⊙ **Where There's Life...**   Soma, 1998

Beautifully emotive Techno ranging from the trippy dancefloor architectonics of "Sexdrive" to the soaring string-driven melancholy of "Dark Manoeuvresa". A future classic.

Thomas Fehlmann

Thomas Fehlmann's musical career began in the late '70s when a chance encounter with Robert Fripp inspired him to form the experimental electronic group Palais Schaumburg, with Holger Hiller and Moritz Von Oswald (better known as Maurizio of Basic Channel/Chain Reaction fame). Blending Cabaret Voltaire-style proto-sampling techniques and tape loops with a disco-influenced rhythm, they clearly anticipated the *modus operandi* of both House and Techno, but constant personnel changes and limited record sales eventually led to the group's dissolution in 1985.

Fehlmann then moved to Berlin and was introduced to House music through Rhythm King Records, who released his first solo project, "Ready Made". In 1988, he began producing tracks for Berlin-based House acts, such as Marathon, Sun Electric and Fischerman's Friend. It was at this time that he met Alex Paterson, then an A&R man at EG Records, who was in the process of setting up his own label, WAU/Mr.Modo. The label released a Ready Made mini-album, **URO Breaks** (1990), as well as Sun Electric's first release, "O'Locco" – a record that defined a new genre: Ambient House. In return, Fehlmann began collaborating with Paterson in The Orb as co-writer and co-producer, a role that has continued to expand with each subsequent Orb release to date.

At the same time, the first wave of Detroit Techno was breaking in Berlin clubs. Brought together by a love of this strange new music, Fehlmann once again teamed up with Von Oswald, and, as early champions of the scene, they were instrumental in bringing a number of these artists to Europe for the first time, forging a Berlin/Detroit axis that is still strong today. Linking up with the Tresor label, the duo also collaborated with a number of these Motor City pioneers under the name 3MB, recording **Techno Soul** (1993) with Eddie "Flashin'" Fowlkes and, most notably, the sublime **Jazz Is the Teacher** EP with Juan Atkins.

As the Berlin scene got harder and Von Oswald reinvented himself as Maurizio, Fehlmann chose to distance himself from all of this, releasing the quirky **Flow** EP in 1994. As things came full circle, he also collaborated with his original inspiration, Robert Fripp, and The Orb on the "Ambient supergroup" album, **FFWD** (1994).

Between 1994 and 1997, he was constantly in the studio, working with The Orb, producing Erasure's eponymous LP, as well as maintaining his input to the development of Sun Electric. In 1996, he became heavily involved in Berlin's Ambient Ocean Club, out of which developed a weekly radio show, presenting obscure music from all parts of the globe. Finally, he released his first solo album, **Flowing NineZeroNineEight** (1998), a compilation of tracks recorded between his seemingly invisible, yet highly influential engagements over the last eight years.

⊙ **Flowing NineZeroNineEight**   Apollo, 1998

A beautiful summary of electronica's ability to soundtrack all moods, which finally sees Fehlmann stepping out of the shadows to reveal his considerable talent.

Peter McIntyre

Female

Peter Sutton is an integral player in the development of the so-called "Black Country sound" which was initially associated with Birmingham-based producers such as Surgeon and Regis. His own records have attracted an international underground following, while the Downwards label which he formed with Karl O'Connor in 1994 has provided a platform for exploring the intersection between the industrial textures of their home city and the minimalist funk of Detroit Techno.

Sutton and O'Connor were schoolboy friends who eventually

formed their first band together in the mid-'80s, inspired by a range of front-line influences including Kraftwerk, Cabaret Voltaire, Throbbing Gristle and the long-forgotten synth experimentalist Fad Gadget. As England succumbed to dance culture, the pair began setting up their own studio, releasing their first single – a self-financed 7" – in 1990 and issuing several others as the decade wore on.

They set up Downwards in 1994, providing an outlet for O'Connor's solo productions as Regis, several ground-breaking 12"s by Surgeon and Sutton's own releases as Portion Control and Female, including the much-sought-after **Pelotone** EP.

Into the Exotic (1997) was a solid debut, though it failed to attract the kind of critical admiration which surrounded long-players from both Surgeon and Regis. Yet Sutton was operating in similar territory to both, stripping back arrangements to a framework of tensile grooves and evocative electronic atmospheres that touched at times on the experimental, industrial funk of Cabaret Voltaire and Throbbing Gristle or the clanking quirkiness of Foetus and DAF. "Fusing the automated sound of

Birmingham's factories with complex rhythmic textures culled from the city's cultural variety," was how Sutton earnestly described his sound, though there were enough well-respected DJs who were also willing to testify to the album's potential for propelling the dancefloor into as yet undiscovered spaces.

Female singles like "Human Remains Human" provided another twist on the sound, though Sutton's only release under his own name, "Prologue", confirmed that he was capable of pushing into new territory almost effortlessly. A second album, **Angel Plague** (1999), demonstrated Sutton's talent for crafting muscular and absorbing tracks such as "My Untied Hands" or "Drawing Me In" which pushed the envelope of minimal, dancefloor Techno in fresh directions. But Sutton – who continues to maintain a day-job in order, he says, to avoid having to conform to commercial pressures – seemed relatively uninterested in pursuing the kind of promotional activities which would have transformed such an obviously exceptional record into a critical triumph.

⊙ Angel Plague   Downwards, 1999

Minimal, percussive Techno with elements of synthetic experimentalism, industria and compelling tribal grooves, this is the perfect example of why Birmingham is now a major force on the Techno underground.

Final Cut

F inal Cut occupy a strange place in the history of Techno. As the first group to boast the active involvement of Jeff Mills, they are the subject of intense speculation. Yet none of the records they made together during their brief career would merit close inspection were it not for Mills' subsequent activities as a member of Underground Resistance and the ground-breaking DJ and production skills he has brought to bear on his successful solo career.

Initially a collaboration between Mills and Tony Srock, Final Cut began their recording career with True Faith, whose singer Bridgett Grace was the central presence on 1989's "Take Me Away". Signed to Jerry Capaldi's Paragon label (also one-time home to Suburban Knight's James Pennington) the group started out following a path that was radically different to their later incarnation as an industrial outfit along the lines of Nitzer Ebb and Skinny Puppy. And on "Take Me Away", the only mention of Detroit Techno was on a mix done by Pennington and Santonio Echols (Mills and Srock did, however, provide an Acid mix).

"You Can't Deny the Bass" also boasted a session keyboards player who would later become a significant player in Mills' forward trajectory. Credited with "additional keyboards", Mike Banks was a crucial link with Mills' future activities. This time around, Final Cut provided their own "Detroit Techno mix" though a version by a well-known local DJ, Duane "In the Mix" Bradley, was reckoned by Capaldi to be a safer bet for club play.

Inevitably, problems arose between Paragon – whose reputation in Detroit was akin to that enjoyed by Trax in Chicago during the late '80s – and Final Cut. After leaving the label, Mills and Srock, perhaps influenced by the distinct industrial phase that Detroit experienced while Techno's main players were enjoying the first flush of success in Europe, began moving more towards the sound that they are best remembered for.

After setting up their own Full Effect record label, Final Cut set about articulating their new direction. **Deep Into the Cut** (1990) was a brutal, bruising record that ambitiously declared itself (optimistically, as it turned out) "the future of dance music", though tracks such as "She Destroys" and "Temptation" bore several hallmarks of the sonic extremism which were later to emerge on Mills' post-UR projects. Released in Europe by Dimitri Hegemann's Interfisch (a precursor of Tresor), **Deep Into the Cut** provided a calling card that resulted in the group playing Berlin's Atonal festival alongside 808 State and Peter "Baby" Ford.

A single from the album, "I Told You Not to Stop", proved to be Mills' swan song with the group. As Srock steered the group towards the more rock-oriented direction then being pursued by the industrial scene as a whole, Mills tendered his resignation and began mapping out his plans for Underground Resistance with Mike Banks. A second Final Cut album, **Consumed** (1991), emerged on the Canadian label Nettwerk, but with Mills out of the picture the group seemed to have lost a vital element and the album failed to captivate.

⊙ **Deep Into The Cut**   Full Effect/Interfisch, 1990

Abrasive, often brutal, Final Cut's debut sounds like the bastard child of Techno and industrial. For committed fans only.

Peter Ford

When Peter "Baby" Ford's first single, "Oochy Koochy", began travelling up the UK charts in September 1988, copies of the record were issued with a sticker warning about possible speaker and amplifier damage due to the extreme levels of bass it contained. Baby

Ford was the first great white hope of the UK's Acid House revolution. He had arrived in London in 1985 and, notoriously, spent his first few months there living in a car. Tracking developments from "Pump Up the Volume" by M/A/R/R/S to Mark Moore's "Theme From S'Express", he eventually became a regular at the legendary Shoom before booking studio time to record "Oochy Koochy". It was followed by a series of increasingly dislocated, Acid-influenced singles including "Chikki Chikki Ahh Ahh" and a weird cover version of Marc Bolan's "Children of the Revolution", but Ford was also soaking up the influence of Detroit and shaping a sound that embraced Deep House, the more playful elements of the London scene and his own variant of Techno.

Ford Trax (1988) provided a better picture of where Ford was coming from than the idiosyncratic singles, although the subsequent **OOO – The World of Baby Ford** (1989) reverted to his original exuberant prototype. From the outside, it seemed like Ford had decided to actively pursue a more commercial direction after **Ford Trax**, though a single with Ian Loveday, "Fetish", marked a return to Techno which was continued on their Minimal Man collaboration throughout the early '90s.

BFord9 (1992) fused oddball disco, hard Techno and dub to create Ford's most ambitious album to date, anticipating a sound which wouldn't gather momentum until later in the decade. Unsurprisingly, it proved too difficult for critics and was overlooked in favour of more easily assimilable fare. Ford then disappeared from view until he reemerged with his own Ifach label, a vehicle for the heavily experimental Techno he had begun working on with Mark Broom, in 1994. This time around, the critics had caught up and, within a year, the label had developed a significant cult following. Ford subsequently set up two more labels, Trelik and PAL-SL, which debuted in 1996 with his first release as Baby Ford since **BFord9**.

A project for Mo' Wax's "Excursions" series, under the name Twig Bud, saw Ford exploring a more downbeat, jazz-oriented mood, though he continued to use his own labels for a sound that was developing along more abstract lines. The arrival of **Headphoneasy Rider** (1997), which reworked some previously released material on Ifach with a number of new tracks, confirmed that Ford's closest point of reference was now the kind of avant-Techno being released by Finland's Såhko and Germany's Mille Plateaux.

Soon after, a single for David Moufang and Jonas Grossmann's Source Records, "Tall Storey", marked the highpoint of Ford's abstract endeavours. His work since then — including the excellent **Normal** on Rephlex, a collection of tracks recovered from the **BFord9** sessions — has opted for experimentation in equally alternative, but perhaps more accessible sonic spheres.

⊙ **Headphoneasy Rider**   Black Market, 1997

An abstract but compelling album that explores the nexus between ambience and funk.

Eddie "Flashin'" Fowlkes

T here are those who say the Belleville Three (Juan Atkins, Derrick May and Kevin Saunderson) should more acurately have been described as the Belleville Four. A one-time room-mate of Saunderson's and a close friend of Atkins, Eddie Fowlkes had been experimenting with music since high school and was one of the first recruits

DOUGLAS COOMBE

to Atkins' Deep Space DJ crew (along with May, Saunderson, Art Payne and Keith Martin – in fact Saunderson admits he was only inspired to become a DJ and join up after watching Fowlkes spin). After Atkins set up his Metroplex imprint, Fowlkes was the first artist to record for the label with 1986's classic "Goodbye Kiss" and was later one of the contributors to Neil Rushton's seminal Virgin compilation **Techno! The New Dance Sound of Detroit** (1988).

But while Atkins, May and Saunderson have been celebrated as Techno's originators, Fowlkes has enjoyed a more subdued reputation, largely due to an intermittent release schedule that focused on one-off singles for a diverse range of underground labels. His longest-running relationship, with Berlin's Tresor Records, coincided with his most productive period and included a collaborative venture with Blake Baxter (as The Project), an influential compilation in the shape of **Detroit Techno Soul** (1993) and, finally, his only solo album to date, **Black Techno Soul** (1996).

Fowlkes' concept of "Techno soul" was, in part, a crystallisation of his earliest musical influences – Stevie Wonder, Marvin Gaye and Motown – but it was also the most significant indicator of the kind of emotional contact he was striving for in his music. The concept was best articulated on two tracks which appeared on the Belgian imprint, SSR. "Black Soul" was one of the high points of the label's boundary-warping **Freezone 5** (1998), while "Soul Spirits" – a warm, emotional confection of beats 'n' bass – was a stand-out on **Moving House 3** (1998). Both tracks marked the apex of Fowlkes' search to weld the adventurism of Techno with more traditional forms of African-American music. The most obvious impact of this drive, though, was to bring his sound closer to House than to the oblique, angular and transgressive shapes of Detroit.

Though Fowlkes initially began his career behind the decks (playing the scratch-heavy style known in Detroit as "flashing", hence the epithet which he has enjoyed since the mid-'80s), in recent years he's preferred to rein back his activities as a DJ in favour of focusing on studio work and running his label, City Boy Records. The label's most significant release so far, **Niko Marks & City Boy Players Feat. Mr. Eddie Fowlkes** (1999), evolved from Fowlkes' gigs around Detroit, playing keyboards and writing with live band City Boy Players. Fusing hardcore funk, jazz and electronics, the album finds Fowlkes sounding increasingly comfortable in the ambitious and eclectic range of tracks such as "It's Yo' Turn Sista" and "Got to Be". The new sound represents a radical shift for Fowlkes, but it may yet germinate his most convincing work so far.

⊙ **Black Technosoul**   Tresor, 1996

At times overly brash, Fowlkes' debut steers away from the deep spaciness of Detroit's mid-'90s sound towards a more retro fusion of funk, synth-pop and chunky percussives.

127

Freddie Fresh

Shuttling between his home town of St. Paul, Minnesota and the Bronx, Freddie Schmid was originally a hip-hop DJ and producer (his first production was a KRS1 remix on 1988's Scott La Rock tribute **The Man and His Music**) who rerouted to Techno through an enduring passion for Electro. A regular fixture at Woody McBride's Depth Probe nights in Minneapolis, as Freddie Fresh he has been one of the most prolific Techno producers in the Midwest, responsible for over 150 releases on labels such as Drop Bass Network, Emergency Broadcast and his own Analog imprint.

Under the name Modulator, he released two early classics on Damon Wild's Experimental label – "Modulator" and the **Painkiller** EP – that deftly articulated both his own wide-ranging musical tastes and the blitzkrieg hard Acid sound that earned Fresh and a number of other producers from the region the soubriquet of "the Midwest Hardcorps". Later singles on Communiqué, Proper and Eye Q pushed in a variety of different directions, though Fresh's trademark taut drums and bass formula survived intact.

It was producer Tim Taylor who told him that, someday, he would make a classic by accident. The chance remark translated itself into the title of his debut for Harthouse/Eye Q, **Accidentally Classic** (1996). Written after a trip to Puerto Rico, the album drew on a mix of influences ranging from the Latin Rascals to Electro and Techno, though his collection of vintage analogue synths (Fresh still records everything live to tape without the aid of computers or sequencers) was also much in evidence.

Under the name Nitrate, Fresh recorded the more straightforward **Acid Stuker** (1996) for Labworks though the fascination with mutoid Electro was still apparent. As the Electro revival got firmly underway,

Fresh became an increasing presence on European dancefloors with releases such as "Drum Lesson", the **Barrio Grooves** EP and "Quiver" all becoming minor underground hits. A collaboration with Fatboy Slim on "Sound of Milwaukee" helped to provide an entry into the mainstream, but it was a show for Radio One's *Essential Mix*, early in 1998, which provided the best introduction to his singular talent. Blending classic Electro from Warp 9 and Doug E. Fresh with his own tracks and an eclectic fusion which included everything from Jeff Mills to Art of

AMY TANVEER

Noise, it was a spell-binding set which was nominated by *Muzik* as one of the year's best.

The Last True Family Man (1999) was a solid follow-up to his Eye-Q debut, though Analog Space Funk (1999) – a collection of excerpts from Fresh's Analog label – also provided a worthwhile document of the producer's musical whereabouts during the intervening years. It remains to be seen, however, whether or not, with access to a bigger budget (he still delivers pizza part-time to help support his family), Fresh can translate the full width of his eclectic musical vision onto disc.

⊙ **Accidentally Classic**   Harthouse/Eye Q, 1996

Ranging from moods that suggest summertime in the Bronx ("Gimme") to darker, spacier, Detroit-inflected grooves ("Barogue"), this is the best available introduction to Freddie Fresh's eclectic sound.

Funk d'Void

After a conversion experience in 1987 listening to Rhythim Is Rhythim's "Nude Photo", Lars Sandberg went on to become a key player in the scene which mapped Glasgow alongside London, Frankfurt, Berlin and Brussels as crucial cities in Techno's dissemination across Europe. By 1989, he was resident DJ at UFO, playing a mix of early Detroit Techno and the wilder elements of Chicago's feverish jacked-up House. From there, he took over the turntables at The Tunnel, a lavishly-designed venue which opened just as the city's dance scene exploded out of the underground and into the mainstream.

But while other DJs in the city, including Slam, were quick to move into the recording studio, Sandberg adopted a more leisurely approach. It was 1993 before his first release – a collaborative effort with Ken Sharman under the name United States of Sound – emerged. "Kiss the Baby/Oscillator" sounded like it had been forged on the dancefloor of the city's Sub Club, though it was actually recorded in the more sedate environs of a bedroom studio in Park Circus. The track was successful enough to warrant a follow-up, but though a few white labels appeared, the second United States of Sound single was never officially released.

It was two years before Sandberg's next release, this time on his own, under the name Funk D'Void. "Jack Me Off" had its roots in the mix of early Trax and Transmat releases Sandberg had played as a DJ, but other tracks – particularly the blissed-out "Thank You" – hinted at the music he'd been introduced to by his jazz pianist mother: it sounded like Joni Mitchell jamming with Derrick May and Herbie Hancock. A year later, "Soul Man" proved to be a equally essential follow-up, by which time Sandberg was also working on the Chaser project with another Glaswegian DJ, Nigel Hayes.

Technoir (1997) was a stunning debut. It touched points somewhere between Steve Rachmad's early Sterac output, R&S-era Dave Angel and Detroit producers like Kenny Larkin and Claude Young. But it was also shot through with a unique vibe that connected to the old days when "Street Life" by The Crusaders, "Nude Photo" and "Sexual Healing" all fought for space on Glasgow's dancefloors. While Sandberg focused on the drums, his mother stepped in for a cameo role, playing gorgeous liquid jazz keys on the superb "Herbie on Rhodes".

⊙ **Technoir**   Soma, 1997

Classic machine percussion and soundscapes that weave from lush Detroit-edged synthetics to darker, weirder dancefloor nuggets like "Bad Coffee".

Funkstörung

Funkstörung (meaning funky distortion), the Munich-based duo of Michael Fakesh and Chris DeLuca, met in 1992 when Fakesh was organising the first Techno events in his small hometown of Rosenheim in Bavaria. DeLuca was the DJ at one of these events and they quickly struck up a friendship, which turned into a working relationship two years later when they began buying equipment from the proceeds of these parties and making tracks.

A demo sent to Holland's Bunker Records resulted in the immediate offer of a six-album deal. But it was over two years before their debut album, **Musik Aus Strom** (1994), saw the light of day. Frustrated by this, the duo decided to form their own label to prevent a similar occurence in the future, retaining their Bunker project names, Funkstörung and Musik Aus Strom, and naming their label MAS. In the two years that they had been forced to wait, they had built up an enormous backlog of material, with which they extricated themselves from their existing contract by simultaneously releasing five albums' worth of music.

Now free to record as they chose, the duo followed up this mass of old material with the first release on their own label, the **Oszillator** EP in June 1996. The difference between the old and the new couldn't have been more pronounced. Where the Bunker material had been largely simple electronica, these four tracks displayed a quantum leap, characterised by highly intricate rhythmic programming and deep melancholy melodies – a combination that has often led to them being called the German Autechre. A second MAS release followed quickly, the **Break Art** EP, as did material on labels as diverse as Interferred Communications, Chocolate Industries and Compost, who have put out their most successful release to date, the **Funkenstört** EP. A planned release on Aphex Twin's Rephlex imprint sadly came to nothing, but there have been three collaborations with the Autechre-related Skam Records. These records, which have crept into specialist record shops in ultra-limited quantities under the label name Mask, have featured, amongst others, Gescom, Jega and Boards of Canada. The duo has also surfaced on the Fat Cat label, remixing Björk out of all recognition. Michael Fakesh himself has released three MAS EPs (**Demons 1–3**) under his own name which have been compiled onto a CD. With heavy media attention focused on Funkstörung, and Warp Records leading the race to sign them, it would seem that Germany may well be the birthplace of a new strain of Artificial Intelligence.

⊙ **Sonderdienste**   Compost, 1998

Funk split into barely recognisable fragments layered with strange sounds from alien radio stations. Complex melancholia never sounded so appealing.

Peter McIntyre

Future Sound of London

Future Sound of London's "Papua New Guinea" is perhaps one of the most alluring Techno records ever made. Yet its constituent elements — including an ethereal vocal lifted from avant-indie outfit Dead Can Dance and a bassline from Meat Beat Manifesto's "Radio Babylon" — were scavenged from outside sources. It's a measure of the FSOL partnership's talent for appropriating fragments of the pop fabric and recontextualising them within their own exotically blurred and slightly disorientating aesthetic. A talent which has made their records, their revolutionary radio broadcasts and their stunning visuals a crucial link in the development of modern electronica.

Brian Dougans was studying sound engineering in Manchester when he first crossed paths with Gary Cobain, a student who'd moved from Bedford to study electronics at the city's university. On the surface they made an unlikely pairing. Cobain was a mouthy, hyper-confident kid from middle England while Dougans was painfully reticent, the son of a one-time BBC employee from Glasgow, with a taste for hot knives and weird experimental music. But after they began making music together in Dougans' bedroom, early in 1985, it was obvious that they shared a similar interest in the outer peripheries of sonic adventure.

Acid House provided the pair with a focus for their experimentation. In 1988, Dougans delivered a seminal moment in the shape of Stakker's "Humanoid", a blistering wedge of wasp-buzz mayhem that quickly became acknowledged as a classic. By this time, Dougans and Cobain had formed a loose alliance with visual artist Buggy G. Riphead, FSOL's unofficial third member, and were already developing a more expansive group concept in which music would be just one of a number of different creative territories they explored.

Singles by Dougans and Cobain appeared under a number of different names — Yage, Smart Systems, Mental Cube and Indotribe — over the next few years until **Accelerator** (1992) and "Papua New Guinea" provided them with both their most sublime creative peak and some significant chart success. The chart appearance led to a unique deal being brokered with Virgin Records, which gave Future Sound Of London unprecedented autonomy and a sizeable advance which they immediately ploughed into a state of the art studio that included video editing and high-end image manipulation equipment alongside the synths and samplers.

A second album, **Tales of Ephidrina** (1993), emerged, this time under the name Amorphous Androgynous. A more ambient affair, it was the sound of Cobain and Dougans leaving the dancefloor far behind. Tracks such as "Liquid Insects" and "Auto Pimp" were typical: seductive concatenations of sound that managed to be both effortlessly beautiful and disturbing at the same time.

While **Accelerator** and **Tales of Ephidrina** hinted at exceptional promise, it was the breathtaking nineteen-track double album **Lifeforms** (1994) which articulated FSOL's vision in its entirety. **Lifeforms** combined a sense of queasy, dystopian bleakness with moments of sharply exquisite beauty, as on the title track or the inspired "Flak", to create what is one of Techno's most ambitious masterpieces. Cobain gleefully explained Virgin's discomfort in discovering that they had signed a group whose music was just one element in a vast multimedia project that embraced film, radio, graphic design and sundry other activities. On no account would they play live, he declared; that was a retrograde, rockist step. Instead they'd pipe material live from their studio down ISDN cables to any radio station that wanted an FSOL broadcast. Instead of a tour, he explained, they would broadcast on radio stations around the country.

In typically contradictory fashion, however, the follow-up, the limited-edition **ISDN** (1995), tumbled out into the public domain with little fanfare and the sound had mutated. On tracks such as "Just a Fuckin' Idiot", "Eyes Pop – Skin Explodes – Everybody Dead" and "Hot Knives", the mood was darker as sounds smudged, blurred and metamorphosed through the hiss of static, ancient circuits and half-obscured pulses that wove themselves through the asthmatic production. Unsurprisingly, the low-key release failed to generate the enthusiasm of its predecessor, yet **ISDN** offered conclusive proof that FSOL continued to inhabit a unique sonic zone that few others had stumbled upon.

Dead Cities (1996) seemed to skid across the entire wavelength of pop iconography. The opening sequence of "Herd Killing" and "Dead Cities" offered fractured guitar licks, speed-drill scratching, frenetic breakbeats and the kind of monotonal synthology that suggested the pair had, in their spare time, been mainlining on the recondite avant-synth pop of Fad Gadget. Elsewhere they created a hybrid of free-form jazz and Durutti Column guitar poetry ("Her Face Forms In Summertime"), mutant hardcore ("We Have Explosive") and strange, skin-crawlingly scary ambience ("Everyone In the World Is Doing Something Without Me"). It was their most difficult, yet deeply shaped release so far — an alternate reality constructed, so it seemed, from the detritus of other musics.

⊙ **Accelerator**   Jumpin' & Pumpin', 1992

Though "Papua New Guinea" has appeared on numerous compilations, it's still best heard in context on FSOL's excellent debut album which offers plenty of glimpses into the brilliance that was to come.

⊙ **Lifeforms**   EBV/Virgin, 1994

Though FSOL had almost completely disengaged from the dancefloor, this still stands as one of Techno's greatest, and most disturbing, masterpieces.

Russ Gabriel

With a diverse range of influences stretching from Juan Atkins to Miles Davis, it perhaps shouldn't be surprising that Russ

Gabriel has become one of British Techno's most consistently compelling producers. His debut album, **Voltage Control** (1995), was an underrated masterpiece, full of supernaturally beautiful electronic melodies and machine-code percussives. His aim, he says, is to make a Techno album that will eventually stand up alongside classic releases by Marvin Gaye, Herbie Hancock and Thelonious Monk.

Gabriel's career began with several well-received singles on Dave Clarke's Magnetic North label under the name VCF. A move to the Essex-based GPR imprint (erstwhile home of Black Dog amongst others) coincided with his growing reputation on the underground scene and resulted in the **Future Funk** EP which confirmed him as one of the UK's most promising talents.

In 1993, Gabriel set up his own label, Ferox Records, to provide an outlet for other like-minded producers including Affie Yusuf, Cristian Vogel and Mark Broom. In keeping with Gabriel's notorious perfectionism, Ferox's output has been relatively small though the quality of the label's releases – including Paul Hannah's essential "Adventures In Techno Soul" 12" and Ian O'Brien's **Intelligent Desert** EP – is evident. The label has also provided a platform for some of Gabriel's best work. His **Peace** EP, released soon after Ferox's inception, was a breathtaking combination of aching melodics, gorgeous sequences and weightless Detroit-inflected string patterns while the **Darwinian** EP, released the following year, marked a shift towards the more fully realised sound which would eventually surface on his 1995 debut album.

Since the release of the **Darwinian** EP in 1994, Gabriel's name has been absent from the Ferox roster, though he has recorded for the label under pseudonyms such as Too Funk and Fusion. Some of this output was subsequently collected on an excellent Ferox compilation, **Adventures In Techno Soul** (1996), and its follow-up, **Further Adventures In Techno Soul** (1998), but Gabriel is currently only to be found recording under his own name for the Ferox subsidiary, Soul On Wax. Gabriel's 1998 single, "Orange Mécanique", offered a good indication of the jazzier direction which is likely to dominate his long-awaited second album.

⊙ **Voltage Control**   Input Neuron/GPR, 1995

Simply essential. One of the most inspired and innovative albums that the UK Techno scene has produced.

Laurent Garnier

Though he's better known these days as one of Europe's favourite DJs, it was Laurent Garnier's day-job in catering that landed him in the right place at the right time. Having left France to work in the UK during the mid-'80s, Garnier wound up as head chef at Tony Wilson's Dry Bar. Given his employer's connections with Factory Records, it was inevitable that Garnier would end up at the Haçienda – the club owned jointly by the label and its biggest act, New Order. It was at the Haç that he heard Mike Pickering spin House for the first time, saw Derrick May, Marshall Jefferson and Adonis play and where he took his own first steps as a professional DJ, playing everything from Washington Go-Go to slick, R&B/soul fusions and, ultimately, the new dance sounds flooding out from Chicago and Detroit.

After returning to France, Garnier began playing in House, gay and new beat clubs around Paris, finally returning to Manchester in 1990 for a six-month residency at the Haçienda where he began to refine his eclectic, but highly charged, sound. Back in Paris, he opened his own club, the semi-legendary Wake Up!, and embarked on a number of

THE ITALIAN JOB

studio collaborations – the best-known being 1993's "Acid Eiffel" recorded with French House producer Shazz under the name Choice.

A Shot In the Dark (1994) was Garnier's first solo endeavour and its release coincided perfectly with a growing appreciation of his talents behind the decks. Released on F Communications (the label set up by Garnier in partnership with Eric Morand) the album traversed minimalism, Trance, deep 4am Techno and a skittish Ambient hybrid – much the same trajectory in fact, as his extended DJ sets – to provide a solid, though relatively unchallenging, debut. In contrast, his marathon seven-hour stints behind the decks swooped and shuddered with white-hot moments of inspiration, igniting enough hyperbole in the dance media to place Garnier firmly among the top five in any list of the world's best DJs.

Laboratoire Mix (1996) was a double album, capturing at least a glimpse of Garnier's talents behind the decks. Combining House classics such as Jungle Wonz's "The Jungle", hard minimal Techno by Fumiya Tanaka and Neil Landstrumm, the ghetto stylings of DJ Deon and a sizeable representation from Detroit (including Juan Atkins, Rhythim Is Rhythim, Aux 88 and Stacey Pullen), it was an expansive affair, though the more concise **Mixmag Live! – Laurent Garnier** (1996) provided an equally convincing snapshot of Garnier's eclectic tastes.

On **30** (1997), his second full-length offering, Garnier opted for a more experimental approach, grafting the languor of French House genius Ludovic Navarre onto a version of Detroit Techno that was part muscular minimalism of the Robert Hood school and part blistering Electro. On tracks such as "For Max", Garnier did attempt to step away from the dancefloor, offering a downbeat experimentalism that owed much to the gentle melancholy of Navarre, but ultimately **30** remained a collection of disjointed moments rather than a fully realised and cohesive album experience.

Meanwhile Garnier and Morand's F Communications label has continued to deliver outstanding releases by producers such as Navarre (under his St Germain alias), Jori Hulkkonen and Aqua Bassino, gaining itself a deserved reputation as one of France's most influential imprints. Always at its best when exploring introspective terrain, F Communications may yet turn out to be Garnier's most significant legacy to dance music.

⊙ **Laboratoire Mix**   React, 1996

It's behind the decks that Garnier really shines and this excellent double album is a comprehensive guide to the best of his inventive and expansive club sets.

Morgan Geist

A s a teenager growing up in New Jersey during the '80s, Morgan Geist was something of a square peg in a round hole. While his peers were digging the likes of Blue Oyster Cult and Bon Jovi, Geist was locked in his bedroom, listening to electronic pioneers such as Devo, Severed Heads and Depeche Mode.

At the end of the decade, these fleeting glimpses of an alternative electronic future broadened out into the widescreen surround sound of Britain's drum machine revolution personified by 808 State. Their oft-quoted desire to drill holes in every guitar would have seemed like heresy to the rock-oriented majority of American youth, but to Geist it was a logical progression. While studying at college, he embraced Techno through British import tracks by the likes of Black Dog and B12, eventually discovering the beauty on his own doorstep of such labels as Transmat and Metroplex, which, ironically, languished in even greater obscurity than their UK counterparts.

It wasn't long before his appreciation of this type of music turned into a desire to emulate his heroes. Armed with such traditional Techno weapons as a cheap sampler and a 909 drum machine, he began producing his own music. Transmat was clearly the defining influence on his earliest efforts, released first on Dan Curtin's Metamorphic label, and then on his own Environ imprint. The four EPs released on the label, three featuring Geist solo, the fourth a collaboration with upcoming talent Titonton Duvante, were full of lush melodics, robo-funk percussion and a rich, creamy bass sound. Available on a compilation album, **Morgan Geist Presents Environ – Into a Separate Space** (1997), they form the missing link between the deep space transmissions of Derrick May and Juan Atkins and the sky-gliding disco dubs of François Kervorkian.

Disco has become an increasingly prominent influence on Geist's music. In fact, he's one of the few producers to acknowledge Techno's debt to the form. Nowhere is this influence more pronounced than on his debut LP, **The Driving Memoirs** (1997), released on Clear Records. Dedicated to his sister, who died in a car crash the year before, the album grooved along at a more House-influenced tempo than his earlier material, evoking the glory days of such pioneers as Larry Levan and Walter Gibbons, in its use of echoplex and delay to create a dubbed-out, ethereal sound.

⊙ **Into A Separate Space**   Environ/Phono, 1997

Coming on like Derrick May's early Rhythim Is Rhythim classics, this is an essential masterpiece of extra-terrestrial longing, alien funk and hot-wired grooves.

Peter McIntyre

Gerd

With influences ranging from Herbie Hancock and Donald Byrd to Acid House and hip-hop, it was a safe bet that Gert Jan Bijl would deliver an interesting take on Techno. His solo productions as Gerd, including the exceptional **This Touch Is Greater Than Moods** (1997), connect with liquid ambience, Tech-jazz and soft romance, sometimes sounding like a less spaced-out Deep Space Network or Detroit's more abstract excursions. Along with his production partner, Dirk Jan Hanegraaff, he's also responsible for a range of projects including Marvo Genetic, Sunshower, Metro Dade and BSO Research, though it's as Sensurreal that the pair are best known. Releases for Speedy J's Beam Me Up! label, including **Never to Tell a Soul** (1994) and **The Occasional Series** (1996), have provided Sensurreal with a cult following for their intriguingly experimental rewrite of the Techno blueprint.

Bijl and Hanegraaff embarked on their production career after visiting Speedy J's studio. Their first release, 1991's "Mild at Heart" as It's Thinking on Plus 8's short-lived Malego subsidiary, was the beginning of an avalanche of singles under a variety of aliases including a series of releases between '93 and '95 as Perez & Dowell.

Bijl's solo debut was Gerd's "Vorpal Blade" on Brave New World in 1994. Since then he's continued to explore a seam of Techno that's both gently poetic (as evinced by a taste for evocative titles such as "Non Velvet Mornings", "Nautiloïdea" and even "Offering a Peach to Celebrate Longevity") and fusion-led. Elements of jazz, House, Latin and funk spiral through his releases, sometimes separately, sometimes together, though Bijl's talent for crafting exquisitely shaped sounds unfailingly lends the end result a cohesive sheen.

1999 began with a re-release of Sensurreal's "No White Clouds In My Blue Sky" (previously on Universal Language) and the promise of a more dancefloor-oriented Sensurreal album. Bijl is currently preparing a second Gerd album with a number of live musicians. The result, he says, will be "a strong mixture of electronica and acoustic music" though, since the untimely demise of Universal Language, it's unclear where or when the album will emerge. Other projects such as the "Aftershower Funk" single on CC Records (as The Juice), a new Perez & Dowell single, "Body Music", and Metro Dade's "Lights of Metro" are scheduled in the meantime.

PERSFOTO / SENSURREAL

⊙ **Gerd – This Touch Is Greater**
   Than Moods   Universal Language, 1997

Spaced-out jazz, gently chilled atmospherics and tough funk all wrapped up in a superb electronic sheen.

Fred Giannelli

Boston-based producer Fred Giannelli has carved an individual and inspired path through electronic music since his days with Psychic TV. His work with Richie Hawtin and Dan Bell on the Spawn project for Plus 8 and the material he does on his own Telepathic label under names such as Mazdaratti and Deneuve form just part of a cutting-edge legacy which stretches back to his pre-PTV solo work as Turning Shrines through to classically Ambient works like last year's **Telepathic Romance** album on the Finnish Sahko label.

Giannelli's releases as The Kooky Scientist on Plus 8 have distinguished themselves by lacing superb dancefloor grooves with weird abstract electronics and deep – sometimes even oppressive – atmospherics. Early outings, like the vibrant "Blue Movie" and the characteristically off-the-wall "Rambunctious", were loaded with an inspired, and deeply funky, experimentalism which embraced both odd shapes and beautifully constructed analogue melodies.

It's this combination which made Giannelli's debut album proper, Kooky Scientist's **Unpopular Science** (1996), such a successful proposition. Dreamy minimal grooves like "Nite Glide" or the epic "Glitterbug" were warm affairs, floating impossibly delicate pads over clanking rhythms and fat-ass bass, while Giannelli pushed sequencers and rhythm boxes into spaced-out syncopations on deep, trippy episodes like "Organ Donor" and "Bad Chemistry 2". The overall feel was less introspective and more immediate than Giannelli's considerable number of armchair fans might have expected, particularly on stand-out cuts like the opener, "Cash Flow", or the equally fine "Discombobulate", but Gianelli is planning a return to the mellower moods of his other alter egos. That may not be for a while, however, since with

Kooky Scientist, he seems to have spawned a monster which threatens to dominate his career for the foreseeable future.

⊙ **Unpopular Science**   Plus 8, 1996

Kooky in places, but not nearly as much as you'd imagine, this was an accomplished dancefloor record which still demands attention.

Global Communication

As the partner of Richard James in the original incarnation of Aphex Twin, Tom Middleton was already surfing an experimental wave when he met Mark Pritchard, a one-time guitar player turned DJ, at a club in Taunton. Inspired by a shared love of Detroit Techno, Brian Eno and Herbie Hancock, the pair quickly set up their own label, Evolution Records (named, appropriately enough, after a Carl Craig track), and began recording together under a variety of pseudonyms — including Reload, Link and The Jedi Knights — though perhaps their best-known identity is that of Global Communication, purveyors of Ambient Techno's most liquid, gorgeous and alluring moments.

Middleton, a classically trained pianist, had already explored Electro, graffiti and skating before being seduced by the weird-out electronic lure of Acid House which made him the perfect foil for Pritchard's equally visionary sensibilities. Signed to Creation subsidiary Infonet under the name Reload, Middleton and Pritchard recorded **A Collection of Short Stories** (1993). Quickly establishing itself as a cult classic, the album was a brooding mix of intense atmospheres, bleak

146

minimalism and post-industrial experimentation that hinted occasionally at the lustrous trippiness of their later Global Communication material and the kind of rhythmic propulsion that would subsequently emerge in drum 'n' bass.

A remix project for Chapterhouse, **The Pentamerous Metamorphosis** (1993), provided the first sustained glimpse of Global Communication's luxurious rewrite of ambience and Detroit Techno. It was the astonishing **76:14** (1994), though, which captured the pair at their best. Tracks such as "4:02" and "14:31" were compounds of synthetic orchestration and deep, swooning atmospheres that suggested a hybrid of Derrick May and Vangelis. Impossibly lush but gently bittersweet, the album was a significant critical success and quickly placed Global Communication alongside Black Dog and Aphex Twin at the leading edge of experimental Techno. As if to confirm the album's achievement, a remix of Warp 69's "Natural High" followed some months later. Draped in thickly opulent strings and dense, extravagantly orchestrated melodics, the mix marked a creative peak in Ambient Techno that has only rarely been surpassed.

Middleton and Pritchard also experimented with a languid, equally dreamy, version of drum 'n' bass under the name Chameleon, signing to LTJ Bukem's Good Looking imprint early in 1995 and scoring two significant underground hits with the singles "Links" and "Close Your Eyes". Twelve months later, their Electro-based project, The Jedi Knights, turned out **New School Science** (1996), which played a notable part in triggering the Electro revival of the late '90s.

Though a compilation of early Evolution releases, **The Theory of Evolution** (1995), had been modestly successful, in 1996 Middleton and Pritchard relaunched their label under a new name. As Universal Language, it provided a platform for artists such as Max 404, Sensurreal, The Horn and Matthew Herbert's Wishmountain project alongside the duo's own material until the label's eventual termination early in 1999.

Global Communication produced just one surprisingly low-key release, "The Groove", in 1997, before an extended hiatus. Pritchard took two years out to produce an album, **Out** (1998), for fiancée Kirsty Hawkshaw, while Middleton worked on a series of solo productions which included his well-received Modwheel singles on Heard and a planned soundtrack project called Amba which is, as yet, unreleased.

The pair reconvened early in 1999 to work on a second Jedi Knights album though, due to legal difficulties with the *Star Wars* franchise, they now found themselves known simply as Jedi. The working title of the new album — **The Return of...** — seemed a typically defiant gesture from a duo whose talent has, so far at least, shown little regard for the constraints of convention.

⊙ **Reload – A Collection of Short Stories**   Infonet, 1993

Not quite the starting point of Middleton and Pritchard's electronic adventures, but a bona fide classic nonetheless.

⊙ **Global Communication – 76:14**   Dedicated, 1994

Redolent of the same bittersweet terrain as the Reload album, but this time draped in gorgeous, drop-dead melodies and wonderfully lush textures.

Kelli Hand

Kelli Hand grew up wanting to be a newscaster. An addiction to computer games like PacMan, Millipede and Galaxian thwarted that ambition by bringing her into contact with Derrick May who, at the time, was working in a video game arcade but harbouring dreams of his own. When the music bug bit, it bit hard. Soon after getting her first job she was spending most of her wages on records and flight tickets to New York to go dancing and record shopping. She went to the Paradise Garage, checked out Grace Jones and Robert Owens playing live and carefully noted what the DJs were doing so she could transfer what she learned into her own turntable experiments back home.

It took a long time before Hand admitted to anyone that she was a DJ. But in 1990, she began spinning at a Detroit club called Zippers. A few months later she launched her own label, UK House Records, and her first single, Etat Solide's "Think About It", though understandable confusion about the origins of the label soon led to a change of name to Acacia – named after the street where she lived. Acacia has since become one of the Motor City's cult labels – though its most visible success has been with Atlanta's Wamdue Kids and Hand's own ghetto-House-influenced material such as "Beat That Bitch With a Stick" and "Freak Them Hoes".

As a producer and remixer, Hand has remixed tracks such as Paperclip People's "Throw" and Dan Curtin's "I'll Take You There". It wasn't until 1996, though, that her long-awaited full-length debut arrived. **On a Journey** provided the room for Hand to stretch out and give free rein to the more soulful elements of her sound. **Ready for the Darkness** (1997) was a more assured and accomplished set.

In demand around the world as a DJ (her incendiary turntable performances are full of rock-hard funk, syncopated Techno and freaked-out House), Hand hasn't yet delivered a definitive mix album though **Acacia Classics – Volume One** (1999) served to plug the gap.

⊙ **Ready for the Darkness**   Distance, 1997

Kelli Hand's distinctive sound is best articulated on this, her second album. Seductive grooves, carefully sculpted atmospherics and a sense of soulfulness are the order of the day.

Beaumont Hannant

F rom the moment Andy Weatherall dubbed Beaumont Hannant "the great white hope of British Techno", it looked like the painter-turned-producer was intent on pushing the button marked "self-destruct" on what was a promising career in music. Once the darling of the music press, fêted alongside the likes of Autechre, Higher Intelligence Agency and The Black Dog as a pioneer of fresh directions in Techno, his subsequent embarrassment over the disproportionate coverage accorded to his releases led to well-publicised disputes with journalists, magazines and other producers. After dismissing Autechre as being "scared to scare", describing the editor of one of the most influential dance music 'zines as "a wanker" and engaging in a very public falling out with *Melody Maker*, it didn't take the opinionated Hannant very long before he ensured the demise of his career.

Hannant's first release, 1993's **Tastes and Textures: Vol.1** EP on Wayne Archbold's GPR label, was a luxurious tangle of electronic cadences and warping beats. This was quickly followed by an ambitious album, **Basic Data Manipulation** (1993), full of intriguingly seductive experimentalism like "Basic Dialog" and "T-GH6493" that led to comparisons with Aphex Twin. Though he later claimed that at least some of the material on his early albums was never meant to be released, Hannant's prolific output resulted in the well-received **Texturology** (1994), **Tastes and Textures: Vol 3**, an album of brilliantly spiky Techno as Y03 with Cherry Bomb's Richard Brown, and **Sculptured** (1994) all in a matter of months.

Notions of Tonality, a four-track EP of exquisitely fractured electronica, emerged during 1995 (though not before Hannant had provided a lushly packaged series of remixes of "Psi-Onyx" from his first EP), but the relentless railing against clubs, the press and other artists had taken its toll. Instead of the reverence which had once greeted his releases, Hannant, though still a creative force to be reckoned with, now found himself in the wilderness.

Together with Richard Brown, Hannant signed to the One Little Indian label in 1996 under the name Outcast. Aiming for eclecticism, Outcast delivered **Out of Tune** (1996) and provided remixes for Jhelisa and Björk, but the magic that Hannant had so effortlessly displayed on his earlier projects was noticeably absent. A vapid contribution to **Trance Europe Express 5** (1997) confirmed the suspicion that whatever gifts Hannant had enjoyed had now been squandered. "I took myself too seriously," he claimed in an interview with music journalist Carl Loben. But by then, to paraphrase a classic House hit, he was too far gone for there to be any way back.

⊙ **Basic Data Manipulation**   GPR, 1993

Almost all of Hannant's releases during '93/'94 were classics but this was the one that more than justified the hyperbole.

Rei Harakami

Alternately brilliantly spiky and beautifully soft, Rei Harakami's music lies somewhere between the brittle surfaces of Ken Ishii and the sentimentality of Susuma Yokota's Prism project. Harakami's first musical experiments began at age 13 when, armed with what he describes as "toy keyboards" and a guitar, he developed his own embryonic version of synth-pop. Like many other Japanese producers, he initially found inspiration in the glossy, hi-tech grooves of Yel-

KUNIHIKO SATAKE

low Magic Orchestra, but these days he cites everyone from Steve Reich to Van Dyke Parks as an influence on his lush, impossibly pretty Techno. Perhaps because he spent time at Kyoto University, studying film and working on video scores, Harakami's music often sounds impressively filmic and emotive. His tracks flirt with wild dance-floor moods and cotton-wool chill-outs, sometimes in the space of a few sparkling beats, layering weightless sounds against heavy dub rhythms and punching drum licks as if he's orchestrating with electronics.

Harakami's debut release was the exceptional **Damning Evidence** six-track EP on Sublime which harnessed House, Techno and breakbeat to his beautifully compelling, bittersweet melodies. Tracks like "Vice Versa" and "Objective Contents" played with Ambient shapes and gentle atmospherics while other cuts, like the break-driven "Pass" or the cool House fusion of "On", explored deep grooves and sub-bass chasms.

The romantic feel of his early work was confirmed on Harakami's elegantly seductive debut album, **Unrest** (1998). Combining the material from **Damning Evidence** with a handful of new tracks, the album was laden with tender and achingly pretty moments such as "Code" which saw him swimming deep in the kind of emotions which suggested summer days, first kisses and a boundless lust for life. A second album, **OPA*Q** (1999), developed the themes of its predecessor.

⊙ **Unrest**   Sublime, 1998

Though, at times, it overplays the sentimentality, Harakami's debut album is still a masterpiece of subtle, Detroit-inflected shapes and truly gorgeous moments.

Hardfloor

In 1992, Oliver Bondzio and Ramon Zenker deployed their arsenal of vintage TB-303s to create a nine-minute epic which impacted on dancefloors like a neutron bomb. The track was Hardfloor's "Hardtrance Acperience" and it single-handedly rehabilitated the Acid sound, blazing a trail for a million 303-driven Trance records which leaked out of Germany over the next three years.

On the face of it, Bondzio and Zenker were something of an odd couple. Bondzio was a DJ on the Düsseldorf-Cologne beat with a taste for raw Chicago House and the harder end of Detroit Techno. Before meeting Zenker, his only previous release was a bootleg megamix of dance classics. The quiet, reserved Zenker, on the other hand, had already notched up a lengthy career in music. Citing Tears For Fears and Howard Jones as prime influences, he had formed an electro-pop duo while still at school, eventually landing a job at a major commercial studio in Düsseldorf. After setting up his own studio with Jens Lissat, the pair recorded "The Techno Wave" as Interactive.

After meeting in a Düsseldorf club, Zenker and Bondzio got together and began plotting Hardfloor around Bondzio's fascination for Phuture's "Acid Trax" and the TB-303. Zenker's musical experience and Bondzio's understanding of both dancefloor dynamics and the MDMA experience locked together brilliantly. By the time of their third single, "Hardtrance Acperience", they had perfected the formula: off-kilter bass groove, relentless hi-hat rhythm, three separate 303 lines providing melody and counterpoint and a pattern of tense repetition that built towards almost unbearable intensity before the inevitable release.

Having discovered the formula, Zenker and Bondzio found it irresistible. Subsequent singles such as "Trancescript" and "Into the Nature" simply reshuffled the elements that had featured on "Acperience", but they were still huge underground hits and soon Hardfloor had the most instantly recognisable sound in Techno. The pair didn't forget the machine on which their success was based, dedicating their debut album, **TB Resuscitation** (1993), to "the inventor of the Roland TB-303." They even opened the album with a track called "Lost In the Silver Box". **TB Resuscitation** was a fine declaration of intent, but it succeeded almost too well. Soon the sound of the 303 was all-pervasive and, by the time of **Respect** (1994), Hardfloor's unique selling-point was well on its way to becoming a cliché. Zenker and Bondzio seemed trapped inside their own formula and, despite reasonable success, the album's solitary single, "Mahogany Roots", suggested that the cracks were beginning to show. A half-hearted attempt to change direction was suggested by 1995's "Da Damn Phreak Noize Phunk", but by then, the Techno scene was engaged by more minimal pleasures and, next to the innovations of drum 'n' bass, Hardfloor sounded distinctly pedestrian.

Zenker's more commercially oriented side-projects – including the execrable "Acid Folk" under the name Perplexer – weren't entirely blameless in devaluing the Hardfloor sound. Bondzio, however, was increasingly drawn to the muscular, minimal Techno of producers like Steve Stoll. The tensions were apparent on the charmless **Home Run** (1996) which pulled in opposing directions without capitalising on the duo's mastery of dramatic dancefloor dynamics. Significantly, Hardfloor's next move was a greatest hits selection. **Best of Hardfloor** (1997) brought together tracks such as "Hardtrance Acperience" and "Into the Nature" with the choicest moments from their remix work.

While **Home Run** had been themed around baseball, Bondzio and Zenker decided to use pinball as the concept for **All Targets Down** (1998). This unpromising beginning translated into a release which was every bit as uninspired as this desperate gambit suggested. The formula was firmly back in place, though the defiant "Hardfloor Will Survive" featured a guest appearance from Phuture 303. Few were convinced. Dispensing temporarily with the Hardfloor moniker, Zenker and Bondzio reappeared with **Electric Crate Digger** (1999) under the name Da Damn Phreak Noize Phunk. The album was a relatively standard Big Beat-style samplefest which seemed cynically designed to capitalise on the chart success of artists such as Fat Boy Slim and The Chemical Brothers. The funk guitars and fuzzboxes all seemed a long way from the revolutionary innovations of "Hardtrance Acperience".

⊙ **TB Resuscitation**   Harthouse, 1993

The album which single-handedly revived the Acid sound and provided the template for countless 303-based releases during the '90s. Still the definitive Hardfloor album.

Hardkiss

Scott Hardkiss (like the Ramones, the members of Hardkiss have all adopted the same surname) was a student studying literature at Oxford when he discovered Acid House in the late '80s. He hooked up with an old friend, Gavin Bieber (later Gavin Hardkiss), for 1989's Glastonbury festival before returning to the US where the pair promoted some of the East Coast's first major raves. Then they turned their attention to San Francisco and drove 3000 miles to meet up with another friend. Having recruited the newly rechristened Robbie Hardkiss, they set about organising a record label and a party crew.

Funding the label initially from parties such as Sunny Side Up and Magic Sounds of the Underground, the trio began alchemising a deeply trippy sound, best exemplified by 1993's "Three Nudes In a Purple Garden" – a hazy, lysergic rewrite of Ambient Techno, Progressive House and their own distinctive musical heritage. One of the mixes from that release, "Three Nudes Having Sax on Acid", became a major UK underground hit thanks to the impact of the burgeoning Ambient scene and a fleeting taste for eclecticism.

Delusions of Grandeur (1994) was a compilation of tracks from each of the Hardkiss protagonists, including the delicious "Rain Cry" by God Within (the alter ego of Scott Hardkiss) before a major label deal with Columbia beckoned and, with it, the distinct undertow of a backlash. Claims that the music had actually been composed by other musicians – including Jon Drukman and Jeff Taylor – surfaced, though the Hardkiss camp steadfastly ignored them.

Namaquadisco (1998) was the first major release from Gavin Hardkiss under the name Hawke. In keeping with the Hardkiss philosophy, it was a strangely stoned and deeply psychedelic transliteration of Techno. Like Doug Rushkoff's *Ecstasy Club* novel, it was a peculiarly San Franciscan take on dance music, though no less compelling for that. Though signs of strain in their relationship are evident, the members of Hardkiss continue to occupy themselves with solo and group projects, though the overall significance of the Hardkiss sound remains locked to the trippy etherealisms of their early releases, in particular the groundbreaking "Three Nudes…" release.

⦿ Delusions of Grandeur   Hardkiss, 1994

Still the definitive guide to the Hardkiss sound – a trippy, stoner amalgam of Ambient, Detroit Techno and Trance.

Havana

Tony Scott and Richard Miller first met when they were 14. Scott also knew Graham Drinnan (aka Gypsy) from a childhood stay in the seaside resort of Ayr. In the wake of Acid House, the three reunited in Glasgow where Millar and Scott were making a living as DJs. They began putting together their own tracks, eventually persuading local record shop owner Billy Kiltie to finance their first release, "Schtoom" – a dense multi-layered groove that nestled somewhere between Leftfield and Gat Decor.

"Schtoom" was hugely successful, providing the launchpad for Kiltie's Limbo label and its unstoppable rise throughout the early '90s. It was followed by the percussive frenzy of "Shift" which sold equally well. Soon the trio were throwing themselves into a variety of side-projects such as Ready For Dead and Sublime. By the time of Havana's third single, "Ethnic Prayer", they were riding high. But while initial copies of

"Ethnic Prayer" sold so fast it seemed set to breach the upper reaches of the chart, the single ran into problems when Phonogram objected to its (uncredited) use of a sample from Tears For Fears' "Change". Unsurprisingly, writs were issued and all remaining copies of the record were destroyed. A re-recorded version without the offending sample still went on to become one of Limbo's best-selling singles.

Suddenly Havana disappeared from view. Miller and Scott set up their own club nights, spinning brutally hard, minimal Techno and inviting guest DJs like Steve Bicknell and Luke Slater because "no one else would". They were openly contemptuous of their earlier releases and dismissed almost all of the numerous side-projects which Drinnan was occupying himself with. Despite this, Havana were still a working creative unit driving themselves to create a sound which would approximate the new music they were listening to – a stripped-down amalgam of Jeff Mills, UR and Planetary Assault Systems.

Condensed eventually arrived in the first half of 1993 and offered a glimpse of the radical overhaul that Havana were attempting. Tracks such as "Skyhat Part IV" or "Nymph" were determinedly underground affairs, fuelled by the wide-eyed, teeth-grinding amphetamine edge of the post-honeymoon Ecstasy rush. But reconciling Drinnan's more commercial sensibilities with the new sound proved impossible and he grew increasingly estranged from the group, eventually focusing entirely on his own solo career which resulted in the **Soundtracks** (1994) album before a major label deal and subsequent obscurity beckoned.

Miller and Scott continued to push the envelope of their rapidly developing sound and began planning an album of their own. They also explored more experimental solo projects under a variety of aliases on Limbo's subsidiary, Out on a Limb. As Manual, Miller released the scorching "In-Sense", while Scott conjured up one of British Techno's finest moments with F2's "Dominica".

Havana's debut album, **Hitch** (1995), also proved to be their swan-song. It was a record of brilliant, radical moments that touched base with the best of Detroit's output. Aimed firmly at the dancefloor, tracks such as "Infinite" and "Sprig" were full of hard, metallic surfaces and kinetic funk, while the swooning "Soul Plate" was shot through with icily romantic melodies and compellingly shaped syncopations. Although it was largely overlooked in favour of more easily assimilable fare, **Hitch** remains one of the highpoints of UK Techno, a classic of innovative, but never self-indulgent, dancefloor smart-bombs that still sounds, years after its release, fresh, exciting and superbly confident. After the album failed to get the recognition it deserved, Miller returned to his job as a courier, focusing only fitfully on his Manual project, and Scott moved to the Soma label and reinvented himself as Percy X.

⊙ **Hitch**   Limbo, 1995

The product of a unique chemistry between two self-taught producers striving to create what they called "the new music", Havana's only album is an essential addition to any collection of dancefloor Techno.

Richie Hawtin

f there is such a thing as a recognisable star in underground Techno, then Richie Hawtin fits the bill. His tall, lanky frame, skinhead crop and rectangular granny glasses constitute an image which has seen extensive coverage in the dance media, while the Plastikman logo (a weirdly expressionist, dancing gremlin) has enjoyed a similarly ubiquitous existence, plastered over record sleeves, record bags, posters and magazines. Like the best corporate design, this imagery is a masterpiece of style as a representation of content. Even if you had never heard Richie Hawtin's music, you'd be able to guess how it sounded from his cool, slightly boffin-ish, skate punk exterior and that liquid, part-funny, part-sinister Plastikman golem. His records are full of gawky, angular shapes that stretch and morph like rubber, but Hawtin's music is also kinetic, strangely unsettling and often deeply narcotic. Before the arrival of weirdbeat and the cerebral aesthetic of Scanner, Squarepusher and μ-ziq, Hawtin attracted the lion's share of Techno chin-strokers, nerds and trainspotters even though his own sympathies are clearly allied with the more vital and instinctive physicality of the dancefloor.

After a childhood in Oxfordshire, in 1979 Hawtin's family moved to Windsor, Canada, a short drive over the border from Detroit. The next few years were spent picking up a new accent, learning to breakdance and exploring the industrial sound of bands like Severed Heads and Skinny Puppy. He soon began tuning into The Wizard and Electrifying Mojo on WJLB, bought himself a pair of Technics decks and eventually found himself meeting Derrick May who – so the story goes – gave him an advance copy of Rhythim Is Rhythim's "It Is What it Is".

Soon Hawtin had landed himself a job as resident DJ at The Shelter in Detroit where he met a one-time indie DJ, John Acquaviva, who'd discovered a passion for Techno, and together the pair began plotting their own records. In May 1990 their first release, "Elements of Tone" as States of Mind, emerged on their self-financed Plus 8 label, named after their habit of playing records with the pitch control on their Technics pushed up against the end-stop. Kenny Larkin, another Shelter regular, provided the label's second release, "We Shall Overcome", and within a remarkably short period of time, Plus 8 was establishing a serious reputation. But the label's success brought with it an unforeseen problem: the first in a series of well-publicised spats with Detroit musicians who felt that "a white kid from Canada" was hijacking their music.

As far back as 1990, Hawtin had been recording solo under the name F.U.S.E. and it was under this name (it stands for Futuristic Underground Subsonic Experiments) that he eventually scored his first significant dancefloor hit with Sheffield's LFO. Billed as F.U.S.E. vs LFO, "Loop" was a close cousin of Ron Trent's "Altered States", mapping an impossibly funky, percussive groove against mood-fuelled Detroit strings and an insistent bass pattern. That single grew out of a long-standing relationship with Warp Records which had begun with leisurely discussions between Hawtin, Acquaviva and the label's Rob Mitchell. The three talked about the concepts behind Warp and Plus 8, surfing ideas about

JOSEPH COLTICE

electronic music and Techno's potential away from the dancefloor. Out of these discussions grew the seeds of the label's Artificial Intelligence series. Hawtin contributed "Spiritual High" to the first **Artificial Intelligence** compilation in 1992 and followed with his own exceptional solo contribution to the series in the shape of **Dimension Intrusion** (1993). A collection of random moments from Hawtin's F.U.S.E. catalogue (including 1991's classic "F.U."), the LP offered a glimpse of Hawtin's abilities across the full-length format. Although his later reputation as the acid-fried auteur of the 303 has overshadowed his F.U.S.E. output, **Dimension Intrusion** was a masterful debut, full of subtle prettiness like "A New Day" and "Dimension Intrusion" itself alongside the warping Hardcore template of tracks such as "Substance Abuse" or "Train Trac".

A few months after the release of the Warp album, Plastikman's **Sheet One** emerged on NovaMute. The basic principle of the album rotated around the reconnection of Chicago Acid House and Detroit Techno, but the record was minimal, polished to a peak of perfection and its shapes suggested a producer in the grip of lysergic freefall. As if to prove the point, the sleeve of the CD release was perforated into tiny squares like acid tabs. **Sheet One** and the subsequent **Musik** (1994) explored sparse, oblique terrain – sometimes, as on "Fuk" (from **Musik**), just Hawtin jamming on 808 and 909 drum machines – but both albums were huge creative and commercial successes. The wired edginess and sometimes overwhelming emptiness of these releases touched a chord with both the dancefloor and the home-listening contingent who recognised something significant in the queasy 303 acid lines of tracks like "Smak" and "Plasticity" (from **Sheet One**) or the dislocated strings of "Ethnik" (from **Musik**).

The Plastikman releases transformed Hawtin from a relatively unknown underground producer into something approaching a star.

Hawtin, however, "began to feel hemmed in" and the result was a three-year hiatus which only ended with the appearance of **Consumed** (1998). Conceptually, the new album was linked to the breathtaking experimentalism of **Sheet One**, but, if anything, it was a darker and bleaker affair, taking the games with space and depth to their outermost limits. **Artifakts** (1998) provided the missing link between **Musik** and **Consumed**. Some of the material on **Artifakts** had been intended for what was to be the third installment of the Plastikman saga, **Klinik** ("Hypokondriak", "Psyk", "Pakard" and "Korridor"), while other tracks had simply been recorded during what Hawtin describes as his "exile" ("Rekall", "Are Friends Elektrik" and "Skizofrenik"), but Hawtin's programming skills ensured that the release still worked as a cohesive and convincing entity in its own right.

Meanwhile, on his Minus label Hawtin was investigating even spacier terrain. The release of **Concept 1 96: VR** – a reinterpretation of Hawtin's 1996 series of monthly 12"s (compiled on **Concept 1 96: CD** early in 1998) by Cologne-based DJ Thomas Brinkmann using a twin tone-arm turntable – confirmed the direction of this fresh experimental phase which was fuelled by a more cerebral, scientific approach to minimalism.

⊙ **Dimension Intrusion**   Plus 8/Warp, 1993

Hawtin's contribution to the Artificial Intelligence series was a classic of perfectly honed electronics and rambunctious grooves.

⊙ **Sheet One**   Plus 8/NovaMute, 1993

Another landmark album that took the 303 back to Chicago and far forward into the future.

⊙ **Consumed**   Minus/NovaMute, 1998

More defiantly abstract and experimental than previous Hawtin outings, the 303s are still there, but this time twisted and mutated into more atmospheric frequencies.

Heavenly Music Corporation

O ver the course of three years during the mid-'90s, San Francisco's Silent Records released a series of four exquisitely crafted electronic albums by Heavenly Music Corporation. In terms of programming, composition and innovation, these releases were light years ahead of Europe's Ambient excursions, comparable only to the spaced output of Heidelberg's Deep Space Network (whose albums Silent licensed for US release). Producer and composer Kim Cascone now describes those years as an "Ambient detour" which punctuated an already distinguished career in music. Cascone studied arrangement, composition and electronic music at Berklee College in Boston before embarking on a career in the film industry, including stints working as a sound designer at George Lucas' Skywalker Ranch and as a music editor on David Lynch's *Twin Peaks* and *Wild at Heart*.

Under the name PGR (Poison Gas Research), Cascone's first album, **Silence** (1986), was also the release that launched Silent. Cascone continued to make records as PGR until the arrival of the first Heavenly Music Corporation album, **In a Garden of Eden** (1993), which keyed in with the more exploratory moods of Ambient Techno. Though the music on **In a Garden of Eden** had a fragile romance, extra-terrestrial beauty and sharp experimentalism, Cascone's academic background in electronic music and computer coding took Ambient Techno into previously unexplored intellectual reaches. However, **Consciousness III** (1994) obscured the theoretical objectives in favour of gently unfolding melodic structures and compelling prettiness.

Lunar Phase (1995) was a compilation of tracks composed especially for a Japanese radio station that based its 24-hour-a-day Ambient programming around tidal movements. The album retained its predecessor's hauntingly ethereal cadences and was, if anything, even more serenely chilled. Tracks such as "Energy Portal" evoked the cyclical shapes of Fripp and Eno's proto-Ambient classic, **No Pussyfooting** (1973), the album which provided Cascone with the Heavenly Music Corporation moniker.

Recorded in an abandoned computer room, **Anechoic** (1996) proved to be Cascone's final album in this temporary guise. Parts of the album were inspired by the vintage computer manuals he unearthed as he ran the wires for his studio, provoking a seam of "straight to the metal" coding adventures which has continued to run through his subsequent work. Following the release of **Anechoic**, Cascone sold Silent Records (which had by then become one of the West Coast's most respected underground labels) and took up a career as a sound designer at Headspace, Thomas Dolby's multimedia company, and work on *Oni*, "a John Woo-style, Japanese anime CD-Rom" released late in 1999.

⊙ **Consciousness III**   Silent, 1993

Stunningly pretty and complex Ambient Techno which provided a new benchmark for the genre.

Thomas Heckmann

Thomas Heckmann is one of a number of artists who are capable of crafting inspired, other-worldly melodies from just a cluster of abstract notes. As Drax, Heckmann has made records which overlay hard, obsessively funky grooves with melodies that sound like planets being ripped apart or, sometimes, seem inspired by the final, tortured sequences of old skool computer games such as Space Invaders and Galaxian.

Heckmann's first release was under the name Exit 100. "Liquid" (1991) was one of the earliest successes for Frankfurt's fledgling Force Inc. label and was licensed to Mute, subsequently scoring a Top 20 placing in the independent charts during 1992 – perhaps one of the strangest, most challenging records ever to do so. Soon after the Exit 100 release, Heckmann came up with "Trope", this time under the project name Age. More linear and less unsettling than "Liquid", the single confirmed Heckmann's talent for shaping and sculpting sounds that seemed to skid across the soundfield before splintering into fragments. The revolutionary bass sound on "Trope" subsequently became a staple of Frankfurt Trance records and Heckmann's output continued to provide a fertile source of inspiration for Techno producers all over the world during the following years.

Throughout the early '90s, Heckmann kept up an exhausting production schedule, releasing records as Exit 100, Age, Skydiver, Spectral Emotions, Purple Plejade and others with the kind of consistency and regularity that few could match. Some of the early Age material was brought together for **Early Sessions & Outtakes** (1993), while **The Orion Years** (1994) provided a useful entry point for those who had missed the 12"s which have formed the main focus of Heckmann's output. **Circuits** (1993) proved to be the last Exit 100 release as Heckmann concentrated on launching his own label, Trope, and a new alter ego, Drax. The feel of this new material was resolutely underground, but it quickly established a cult following. Despite his cult status, Heckmann scored a considerable hit with "Amphetamine", which launched itself into the Top 20 in France during 1994.

Drax's **Tales From the Mental Plane** (1995) was perhaps too far ahead and experimental in style to achieve similar commercial success, but it was an astonishing release nevertheless. Tracks such as "Mental Surface" or the epic "Bath the Room With Light" wired Heckmann's trademark abstract electronics with circular Electro rhythms and alien atmospherics to craft a dramatic, innovative sound that anticipated many of the developments which percolated through Techno in the years afterward.

Prior to the release of the Drax album, Heckmann launched another label, AFU, which provided a platform for yet another alias, Silent Breed. Perhaps the least satisfying of his projects, Silent Breed still cultivated a reasonable underground following, while Heckmann continued to proliferate new names and side-projects at a dizzying rate – between '94 and '98, he released records as TPH, Electro Nation, 8-Bit Science, Stromklang and Metric System. After a four-year gap, he returned to Force Inc. and the Age moniker in 1997 with the appropriately titled "Return to the Force" single and the subsequent album, **Isolation** (1998). Heckmann began 1999 with the third instalment of his "Welt In Scherben" series, an exceptional 12" that proved that his gift for combining extra-terrestrial sounds and melodies with hard dancefloor grooves was as compelling as ever.

⊙ **Drax – Tales From The Mental Plane**   Trope, 1995

Even now, this still sounds like an album from outer space. Hard-as-nails grooves, other-worldly melodies and unconventional imaginative leaps make this the definitive Heckmann release.

DJ Hell

G rowing up in the rural Bavarian district of Chiemgau, Helmut Geier (Hell to his friends) used to sneak night-time listens to the radio under his bedclothes. By the time he was old enough to travel into Munich's record shops with his brother, he had already developed an all-consuming passion for music. After a spell of punk rock evangelism, DJ Hell became a hip-hop/rare groove DJ/party promoter in Munich. Access to Munich's import stores eventually led him to House and Techno and the prevailing influence on his sets at venues such as the Tanzlokal Grössenwahn was predominantly a UK version of Acid House.

Hell's reputation began to spread thanks to incendiary sets which revealed not only an encyclopedic knowledge of music, but an inspired flair for programming on the fly. In 1992, he was invited to play at Berlin's Love Parade. He concluded his set with a single-sided white label. A stunning combination of heavy funk percussion and wildcat orchestration that was the result of his first and only studio session, the track was called "My Definition of House". Based around a cello sample borrowed from a David Byrne and Brian Eno theatre production, the track sounded like a cross between X-102 and Baby Ford and it was good enough for R&S boss Renaat Vandepapeliere to offer him a record deal on the spot.

"My Definition Of House" became a landmark release, drawing comparison with seminal classics such as Rhythim Is Rhythim's "Strings Of Life" (partly because of the similarity of Byrne and Eno's cellos to May's icily robotic Ensoniq string samples) and Ron Trent's "Altered States" masterpiece. Although more records followed – like the stuttering distortion workout of "Three Degrees Kelvin" on Magnetic North – Hell didn't maintain a lengthy relationship with R&S. Instead, the association which has dominated most of his recording career dated back to his days on the punk scene. Disko Bombs was a label set up initially as a dance counterpart to the punk label run by Optimal Records in Munich, the shop where Hell had bought many of his punk singles in the late '70s. And, just as Helmut had shortened his name to

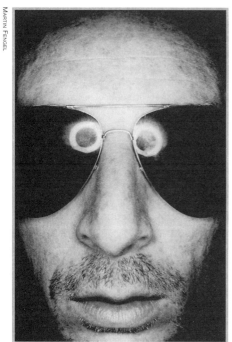

MARTIN FENGEL

Hell, Disko Bombs quickly became just Disko B.

With Disko B, Hell began to explore a dark, almost gothic strain of Techno that had its roots in the explosive energy of punk. Tracks like "Moth-erfunk" or "Risveglio Di Una Citta" were brood-ing affairs that borrowed the hard, minimal feel of Jeff Mills or Robert Hood and invested it with a sense of baleful, barely restrained violence. On "Totmacher" (lit. "Dead Maker") he blended *film noir* soundtracking with deep, punishing grooves, while 1994's "Allerseelen" (which was remixed by Mills) became one of the year's most name-checked underground hits.

Recorded with Mijk van Dijk in Berlin and Disko B label-mate Richard Bartz, Hell's debut album, **Geteert & Gefedert** (1994), was suitably intense, throwing tough Detroit grooves and hard-ball dynamics across tracks like "I Feel Love" and "My Life Is Hell". Though the influence of his collaborators was certainly traceable, the album proved that Hell had settled into his stride as a producer. A contribution to the X-Mix series, **Wildstyle** (1995), provided international audiences with a taste of Hell's skill as a DJ. An impressive mix of old and new classics, it remains a key release for anyone who's interested in the reasons behind Hell's reputation as Germany's premier DJ during the mid-'90s.

As evidenced by **International Deejay Gigolos Vol. 2** (1998), his own International Deejay Gigolos label has focused on a playful, deliciously retro style of Electro that harks back to the golden age of Kraftwerk and – thanks to the input of Australian/American art students Chicks On Speed – Gina X Performance. Hell's second album, **Munich Machine** (1998), was a broader, more accessible outing than its predecessor. As the name suggested (Munich Machine was originally the name of one of Giorgio Moroder's mid-'70s projects), the album saw Hell plundering computer disco with tracks such as "For Your Love" and "Berimbau" being little more than thinly disguised pastiches of classic Moroder/Donna Summer workouts. However, the album also contained credited cover versions including an intriguing version of The Normal's "Warm Leatherette" and an electronic reworking of "Suicide Commando" by obscure Hanover guitar band No More, a single which Hell had played non-stop during his early career as a punk DJ and which, symbolically at least, brought Helmut Geier's musical trip full circle.

⊙ **X-Mix 5: Wildstyle**   Studio K7, 1995

This is an indispensable mix album for those who like the occasional classic to punctuate the adrenaline rush of new sounds by artists such as Richard Bartz, Mike Dearborn and Surgeon.

⊙ **Munich Machine**   Disko B/V2, 1998

With major label backing from Richard Branson's V2, Hell painted a broad canvas full of accessible synth hooks, sex-kitten vocals and – gulp! – just a dash or two of Giorgio Moroder.

Higher Intelligence Agency

Birmingham's Higher Intelligence Agency evolved around the same time as the city's experimental Ambient club night, Oscillate, and involved many of the same people, though the group's activities are largely centred around producer Bobby Bird. The Higher Intelligence Agency/Oscillate collective were also influential in the formation and development of the Beyond Records label which provided a platform for the group's own releases and a number of groundbreaking compilations such as **Ambient Dub Volume One** (1992), which featured Higher Intelligence Agency's debut, "Ketamine Entity" – an almost evanescent exploration of shifting atmospheres and subtle melodics rather than beats and basslines.

A single, "Speedlearn", followed and Higher Intelligence Agency soon became a staple contributor to the flood of Ambient compilations which emerged over the following years. The debut album, **Colourform**

(1993), featured Bird in association with other members of the Oscillate team such as Steve Savale and Dave Wheels and remains one of the British Ambient scene's landmark releases.

While other Ambient artists were content to confine themselves to the studio, Bird developed a compelling live show (aided and abetted by Dave Wheels) based around improvisation and variation rather than straight renditions of albums and singles. Shortly after the release of **Freefloater** (1995), Bird teamed up with Biosphere's Geir Jenssen for a concert in Norway. The location they chose was as extreme as their methodology – the top of a mountain, accessible only by cable car, in Jenssen's home town of Tromsø, which lies inside the Arctic circle on the northernmost tip of Norway. The music they improvised for the concert was made from samples taken in the surrounding area – the noise of cable cars, the shrieking of the polar winds and the glacial sounds of the Norwegian winter. A recording of the concert was subsequently released as **Polar Sequences** (1996).

Following the success of this venture, Bird embarked on a number of collaborations – with Heidelberg's Deep Space Network on **Deep Space Network Meets Higher Intelligence Agency** (1996) and Ambient guru Pete Namlook on **Shado** (1996). A second concert with Biosphere, this time in the less extreme environs of Birmingham, took place the following year.

While Bird continues to operate as Higher Intelligence Agency, he has also set up another label, Headphone, as a vehicle for his own productions and collaborative efforts with other artists. The first release on Headphone, **Nothing** (1997), was a collaboration with Brian Duffy under the name System Error. A follow-up to **Shado** emerged in 1999, with Bird also mapping out a third Higher Intelligence Agency long-player.

⊙ **Freefloater**   Beyond, 1995

Carefully sculpted textures, warm ambience and elegantly chilled moods make this the definitive HIA album so far.

Robert Hood

A long with Alan Oldham (DJ-T1000), Robert Hood (then known as Rob Noise) was an early recruit to the fledgling Underground Resistance organisation. Operating as self-styled "ministers of information", Oldham and Hood constructed press releases, mission statements and took care of whatever day-to-day business came their way. As The Vision, Hood later became an integral part of the UR infrastructure, adopting the role of MC for the group's live shows and contributing to releases such as the **Riot** EP, "The Punisher" and **X-102 Discovers the Rings of Saturn** (1992). During the same period, his first solo release as The Vision, "Gyroscopic", also emerged on the UR label.

Subsequently, Hood began collaborating with Jeff Mills on the fledgling Axis label. Early releases such as the **Tranquilizer** EP and the **Drama** EP extrapolated the experimentalism they had already explored together as part of Underground Resistance, though Hood's **Waveform Transmission Vol. 2** (1993) demonstrated a distinctive and restless creativity that was all his own.

The release of **Minimal Nation**, an astonishing double-pack of individual, stripped-to-the-bone grooves, provided Hood with a considerable underground success and cemented his reputation as a sonic trail-blazer. **Minimal Nation** became the catalyst for a sound which would increasingly dominate Techno over the years that followed. Hood's own label, M-Plant, continued to explore the minimal theme with releases such as "The Protein Valve" and the limited edition "Advance Model", reaching its creative apex with the stunning **Internal Empire** (1994). Hood had jettisoned the raw, bruising feel of his earliest work to focus on a taut, precision-engineered sound that has rarely been replicated. Tracks such as "Master Builder" or the glittering "Multiple Silence" were painstakingly rendered examples of syncopation and repetition enveloped in a sharply defined production patina that set an as yet unsurpassed benchmark for minimalist Techno.

The releases that followed **Internal Empire**·seemed to admit the impossibility of refining the formula any further as Hood's sound began to expand and broaden. While his output on M-Plant and Hard-wax (as Missing Channel) became increasingly celebrated on the underground, Hood's interest in a more identifiably "soulful" sound began to assert itself. **Nighttime World** (1995) opened with the kind of carefully tempered musical figure that could have been lifted direct-ly from **Internal Empire**, but the new direction was swiftly established as the introduction flooded with warm, embrasive strings and a live-sounding bassline. On "Episode #19", Hood juxtaposed an exuberant pizzicato melody against a languid bass pattern, elsewhere "The Color of Skin" was as dreamily melancholic as anything Detroit had yet produced.

Though his output since the mid-'90s has been sporadic and the increase in the number of artists exploring minimalism has tended to obscure his significant contribution to the development of the sound, Hood still enjoys a position as one of the most revered producers on the Techno underground.

⊙ **Internal Empire**   M-Plant/Tresor, 1994

A defining moment in the trajectory of minimal Techno, Hood's masterpiece has yet to be surpassed.

Mike Ink

aybe it's something in the water, but Cologne seems to have a sizeable gene pool of talent, ranging from the producers and artists who orbit Dr. Walker's Liquid Sky bar in the city centre to those who are more likely to be found hanging out in record shops such as A-Musik and Delirium. But, along with his erstwhile partner, Jörg Burger, the producer most associated with Cologne's distinctive brand of syncopated dancefloor Techno is Wolfgang Voigt, better known as Mike Ink. Ink's sound is an odd, often quirky transmutation of Germany's Trance sound. Based more on offbeats and rhythmic interplays than its more linear cousin and featuring elastic grooves and playfully sharp Acid sounds, his music falls somewhere between Frankfurt and Detroit.

He describes music as his "lifetime mission" and reveals a complex nexus of influences that includes Wagner, Miles Davis, Palais Schaumburg, Scritti Politti and Schoenberg, though he does admit to a taste for *schlager* (Germany's version of the cheesy pop hits that dominate music charts worldwide). The overwhelming impact on his musical career, however, remains Acid House. Ink's fondness for the Roland TB-303 is evident in all but a handful of his most classic releases. Tracks such as 1993's "Five Years On Acid", "Accident In Paradise" and "Living In Pain" are fuelled by warping Acid lines and vertiginous peaks of swooping sound that suggest a continuing love affair with the silver box. Even his publishing company is called Three-O-Three Music.

Yet his best-known track, 1994's "R.E.S.P.E.C.T", dispensed with the 303 in favour of a bruising Detroit groove and metallic strings while the output of his Profan and Studio One labels veers towards more experimental territory. His most extreme releases, as Gas, are dislocated Ambient excursions such as 1999's **Konigsforest** or 1997's **Zauberberg**.

While Ink has a long involvement with collaborative projects (most of his early releases were done in partnership with Jörg Burger, up to and including 1996's Burger/Ink album, **Las Vegas**), he has managed to build a significant cult following thanks to a distinctive style and a seemingly limitless creative energy. Ink's quirky sense of humour has led to some odd releases, such as the 1995 EP that included tracks named after more famous pop outings: "How Deep Is Your Love", "Young Americans" and "Viva Hate" (tucked away somewhere in Ink's extensive catalogue, Techno sleuths may also discover "99 Red Balloons").

Life's a Gas (1996) brought all of this together. It remains one of the essential moments in German Techno – an upbeat, insanely funky offering that gave free rein to Ink's passion for supple grooves and compelling dancefloor angles. Since then, Ink has focused on increasingly experimental projects such as Gas and work for his own labels. However, given the fact that it took five years between his early releases on Transatlantic (including the sought-after **Dialogue** EP) and the arrival of his debut album, fans of Mike Ink would be best not to expect a follow-up anytime soon.

⊙ **Mike Ink – Life's a Gas**   Force Inc., 1996

Ink's trademark elastic groove underpins a series of tracks that are alternately beautifully quirky and brilliantly danceable.

⊙ **Gas – Konigsforest**   Mille Plateaux, 1999

Queasy ambience, distorted textures and atmospheric dislocation, sometimes reminiscent of Thomas Köner and just as good.

Ken Ishii

Ken Ishii's introduction to electronic music came through Japan's Yellow Magic Orchestra and European industrial/Electro bands like Cabaret Voltaire and Nitzer Ebb. When the first House and Techno records reached Tokyo, Ishii began crafting his own unique take on the sound, first on borrowed equipment, then with a cheap second-hand sampler and a Korg synth. The results were stunning. He was still a student at Hitotsubashi University when Renaat Vandepapeliere offered him a contract with R&S Records. A cluster of singles for R&S, Plus 8 and ESP emerged, defining Ishii's music as silkily abstract (R&S material like "Garden on the Palm" and "Pneuma"), spikily percussive (his "Samsara" track under the Utu banner) or seductively dreamy (his music for ESP under the names Rising Sun and Yoga).

His music drifts on liquid structures, focusing as much on sounds and timbres as it does on melodies. When R&S collected his early releases for **Innerelements** (1994), critics found it difficult to classify his music, often choosing to describe it as "Ambient" rather than anything remotely close to Detroit Techno. Ishii's ideas had more in common, it seemed, with the beatless, gradual shifts of ambience than the raucous thump of the dancefloor, yet he cited Chicago producers like Lil' Louis and Tyree, Detroit's Derrick May and the avant garde experimentalism of Krautrockers Neu! as influences.

In 1995, when Ishii's "Extra" single was released (accompanied by Koji Morimoto's gorgeous manga animation video), it quickly became apparent that his music had moved onto a whole new level. The introspective, mood-based tone poems of **Innerelements** had matured into a wild, strange brew full of imploding sounds and sudden dramatic shifts. **Jelly Tones** (1995) confirmed this development with a series of fractured symphonies like "Moved by Air" and "Stretch" which pushed the envelopes of funk, Techno and abstract electronics into previously unexplored terrain. **Reference to Difference** (1996), which Ishii recorded for Sublime as Flare, followed suit. Tracks such as "Morceau" (from **Reference to Difference**) or "Cocoa Mouse" (from **Jelly Tones**) flirted with Ambience, Detroit Techno and the futurist dream-pop of YMO to

R & S RECORDS

create something that both acknowledged its influences and transcended them.

On his second Flare album, **Grip** (1996), intervals from Korean, Chinese and Balinese music overlapped with the minor seconds and tritones of Acid House. His intuitive compositional style ebbed and flowed, following feelings not formulas on real moments of genius like "Curved Flow" or the warped motorik funk of "Clinch". **Re-Grip** (1996) enlisted the remix services of a number of Japanese

producers – including Akio Milanpaak, Rei Harakami and Co-Fusion (with whom Ishii was later to co-produce the "Game Over" single for R&S) – to rework a selection of **Grip** tracks such as "Turbinates" and "Sweet Kathar-sis", but ultimately, like most such exercises, the results were variable with only Harakami's interpretation of "Curved Flow" providing any real compe-tition for Ishii's oddly crafted originals. Since then, however, Ishii has been relatively quiet, with only a clutch of singles – "Overlap", "Echo Exit" and "Game Over" – punctuating the silence.

⊙ **Innerelements**   R&S, 1994

Tiny spikes, cool atmospheres and disturbing melodies combine on this collection of Ishii's early R&S releases. Loaded with innovative cuts like "A.F.I.A.C." and the epic "Fragments of Yesterday", which layered cut-glass sounds against bright, abstract grooves to devastating effect, this album offered positive proof of Ishii's radical talent back in 1994. It still sounds ahead of its time now.

⊙ **Jelly Tones**   R&S, 1995

Twisting spirals of sound through sudden rhythm shifts and brilliant surfaces, Ishii's official debut album redrew the codes of Detroit Techno into a thrillingly original digital landscape.

Takkyu Ishino

A founder member of Japanese techno-pop outfit Denki Groove, Takkyu Ishino's solo career as an underground DJ and produc-er for labels such as Torema and Frogman runs parallel to his more mainstream activities. Outside Japan, he's best known for a sound that embraces both hard, minimal Techno and the softer angles of Trance. However, the domestic success of Denki Groove leaves him in a similar position to The Shamen's Mr. C: well-known in the mainstream thanks to a series of pop hits, but operating a simultaneous underground career as a DJ, producer and promoter.

Ishino's musical career began with a group called Zinsei (also featuring Denki Groove's Pierre Taki) in the mid-'80s. After Zinsei's break-up, Ishino and Taki formed Denki Groove, recording their first album, **662 BPM** (1990) for SSE before recruiting Yoshinori Shimada and heading to Manchester to record **Flash Papa** (1991). During the sessions for the album, Ishino was introduced to the city's club scene and, though there were few obvious traces on Denki Groove's next album, **UFO** (1991), the influence of dance culture became increasingly apparent, culminating in 1994's Techno-oriented **Dragon** and a series of Denki Groove remixes by artists such as Ken Ishii and Hardfloor as the '90s wore on.

A working holiday from Denki Groove resulted in **Dove Loves Dub** (1995), Ishino's first solo album, though it was a subsequent mix set, **International DJ Syndicate Vol. 1** (1996), which demonstrated how convincingly he'd assimilated Techno. Featuring tracks from Joey Beltram, Jeff Mills and Basic Channel, the album veered towards the harder and more minimal amalgam which had developed into the leading edge of dancefloor electronics over the previous eighteen months and provided Ishino with growing recognition in Europe.

By now running an increasingly successful underground career, Ishino embarked on a collaboration with Westbam (later released under the name Takbam) and signed a deal with Low Spirit which resulted in **Berlin Trax** (1998). Tracks such as "Taxi Funk" and "Alles Nach Nippon" made **Berlin Trax** a solid follow-up, though again it was hard to resist the idea that Ishino articulated his grip on Techno more convincingly as a DJ than as a producer.

Throbbing Disco Cat (1999) combined the previous year's **Montag** EP with all-new tracks and a bonus disc featuring a grab-bag of earlier material. It found Ishino busily trying to reconcile the disparate elements of his sound — Trance, hard minimalism and quirky experimentalism — into a single cohesive entity, but remained an awkwardly unsatisfactory package. Momentary flashes of brilliance, however, suggest that when Ishino finally resolves the disparity between his DJ and production activities, he will be more than a force to be reckoned with.

⊙ **Dove Loves Dub**   Sony, 1995

Oscillating between the sledgehammer rhythms of his work for Fumiya Tanaka's Torema label and a more playful sound, this is still one of the most intriguing moments in Ishino's rapidly growing catalogue.

Ismistik

T romsø is situated on the northern-most tip of Norway, inside the Arctic circle. In the summertime, during the months of the midnight sun, it is picture-postcard beautiful, surrounded by glacial mountains and a harbour that overlooks a glittering, impossibly blue ocean. During winter, however, Tromsø is submerged beneath the polar night. From October to March, the city exists in darkness. Maybe that's why it has come to be described as "the Detroit of the north". As more than one producer has pointed out, "There's nothing else to do here in winter except make music and shovel snow…" The city is home to an extraordinarily creative Techno scene – including artists such as Biosphere's Geir Jenssen and Mental Overdrive's Per Martinsen – but one of its most intriguing musical exports was a group who burned brightly for just a few short years during the early '90s before vanishing almost as quickly as they had emerged.

Ismistik was a collaborative venture involving Bjørn Torske, Ole Mjøs and Mette Brundtland. Early singles on Djax, such as "Bonus Bouncers" or 1992's "Oasis", hinted at a rare talent for exploring quietly introspective grooves and atmospheres chilled to sub-zero temperatures. On "3rd Trace", for example, they layered gently meandering rhythms and delicately evolving ambience that suggested both the cold, dark moods of their hometown in winter and the wide open expanse of deep space.

A move to the relatively less severe environs of Bergen preceded the recording of Ismistik's masterpiece, **Remain** (1994). It was a remarkable debut, packed with deep, desperately inventive tracks such as "Woodvibe" or the swooning "Bulb" which threatened to surpass even the most seductive moments of Techno's romantic drift. But Ismistik seemed to possess a talent for encompassing a dizzying array of directions within their seemingly simple, but carefully crafted sound. The wayward experimentation of "Tortoise Thoughts", the dislocated tone poetry of "Daybreak" and the frenetic Detroit groove of "Cassis" each suggested the arrival of a major talent to rival the best of Techno's experimental vanguard.

Yet **Remain** also proved to be Ismistik's swan song. Perhaps Torske and Bruntland (Mjøs had departed some time earlier) felt they couldn't sustain the levels of creative brilliance which they had reached during the album's recording and preferred to leave a legacy which has made the title of Ismistik's sole long-player seem strangely prophetic. Years later, it still stands as one of Techno's most enduring and innovative peaks.

Torske resurfaced eventually with the more House-oriented **Nedi Myra** (1998) on Russ Gabriel's Ferox label. While echoes of Ismistik's bittersweet moods were still evident, it was a more playful, upbeat offering. Now permanently based in Bergen, it seems as if Torske has traded the spirit of his hometown for a less melancholic extreme.

⊙ **Remain**   Djax, 1994

Like Black Dog's **Temple of Transparent Balls** or Move D's **Kunststoff**,
this is one of Techno's most beautiful and accomplished underground
classics. The sound of a group surfing romantic moods,
experimentalism and pure electronic genius.

Jam & Spoon

n 1992, as Hardcore plunged itself into a maelstrom of supersonic
velocities and punishing, hammer-blow beats, a schism which had
been apparent in Techno as far back as 1988 reached its apotheosis.
The dichotomy was underlined by one of that year's biggest dancefloor
tracks, a release by a relatively unknown German duo, Jam El Mar
and Mark Spoon. "Stella" was an airy, blissed-out confection that harnessed a maddeningly infectious melody to a groove borrowed from
Moby's "Go" and, in clubs where the tropes of Hardcore had been
rejected, it quickly became a classic anthem, a ray of instant, absurdly
pretty, sunshine in the otherwise grey landscape of the early '90s.

A classically trained guitarist who had turned to production, Jam El
Mar (Rolf Ellmer) had already engaged with the dancefloor thanks to
his Dance 2 Trance project with DJ Dag, while, in his role as A&R man
for Logic Records, Mark Spoon (Markus Löffel) was in the process of
masterminding the career of dance-lite specialist Dr. Alban. The pair
had previously worked together on sessions for Dr. Alban singles such
as "Hello Africa" and "U and Me", with Spoon as producer/remixer and
his soon-to-be partner fulfilling keyboard duties.

"Stella" was lifted from their first official release as Jam & Spoon, the unpromisingly titled **Tales From a Danceographic Ocean** EP (a suspicious nod to the progressive rock of Yes and their **Tales From Topographic Oceans** album). Despite the sweetness of the EP's stand-out cut, it was clear that the pair had a darker side – one of the release's other tracks rejoiced in the title of "My First Fantastic Fist Fuck".

A remix of Bruno Sanchioni and Giuseppe Cherchia's "Age of Love" followed and quickly became just as much of a fixture on dancefloors as "Stella", acquiring a not entirely proven reputation as the "biggest-selling remix in Techno history". The hyperbole surrounding the pair continued undiminished and perhaps contributed to the grandiose ambition of their simultaneously released twin debut albums, **Triptomatic Fairytales 2001** and **Triptomatic Fairytales 2002** (1993). Despite the obvious suggestion of tracks such as "Neurotrance Adventure" and "Operating Spaceship Earth", the first of these was less a spaced-out opus and more the kind of taut, pop-oriented affair which fused the duo's obvious commercial sensibilities with the shapes of Frankfurt Trance. **Triptomatic Fairytales 2001** yielded a hit single, "Right in The Night", and, for a time at least, became the dance album that even mainstream buyers installed in their collections. **Triptomatic Fairytales 2002**, meanwhile, concentrated on Jam & Spoon's taste for progressive epics, complete with overwrought, often baroque, arrangements such as "I Saw the Future" or "Nocturnal Audio Sensory Awakening".

Jam & Spoon's profile led to remixes for the likes of Pet Shop Boys, Frankie Goes to Hollywood and Enigma, but their affinity with more commercial waters proved stronger than the pull of underground dancefloors and, by the mid-'90s, they were becoming increasingly dislocated from club culture. A side-project as Tokyo Ghetto Pussy attempted to recapture their relevance on the dancefloor, but **Disco 2001** (1996) was largely ignored. A further Jam & Spoon album, **Kaleidoscope** (1998), offered little to recommend it, but did include "So-

Called Techno Track" which, perhaps inadvertently, summed up their approach since the days of "Stella" and "Age of Love".

⊙ **Triptomatic Fairytales 2001**   Sony, 1993

"Stella" still sounds as blissfully dreamy as it always did, but Jam & Spoon's debut hasn't aged all that well. Strictly for Techno-pop archivists.

The Keyprocessor

Where Derrick May and Juan Atkins looked out onto Detroit and sought escape from the urban desolation surrounding them, Wilco Boumans looked around the small Dutch town of Bergeyk and saw provincial boredom. Determined not to spend the rest of his life in a line of chattering garden fences, he moved to neighbouring Eindhoven to study computer science. His interest in computers spilled over into music and he began listening to a number of synthesiser pioneers, including Kraftwerk and Yello. This music seemed as far as possible from the traditional life he was striving to leave behind. At this time, he met a like-minded individual, Erwin van Moll, who owned an Amiga computer, and they began to experiment with the machine's music-making abilities. Van Moll went on to record as Max 404 and Boumans collaborated (often uncredited) on a number of his records, including the classic album **Love & Mathematics** (1995).

Growing in confidence, Boumans struck out on his own. It wasn't long before his tracks came to the attention of Stefan Robbers, owner of Eindhoven-based Eevo Lute Records. Founded in 1992, the label had already gained a reputation for releasing quality, intelligent Techno, by such artists as Terrace (Robbers' own project), 2000 and One, and Bouman's old ally, van Moll. Soon, Boumans joined this illustrious roster with his debut EP, **In the Painful Quest of Beauty**, released in 1994 under the name The Keyprocessor. From the majestic choral synths of "Dirt" to the bubbling, military rasp of "Cabs", it was clear that he felt in no way overawed by the company he was keeping.

Two tracks from this EP appeared on the **Agenda 22** (1994) compilation along with a new track, "A Laughable Death" – a beautiful study in syncopated sadness that saw Boumans and van Moll recording together again. Since that time, Boumans has released only two more tracks, as computer studies turned into a demanding professional career, "Phantom" and "Far Away", both featured on **Agenda 23** (1998). According to Boumans, there are still a number of unreleased Keyprocessor tracks, both in the Eevo Lute vaults, and in his own scorched sampler. Some of these are available on the Internet at www.xs4all.nl/~keyproc/. Let's hope there's more soon.

◉ In the Painful Quest of Beauty   Eevo Lute, 1994

Four tracks, ranging from the hard-edged pointillist starchase of the title track to the widescreen choral ambience of "Dirt". Limited technology, unlimited imagination.

Peter McIntyre

LA Synthesis

Originally from Liverpool and Birmingham, respectively, Tony Gallagher and Carl Grant met on the fringes of the underground party scene in southeast London. Discovering a shared and relatively eclectic pool of influences – ranging from Model 500 and Black Dog to Kraftwerk and minimalist composer Steve Reich – the pair began experimenting with their own tracks, though it wasn't until promotional copies of "Agoraphobia" began to emerge towards the end of 1994 that the duo started to attract attention. "Agoraphobia" was a near-perfect debut, sewing a memorably trippy hookline (an exquisitely beautiful synth riff that was inspired by Reich's explorations in repetition) through a complex backdrop of clanking percussives and Detroit romanticism. Released on Plink Plonk with a Kenny Larkin remix, the single quickly became a fixture in London's clubs, crossing over into both Detroit and Ambient Techno sets.

Though "Frozen Tundra" was recorded for Plink Plonk, the group's relationship with the label proved to be short-lived and the follow-up didn't appear. Aside from live performances, LA Synthesis seemed to disappear for most of 1995, re-emerging eventually in 1996 with the "CMI Wavesequence" single on Mark Broom's A13 label. The backlog of material they had built up during the lengthy break began to filter out slowly, first with the "Zebra/Reich" single on Blue Basique and, soon afterwards, with the previously stalled "Frozen Tundra" single which signalled a new deal with the French label Shield.

It finally seemed as if the pair's stop-start career would now build up momentum, but the release of **Matrix Surfer** (1997) was so low-key that only industry insiders were even aware of its existence. Yet it was a remarkable debut. Fusing ethereal melodic patterns with evolving Detroit-edged grooves, tracks such as "If" and "Positive Negative" suggested that LA Synthesis were likely contenders to fill the void left by the recently disbanded Black Dog.

"Harmonic Disassembly", released on Global Communication's Universal Language label towards the end of 1997, hinted at a more Electro-based aesthetic than previous offerings, though the flipside's

"Skyline" retraced the classic LA Synthesis fusion of heart-stopping melodics and elegant rhythms. The single's release coincided with the arrival of new member Chris Johnson – a jazz pianist who had been drafted in to help realise the "funkier, more live-oriented direction" the group wanted to pursue. Johnson appeared on just one single, 1999's "Doidy Dawg" on Ultimatum, before Gallagher split from the group to pursue a solo project under the name Linear Systems.

⊙ **Matrix Surfer**   Shield, 1997

Perhaps one of the most overlooked UK Techno albums of the '90s, this is a beautiful combination of second-generation Detroit romanticism and sharp, inventive grooves. Hard to find, but definitely worth tracking down.

Neil Landstrumm

In 1992, Neil Landstrumm arrived in Edinburgh from his home in the northern town of Inverness to pursue a degree in Business Studies. But things didn't quite happen the way he'd planned. He started going to Pure (the city's long-running Techno club) and heard DJs like Derrick May and Richie Hawtin. The archetypal bedroom musician, Landstrumm spent his all his time investigating and exploring machines, pushing them to create the sounds he'd heard on records and only occasionally venturing out for nights at Pure or Sativa where the music was becoming harder, more minimal, more tuned in to what was going on in his own head.

Sharing a flat with Edinburgh promoter John Stewart provided Landstrumm with an introduction to Cristian Vogel who was sufficiently impressed with those early sonic experiments to invite him down to Brighton. Working in the studio there, Landstrumm turned out both the **Paskal** EP for Mosquito and a collaborative single with Cristian (Blue Arsed Fly's "Starfish") for the Edinburgh-based Sativae label. The records introduced Landstrumm's diamond-hard, stripped-down style and immediately began picking up critical attention. More records followed, like the **Index Man** EP for Peacefrog, Blue Arsed Fly's "In the Bag" outing for Russ Gabriel's Ferox label and then, finally, his **Brown By August** (1995) debut album.

Landstrumm also attracted attention for his heavyweight live shows, improvising muscular grooves which seemed to expand and contract around simple electrical impulses and enormous, heavily distorted kick drums. He's passionate about the concept of live Techno, arguing that, in the right circumstances, it can provide the music with vast new dimensions.

Landstrumm set up his own Scandinavia label at the beginning of 1996 as a platform for the group of like-minded producers with whom he's surrounded himself. The label's first major release was **Understanding Disinformation** (1996), Landstrumm's second album, and the one that found him moving towards an ever more uncompromising minimalism. It was followed by the brutalist **Bedrooms & Cities** (1997) which merged his love of Sheffield bleep Techno with the original sound of hardcore rave. Landstrumm's continued refusal to be constrained by musical boundaries resulted in the **Pro Audio** (1998) album. Recorded in New York following his relocation there, it fused the sounds of Adam X and Adam Beyer with his own increasingly experimental take on minimalism.

⊙ **Understanding Disinformation**   Scandinavia/Tresor, 1996

Bruising, muscular minimalism wrapped up in a razor-sharp production, this was a Landstrumm *tour de force*.

Kenny Larkin

F ormer USAAF serviceman and stand-up comedian Kenny Larkin is one of the chief innovators of Detroit's so-called "second generation" of Techno producers. Possessed of a distinctive melodic flair which has been much emulated, he has parlayed his considerable talents into two albums — **Azimuth** (1994) and **Metaphor** (1995) — which stand among the finest moments of modern electronics.

It was during a six-month stint as a stand-up that Larkin first discovered Techno. Soon he was a fixture at local clubs such as The Music Institute, The City Club and The Shelter, where he met Richie Hawtin who was in the process of making his own embryonic forays into production. When Hawtin finally got his Plus 8 label up and running, Larkin was eventually recruited to release his first single for the label, "We Shall Overcome".

After the release of a follow-up, "Colonize", Larkin left Plus 8 to set up his own label, Art of Dance, and scored his first major underground hit in 1992 with "War of the Worlds" under the name Dark Comedy. Based around a gently syncopated bass sequence and heavily layered with sparkling melodic flourishes, it suggested an alternate register for Techno. Larkin's contribution to the influential **Panic In Detroit** (1992) compilation, "Serena X" (under the name Yennek), confirmed his interest in music which was as much about listening as dancing. It was his contribution to the unparalleled and hugely innovative **Virtual Sex** (1993) collection, though, which pushed him to the forefront of Techno's romantic drift.

"Tedra" was an exquisitely beautiful, deeply emotive fusion of fizzing, digital textures and rhythmic syncopation. Some of the track's melodic figures were clearly influenced by jazz fusionist Jean Luc

Ponty, but, overall, the effect was pure, inventive Techno. "Tedra" was later included on the superb **Azimuth**, Larkin's debut for Warp. One of the most distinctive and influential of mid-'90s Techno albums, **Azimuth** pinned Detroit's basslines and syncopated drum patterns onto a melodic tapestry of liquid digital synthetics. Stylistically, it represented an evolution of both Derrick May's bright, sharp kinetics and Warp's Artificial Intelligence aesthetic (Larkin contributed the track "Maritime" to 1994's **Artificial Intelligence II**).

LADYBUG / BLACK FLAG

Then, on the night of November 17, 1994, Larkin was the victim of a shooting during what he later concluded had been an attempted robbery at his home in a suburb outside Detroit. Following intensive surgery, Larkin made a full recovery, even travelling to Europe some weeks later to promote his new R&S album, **Metaphor**. **Metaphor** was a darker, more compulsively percussive album than its predecessor. Stripped of the sparkling melodies and breathtaking modal shifts — which this time around had been replaced by painstakingly constructed rhythm patterns, subtle detailing and a lustrous sheen — it was nevertheless a strikingly original release that, once again, limned new territory for Techno. A single, "Catatonic" (the album's original working title), became a sizeable underground hit, confirming Larkin as one of Detroit Techno's point men.

An Art of Dance compilation, **Exhibits** (1995), combined tracks from a number of his different alter egos — Yennek, Pod and Dark Comedy — with contributions from Sean Deason and Stacey Pullen, but the collection seemed strangely muted in comparison with the electrifying innovations of his solo albums. A new deal with the Belgian label Elypsia resulted in the Dark Comedy album **Seven Days** (1997) which allied a selection of older tracks — including "War of the Worlds" and "Without a Sound" — with previously unreleased material. Less obviously listening-oriented than either **Azimuth** or **Metaphor**, the new album was received with puzzlement by critics who expected a continuation of the pristine surfaces he'd explored in 1994 and 1995. **Seven Days** has, however, survived the intervening years in remarkably good shape.

⊙ **Azimuth**   Warp, 1994

Probably one of the most essential Detroit albums of the entire Techno movement, this has power, beauty, grandeur and grooves to shake the house down.

⊙ **Metaphor**   R&S, 1995

Less immediately seductive than its predecessor, this was a darker,
moodier affair, but still ranks in the top ten Detroit albums.

Peter Lazonby

eter Lazonby's highly individual strain of Techno draws variously on Detroit, the UK Progressive House scene, modern com-
posers such as Janáček and Messiaen, choral music, Brazilian samba
and ethnic culture to create complex, multi-layered tracks which bridge
both the dancefloor and the home listening experience.

After a brief career as a studio engineer "making records for other
people and getting paid nothing for the privilege", Lazonby made his
solo debut in 1993 with "The Charm", a compellingly pretty and innovative production that merged warm atmospherics, sub-bass and
sparkling jazz vibes. Though it failed to make an impact on the relatively conservative musical climate of the time, "The Charm" did offer
some clues as to the direction of Lazonby's next single, the breathtakingly ambitious "Sacred Cycles". Arranged in three discrete sections and punctuated by a spoken-word sample of Bhagwan Shree
Rajneesh, the eleven-minute single borrowed elements from a number of different sources, including Frankfurt Trance, systems music
and the rhythms of Burundi to create one of the most original UK
dance records of the mid-'90s. The single became a Europe-wide
dancefloor hit, particularly in Germany where it has enjoyed a number
of equally successful re-releases.

Your Humble Servant (1995) developed the themes hinted at by the singles, particularly Lazonby's avowed interest in creating unusual and evocative atmospheres. One of the album's standout cuts, "Stamina" – a collaboration with Sex, Love & Motion DJ Russ Cox – became an anthem on many London dancefloors. A collaboration with Rad Rice as Deeper Throat provided two singles, "Mouth Organ" and "Peddle Power", though it was 1996's "Song Without Words" which signalled just how far Lazonby had travelled. More abstract and Detroit-inspired than his earlier material, full of wriggling synthetics and an overwhelmingly trippy ambience, it suggested that Lazonby had somehow managed to refine or condense the expansive, sometimes unruly, precincts of his sound into something more individual.

If You Cannot Resist... Why Do You Exist? (1997) was, creatively at least, a *tour de force*. Extrapolating the developments suggested by "Song Without Words", tracks such as "The Chair" or "Asleep" explored calm ambience, clicking, percussive grooves and sophisticated sonic atmospheres, but the release became mired in label and distribution problems, resulting in only a limited number of copies reaching the public domain. Lazonby subsequently moved to New Orleans where he began working on a shifting collaborative project with various singers, songwriters and poets under the name Healing Arts.

◉ Your Humble Servant   Brainiak, 1995

Wide-screen atmospherics and a vast melting pot of diverse influences make for a compelling and multi-layered experience.

Leftfield

nitially the solo project of Neil Barnes, Leftfield's debut single, "Not
Forgotten", appeared in 1989 on London label Outer Rhythm in limited
form. When friend Paul Daley (who had been drumming for A Man Called
Adam and Brand New Heavies) heard it, he immediately clambered
aboard the Leftfield ship and the pair set about remixing the track into
one of dance music's unforgettable moments. From there on the pair set
about restructuring dance music, embarking on a mission that, over the
next few years, would see them tearing up dancefloors and alchemising a
sound that drew intuitively from Techno, House and reggae.

Throughout 1991, legal wrangles with Outer Rhythm prevented
them from using the Leftfield name to record under. Fortunately it did-
n't hinder their remixing career and they set about reworking tracks by
the likes of Superreal, React 2 Rhythm, Inner City, Pressure Drop,
Stereo MC's, Tricky and even David Bowie, using these opportunities
as an outlet for their own ideas and helping kick-start a trend that
would sweep Britain and become known as "Progressive House".

In 1992, frustrated by the major labels' inability to view dance
music with any kind of long-term development and commitment, they
set up their own Hard Hands label. One of its first offerings was Dee
Patten's "Who's the Bad Man?", a tough blend of skanking breakbeat
House that stamped the label's authority on clubland and became a
yardstick for the breakbeat scene. The label has since helped establish the names of Vinyl Blair (featuring DJ Billy Nasty), Pressure Drop,
Bushflange (featuring Leftfield DJ Nick Rapaccioli), Delta Lady (alias
Secret Knowledge), Full Moon Scientist, Small World and Dark Globe.

Later that year, Leftfield issued "Release the Pressure" – the first
track of their own for two years – which featured the distinct vocals of

reggae vocalist Earl Sixteen. This slow dubby, grinding groove was followed by another single, "Song of Life". With its ecstatic chord sequences and angelic voices, it once again placed Leftfield in pole position as a year of club music experimentation drew to a close.

1993 was a year which saw dance music and rock music converge, and Leftfield released a single that, for some, still remains the final word in rock/dance collaboration. "Open Up" featured the vocals of ex-Sex Pistols frontman John Lydon – an old mate of Neil's from the punk era – and it spat itself into the clubs and then the charts, giving Leftfield their highest entry to date at #13. It was gutsy, spunky and energetic; everything that punk had been and which the rock press largely accused dance music of lacking. It was the biggest two-fingered salute dance music had yet administered.

"Open Up" set the scene for **Leftism** (1995), Leftfield's debut album which collected together the three previous singles and surrounded them with another eight shots of sonic skullduggery. A devastating debut, it mixed Techno with breakbeat, ambience, dub and sound-system style toasting with expert ease. It caught the mood of the times perfectly but would set standards for years. Rushing into the album charts at # 3, **Leftism** sold over 100,000 copies in its first six weeks, hanging around for a further 80 weeks and registering over 900,000 sales worldwide to date.

Since then things in the Leftfield camp have appeared quiet, when in reality it's been a behind-the-scenes hive of activity. A new label Offshoot was set up to cater for more DJ-friendly Techno while Paul Daley continues to DJ across the globe. Two tracks from John Lydon's album were given the Leftfield treatment, whilst new tracks appeared in numerous TV adverts and film soundtracks – including *Trainspotting*, *Shallow Grave* and *Judge Dredd*. Most of this period though was concentrated on writing their much anticipated second album, **Rhythm and Stealth,** released late in 1999.

⊙ **Leftism**   Hard Hands, 1995

Leftfield's debut arrived just in time for the superclub era and it's not
hard to figure out why widescreen epics such as "Song of Life" or
"Black Flute" imprinted themselves onto the dancefloor's more Techno-
literate psyche.

⊙ **Rhythm and Stealth**   Hard Hands, 1999

Over two years in the making, the title pretty much says it all. From the
outset of the first track, "Dusted" (featuring hip-hop MC Roots
Manuva), the speakers spew a dark, minimal cacophony of hard-edged
beats. "Chant Of A Poor Man" offers a smoke-heavy dub reply to "Afro-
Left", while "Rino's Prayer" is a stomach-churning collision of sine
waves and cymbal crashes. With guest appearances from dance/rap
pioneer Afrika Bambaata, and long-time collaborator Cheshire Cat,
Leftfield have again reset the parameters of dance music.

Sherman / Peter Buckley

Robert Leiner

The mystery of Robert Leiner who, at one time, was one of the
R&S label's major artists has deepened in the years since the
release of his third and final album, **Different Journeys** (1994). Leiner
originally moved from Gothenburg to Ghent as a studio engineer for
R&S. As Source, one of his early creative successes was "Neuromancer" – a uniquely crafted and distinctive track which layered impeccably detailed electronics with an almost painterly skill. His first major
work for the label appeared under his own name on the more Ambient-
oriented Apollo offshoot. **Visions of the Past** (1992) bore few superfi-
cial traces of Leiner's most significant influences, Jean Michel Jarre and

Tangerine Dream, though the pastoral feel of tracks such as "Full Moon Ritual" and "Northern Dark" suggested an interest that hovered somewhere between the dancefloor and a more classically inspired intent.

Leiner returned to the Source moniker the following year for the groundbreaking **Organized Noise** (1993). Along with CJ Bolland's **The Fourth Sign**, it offered conclusive proof that European Techno was shifting ahead of its antecedents. Tracks like "Eclipse" and "Beyond Time" were full of expertly shaped ideas, forged in what was, at the time, one of the most creative Techno studios in Europe, the R&S Laboratories. **Organized Noise** was acclaimed as a major step forward, but was almost eclipsed a few months later by "Experience", a double 12" that launched Leiner's Source project into overdrive during the early months of 1994.

In November of that year, the lavishly packaged **Different Journeys** emerged, this time under the name The Source Experience. It was a less accessible work than previous Leiner releases, sewing together hermetic tapestries of sound that only revealed the album's magic after repeated listening, but it turned out to be Leiner's most enduring and convincing record. Arranged and mixed live in the studio, **Different Journeys** was charged with dynamic shifts that suggested Leiner had been immersed in Basic Channel, Luke Slater and Jeff Mills, though it retained the distinctive melodic flavours of his earlier material.

Following the required promotion for **Different Journeys**, Leiner disappeared from view, surfacing occasionally over the next two years before vanishing completely. In the wake of '94 and '95's exponential explosion in the dance scene's commercial profile, Leiner's disappearance was overshadowed by seemingly more pressing matters. But the role he played in shaping the creative spirit of current European Techno should not be underestimated. During his all-too-brief years at R&S, Leiner made a significant contribution to Techno's forward trajectory.

⊙ **Organized Noise**   R&S, 1993

Almost every Leiner record made a significant impact, but this one was the big one. A release which shaped the direction of European Techno for years to come.

Cari Lekebusch

Alongside fellow Stockholm DJ and producer Adam Beyer, Cari Lekebusch's musical style has become synonymous with Swedish Techno. Lekebusch has developed the material on his Hybrid label into a fusion of compressed, tribal percussion and rolling loops punctuated by vocodered vox and undulating riffs, while Beyer's Drum-code label has realised a more direct, kick drum loop approach. Both currently now stand amongst the fore-runners of European underground Techno production.

Lekebusch started collecting records at the age of 10 and compiled mix tapes using one cassette deck and the pause button. His first release was an Electro track pressing of 150 copies in the late '80s that he admits to being nothing serious. Persisting with basic drum machines such as Roland's 101 and 303, his first releases of real note emerged in 1991 on Sweden's Ohm Records, who also released early material from Robert Leiner.

Citing his local record store, Vinyl Mania, as a constant source of inspiration, Lekebusch connected immediately with the early Techno sound. Later in 1991 and 1992 he released the series of "Fred" records on Belgium's R&S that hinted at the fledgling direction of his own Hybrid label which he was to set up in early 1994. "Hybrid One"

remained a simple affair in red and black typeface that was to change the shape of his music into a more concentrated style and develop the basis for a dedicated body of work.

With a healthy back catalogue on Hybrid under his belt (ten releases at the beginning of 1999), Lekebusch is presently developing a new label dedicated to a deeper, mellower sound. Djupt, which translates from his native tongue as "deep", is set to continue his Scandinavian legacy of forward-thinking music into the next millennium.

○ "Hybrid One"   Hybrid, 1994

The first tentative step into looped compression and tribal rhythm that was to shape the future Techno sound of Stockholm.

Jonas Stone

LFO

L ike many of the artists, producers and DJs who subsequently found themselves at the heart of rave culture, Mark Bell and Gez Varley were initially drawn to dance music by Electro and hip-hop. The pair first met in the mid-'80s, when they were members of rival breakdancing crews, then lost touch before reconnecting in 1989 when they found themselves enrolled on the same graphic design course in Leeds. In the intervening years, they discovered that they'd both gravitated towards Acid House and, though Bell was already making music with another partner, he and Varley quickly began working on tracks together, inspired equally by the output of Chicago's Trax Records and Detroit's Transmat.

Bell and Varley's Electro roots were still evident in one of the first tracks they put together, a raw amalgam of heavy sub-bass tones and sinewave bleeps called "LFO" (after the universal acronym for a synthesiser's low frequency oscillator) which gave the duo their name. "LFO" was one of a handful of tracks that persuaded Sheffield's Warp Records to sign the pair and it eventually became their first single for the label.

Neither LFO nor their new label were prepared for what happened next. "LFO" impacted on rave with thermonuclear force, becoming a massive dancefloor anthem before finding itself racing up the UK pop charts. Warp hurriedly persuaded the pair to begin work on an album, but it was almost a year before LFO re-emerged with "We Are Back" and the subsequent **Frequencies** (1991) album.

Frequencies was a *tour de force*. Tracks such as "Nurture" and "Mentok" combined weird angular shapes, slippery funk and heavy bass to create a sound that continued to influence the course of Techno in the UK throughout the '90s and inspired numerous producers and artists. Yet despite the creative success, Bell and Varley embarked on an extended "lost weekend" – punctuated only by 1992's "What Is House" and their seminal collaboration with Richie Hawtin on "Loop" – that was to last until their brief return in 1995 with the grinding, lo-fi menace of "Tied Up". Recordings with Kraftwerk's Karl Bartos completed during this period were stalled due to record company disputes and remain unreleased.

The arrival of **Advance** (1996) also signalled the end of Bell and Varley's partnership. Though the album was an inspired update of the LFO sound, it was clear that their working relationship was coming to a natural conclusion. Bell went on to record an album, **Surge** (1996), under the name Speedjack for Belgium's R&S label before beginning a lengthy tenure as Björk's musical director. Varley opted for a different approach, recording as G-Man for Colin Newman's experimental Swim label (including 1996's critically acclaimed **Kushti** album) and later signing to Berlin's Studio K7 for an album of deep, minimal grooves, **Presents Tony Montana** (1997).

⊙ **Frequencies**   Warp, 1991

It's possible to trace the shadows of fellow Yorkshiremen Cabaret Voltaire in LFO's deep, subsonic pulses, but the overwhelming influence on **Frequencies** was a merger between Derrick May and the freakiest of Chicago Acid. One of the most influential albums to emerge from the UK during the early '90s.

Oliver Lieb

There was a time when it seemed like Oliver Lieb was solely responsible for a huge percentage of the Trance records flooding out of his hometown of Frankfurt. A bewildering variety of aliases — around nineteen, including Spicelab, LSG, Ambush, Paragliders, Genetix, Azid Force and True Minds — and the kind of prolific production rate that suggested the only time he emerged from his studio was to check out the spiralling velocities in the city's Omen club fuelled his apparent dominance of the scene throughout the early '90s. A subsequent dispute with Harthouse and the waning popularity of the Frankfurt sound have since taken their toll, though.

Lieb didn't set out with the intention of being Germany's 160bpm Trance king. Initially he was a bass player in soul and funk bands. The lure of technology, however, soon found Lieb experimenting with sampling and he began releasing singles on the ZYX label — scoring an early hit with "System" as Force Legato — before signing his Spicelab project to Harthouse in 1992. Almost immediately, his early EPs for the label, including the menacingly loopy **Spirit of Fear**, garnered critical acclaim and a sizeable following on the dancefloor.

Despite containing just four tracks, of admittedly epic length, **Lost In Spice** (1993) was hugely successful. Coinciding with the rising fortunes of the Frankfurt sound, the release quickly confirmed Lieb as a significant creative force on the Trance scene. His remixes of Sven Vath's "Accident In Paradise" and the surprise underground hit "Amok" by Interactive neatly sketched the boundaries of his multi-layered, slightly bombastic sound. **Constellation** (1993), a supposedly ambient project for Harthouse subsidiary Recycle Or Die, managed to convey a similar sense of wildly accelerating intensity while reining back the stomping kick drums just enough to provide some relative calm.

A collaboration with Torsten Stenzel, under the name Paragliders, resulted in a handful of more formulaic Trance outings. However,

Lieb changed direction again for his first LP as Ambush, **The Ambush** (1994), which built on the success of two EPs released the previous year and found Lieb experimenting with tribal rhythms and a kind of synthetic ethnicity which prefigured the rise of Goa Trance over the coming months. Although the end of his prolific period at Harthouse was in sight, Lieb still found time to work with Dr Atmo on **Music to Films** (1994), an alternative ambient soundtrack inspired by the film *Koyaanisqatsi*, recorded for Pete Namlook's Fax label.

A second Spicelab long-player, **A Day on Our Planet** (1995), suffered from a growing dispute with Harthouse which led to a distinct lack of promotion. By the time of Lieb's most convincing album to date, **Rendezvous In Outer Space** (1995) under the name LSG, he had been forced out of his studio in the Harthouse building and seemed more inclined to talk in bitter terms about his former employers than discuss the music itself. The declining fortunes of the Frankfurt Trance scene, and the acrimonious parting from Harthouse, consigned Lieb to a lengthy period of creative limbo which reached its nadir with his remixes for *Baywatch* star David Hasselhoff. A third Spicelab album, **Spy Vs. Spice** (1996), emerged on Lieb's own label though his ties with Hamburg's Superstition Records continued to provide a platform for a number of overlooked one-off releases. Since then, Lieb has struggled to recapture the glory days of his time at the centre of the Frankfurt phenomenon and he has become increasingly detached from the dancefloor's main currents.

⊙ **LSG – Rendezvous In Outer Space**   Superstition, 1995

Lieb's most restrained and fully rounded set so far tempers the broad strokes of his trademark Frankfurt sound with something approaching, ulp!, subtlety.

Maas

It's perhaps appropriate that Ewan Pearson's first single, under the name Villa America, was called "Motorcade" because he makes the kind of Techno that's best described as stately: a lush combination of swooning strings, rolling Motor City grooves and basslines that exist somewhere in the space between Mr. Fingers and Model 500. As Maas – a name borrowed from Thomas Pynchon's novel *The Crying of Lot 49* – he has built a quiet but considerable reputation.

Pearson had already released "Motorcade" and "The Reason" (as Dirtbox) by the time he came to the attention of Soma Records who heard a tape of six tracks recorded with Cherry Bomb's Richard Brown. The result was 1995's **San Narcisco** which culled four of the cuts from the session. With its mix of shimmering, string-laden textures and liquid grooves, **San Narcisco** immediately impressed critics who recognised the influence of producers such as Carl Craig and Kenny Larkin in the record's beautifully crafted Tech-House shapes.

Soon after the release of **San Narcisco**, Pearson began an MA in philosophy and cultural studies at the University of London, delaying any question of a follow-up until the arrival – more than a year later – of the **Suture Self** EP. There was another lengthy delay before the sinuous House groove of "Another Saturday Night" punctured the silence early in 1997 and announced the impending arrival of a full-length album. Laced with seductive cadences and heady, Detroit-inflected rhythms, **Latitude** (1997) was an extraordinarily romantic debut, full of exquisite tracks such as "Festina" and "Esplanade" which pushed the parameters of machine soul towards jazz, House and hip-hop. One of the album's standouts, "Look at Me Now, Falling", was released as a single with remixes from France's I-Cube to deserved critical acclaim and

LEON CHEW

there were a number of live appearances all over Europe to sustain the momentum.

Soon after the release of **Latitude**, Pearson released the "Cardinal Numbers" single on Ideal, under the name Sulky Pup, but his main musical activities outside Maas are concentrated on his downbeat project World of Apples for the Giant 45 label. A new Maas album was originally slated for release in 1999, but Pearson's creative muse was not about to be coerced and there was to be no further new material until the release of the dancefloor-oriented "Powers of Ten" single early in 1999.

⦿ Latitude   Soma, 1997

Lush machine symphonies meet well-crafted Tech-House grooves somewhere in the space between Kenny Larkin and Ludovic Navarre.

Mad Mike

One of the most revered producers in Techno, less is known about Mad Mike than any other artist working in electronic music. The subject of intense speculation and a dense tangle of rumour, counter claim and supposition, some doubt that such an artist even exists and that he is, in fact, a cipher for a number of different artists who – for a variety of reasons – wish to remain anonymous. If he does exist, then it is as a shifting, nebulous entity whom few people have actually talked to and even fewer have met. Claims that he has occasionally manifested himself as an artist known only as "The Invisible One" have simply deepened the mystery. What has been suggested, at various times, is that Mad Mike was originally a guitar player who operated on the fringes of George Clinton's Parliament/Funkadelic organisation, playing regularly for a spin-off project called Cherubim. Another reported manifestation – in a Motor City funk band called The Mechanics that touched on jazz, rhythm & blues, rock and fusion – has neither been confirmed nor denied.

At times credited simply as "Mad" Mike, sometimes as "Mad" Mike Banks and, at others, just as Mike Banks – it's possible to trace an ongoing production career that has maintained involvement with a number of Detroit's most influential, underground records. Yet of the half-dozen, grainy photographs of him which have been published, none provides a clear picture of the producer – if he exists at all – and the photographs seem recognisably to depict entirely different people.

As the embryonic Techno scene reached its take-off point with the seminal Virgin compilation **Techno! – The New Dance Sound of Detroit** (1988), he was reputedly involved with Members of the House, who contributed the album's most soulful cut, "Share This House". The most celebrated phase of his career has been as a central figure in the Underground Resistance organisation. Yet even this remains a mystery. A 1998 compilation, **Interstellar Fugitives**, was a collective effort featuring artists such as Andre Holland, Marc Floyd and Chuck Gibson with only one track visibly credited to "Mad" Mike and another, "Negative Evolution", to UR – though claims that the mysterious Chamaleon who contributed two of the album's fourteen cuts was another of Mad Mike's multiple aliases remain unsubstantiated.

Whoever Mad Mike is, there is no doubt that he is a figurehead of enormous importance in Techno, due not only to the ground-breaking releases with which he is credited but also to a pervasive and compelling philosophy that has forced the genre to become increasingly self-aware. A series of sleevenotes by an anonymous Detroit journalist known only as "The Unknown Writer" has helped to both perpetuate and articulate this philosophy. Sometimes these writings exist only as brief messages etched into the run-out groove of vinyl releases; at other times the messages are lengthier, printed on sleeves or labels, sketching out a unique value-system that ranges from a positivist support of family, friends and community to the the tropes of Afro-futurism and, most importantly, the notional war – of ideas, thoughts and personal actions – being waged against those who would control, divide, conquer and manipulate, the "programmers" who shape society for their own gain. Mad Mike has also been placed at the centre of a number of philanthropic community projects in his native Detroit, investing the mythology surrounding him with elements of both the Robin Hood legend (the urban jungle of the Motor City translating neatly into Sherwood Forest for the purpose) and the discreetly unpublicised benevolent works of organisations such as Detroit's Shalom Temple.

What remains, however, when the conjecture is finally stripped away is, of course, the music. Tracks credited to Banks such as Underground Resistance's "Jupiter Jazz" (from the **World 2 World** EP), "First Galactic Baptist Church" (from **The Turning Point** EP) and "Base Camp Alpha 808" (included on the essential 1995 compilation, **Origins of a Sound**) have fused Techno with funk, soul and Electro to create some of the genre's most profoundly emotive and innovative moments. With releases as good as these, what matters is not an analysis of motives or inticate biographical detail but the music itself. The message to be drawn from the Mad Mike phenomenon is clear – the records speak for themselves.

◉ Underground Resistance –
Revolution For Change   UR/Network, 1992

Thrilling, militant and super-hard, this combination of live tracks and early releases is a must-have for any Techno enthusiast.

◉ Underground Resistance – World 2   World UR, 1993

Pure electronic genius. "Jupiter Jazz" is up there alongside "Strings of Life", "Altered States" and "Can U Feel It" as one of the most affecting, emotional moments of modern dance culture.

Max 404

Borrowing the name of his creative alter ego from Aaron Lipstadt's 1982 sci-fi flick *Android*, Erwin van Moll has followed an individual path through Techno. His 1995 debut, **Love & Mathematics**, remains one of the high points of European Techno's romantic drift, yet, despite the critical acclaim, he continues to release records only sporadically.

Van Moll grew up near Eindhoven, in Valkenswaard, a small town famous for having the largest number of bars per head of population in Holland. He resisted the temptation to spend all his time drinking, but discovered an equally potent addiction in the shape of records by Arthur Baker and Afrika Bambaata. When Electro's creative impulse began to subside, he became fascinated by the emerging remix culture and its increasing emphasis on texture and sound rather than the linear narrative evolution of conventional pop. Given this fascination, perhaps it was inevitable that when the first Techno records arrived in Eindhoven's import shops he was an early convert.

On a borrowed 12-bit sampler, he crafted his first EP for Stefan Robbers' Eevo Lute imprint. **Recycler** (1992) unveiled van Moll's talent for crafting carefully sculpted tones and grooves. A year later, the follow-up explored more ambient terrain. **The Music of Chance** (released under the name Proteus Generation for the Djax Upbeats label) is just one of van Moll's lost classics, but the heavily atmospheric 5/4 groove of tracks such as "Waiting For You" showed a willingness to push beyond dancefloor conventions towards a more individual take on electronics.

He returned to Eevo Lute for "Faceless Techno Bastards Are a Complete Hype" in 1994. With van Moll posing as Faceless Techno Bastards from Auckland, New Zealand, the single was a tongue-in-cheek attack on clichés which were beginning to surface in Techno. Some reviewers didn't get the joke, however, with more than one declaring that the record had put "the Auckland sound" on the international map.

But it was his Max 404 material which made van Moll a *cause célèbre* on the European underground. In 1994, he contributed two tracks to the highly acclaimed Eevo Lute collection **Agenda 22** (including a collaboration with fellow Dutch producer The Keyprocessor on "A Laughable Death"). The release of **Love & Mathematics** (1995) coincided with a resurgence of interest in the Detroit sound and a vision of

Techno which stretched beyond the dancefloor. Accordingly the beautifully crafted cadences and timbres of tracks such as "I Do Not Feel Like an Alien In This Universe" or "Quidditty" (which inspired a suitably ethereal short film by director Jeffrey Schlags) were given a warm critical reception.

Since then, van Moll has released just a handful of Max 404 singles: 1995's **Void** culled three of the more dancefloor-oriented cuts from **Love & Mathematics,** while the following year's **Convulsion** combined a further two album tracks with the trip-hop salsa of "Infinite Legs" and the harder Techno styling of the title cut. "Awakening" followed on the short-lived Lucid imprint of Amsterdam's Mazzo club, but it was van Moll's only other release in 1996. He continued to record, however, releasing the acclaimed **Before & After** EP on Global Communication's Universal Language label a year later.

⊙ **Love & Mathematics**   Eevo Lute, 1995

A superb debut that weaves lighter-than-air atmospherics, tight chrome beats and haunting melodies into a pristinely romantic vision of Techno.

Derrick May

Juan Atkins was Techno's originator, but the artist who did most to propel the music around the world in the early days of its proliferation outside Detroit was Derrick May. In contrast to the self-effacing Atkins, May — one-time classmate of Atkins' younger brother and video arcade manager — had a more rebellious character that provided the emerging dance media with an endless stream of inspired invective, carefully calculated soundbites and sometimes maddening arrogance to provide Techno with a public persona that was every bit as compelling as the music itself. But May also had the moves to back up his mouth. Between the mid-'80s and the early '90s he released a string of brilliant, ground-breaking records — "Nude Photo", "Strings of Life", "It Is What It Is", "Beyond the Dance" — which altered the course of modern music and provided Techno with a benchmark of inspiration and innovation which has yet to be surpassed.

TRANSMAT RECORDS

May was an only child who moved with his mother to the Detroit suburb of Belleville during the late '70s. He met Kevin Saunderson at the local high school and, through Aaron Atkins, the pair began hanging out with Juan, vibing out on Alvin Toffler, Atkins' studio trickery and his skill behind the decks. After his mother moved to Chicago, May remained in Detroit, occasionally staying with the Atkins family. On visits to see his mother, he'd head down to

Chicago clubs such as The Music Box and The Power Plant where House music was being forged, noting the dynamics of the city's flourishing independent scene and returning to Detroit with ideas about Techno evolving into a similar phenomenon.

By 1985, Atkins and May were operating their Deep Space DJ crew. May picked up a residency at a downtown Detroit club called The Leidernacht where he was spotted by programmers from the local WJLB radio station. They offered him his own show, *Street Beat*. Broadcasting immediately before The Electrifying Mojo's night-time slot, May spun an eclectic mix of early House, Electro, disco and the beginnings of Techno and became an important focus for those who would become significant players on the Detroit scene over the following years.

Inspired by the example of Atkins and Metroplex, May launched his own label Transmat in 1986, initially as a subsidiary of Metroplex. The label's first release was X-Ray's "Let's Go", a collaboration between May, Saunderson and Atkins that also featured Aaron Atkins providing vocals. It was an unpromising beginning which hinted at little of what was to follow. On April 6, 1987 (the date was chosen to coincide with his birthday), May unleashed the seminal "Nude Photo" under his new Rhythim Is Rhythim pseudonym. It was an extraordinary record that updated Atkins' blueprint and stretched it far into the future. Based on the kind of hollow, synthetic bassline pioneered on the records of Mr. Fingers, the track was an abstract combination of melodic counterpoints and rhythmic syncopations that was at once compelling and alien.

May's next release was the equally astonishing "Strings of Life". An ecstatic concatenation of Ensoniq string samples, shuffling rhythm patterns and an unforgettable piano riff courtesy of Michael James (edited down from an eight-minute sequence), the track was radically different from "Nude Photo" (with which it was linked only by its over-whelming sense of alien dislocation) except insofar as it suggested that May was flirting with genius.

"Strings of Life" paved the way for Neil Rushton's seminal compilation, **Techno! – The New Dance Sound of Detroit** (1988). The album opened with another astonishing Rhythim Is Rhythim classic, "It Is What It Is", an acidic yet oddly romantic track that once again demonstrated May's talent for fusing abstract melodies and dizzying rhythm syncopations.

In 1989, having drafted Carl Craig to assist with Rhythim Is Rhythim's live commitments supporting Kevin Saunderson's Inner City, May was once again back in England. With Rushton now acting as his manager, he worked on the S'Xpress album **Intercourse** for his friend Mark Moore and played a legendary gig at London's Town & Country Club, a recording of which was later used as the basis for a controversial remix version of "Strings of Life" released, apparently, without May's consent. May also collaborated with Music Institute DJ Darryl Wynn on the R-Tyme project, delivering another classic in the shape of "Illusion". **Innovator** (1991) brought together many of the tracks May had initially brought with him to England — including "Strings of Life", "Sinister", "Wiggin" and "Beyond the Dance" — and delivered irrefutable evidence of the scale of his talents.

Rushton's move to secure a deal with Trevor Horn's ZTT label for a project featuring both Atkins and May foundered when, characteristically, May told Trevor Horn that he would refuse to appear on *Top Of The Pops*. A further setback occurred when a negative reaction from critics greeted the release of "The Beginning", prompting a lengthy, self-imposed retirement from recording which, with a few exceptions, still continues.

"Icon", May's contribution to the seminal **Virtual Sex** (1993) compilation, was a standout on an album which, even today, still stands as one of the peaks of Techno's excellence. Nonetheless, the semi-retirement continued, punctuated only by the release of System 7's **Fire** (1994) which included two collaborations with May, "Mysterious Traveller" and "Overview". There was also the release of **Relics** (1994), a collection of classic Transmat material interspersed with out-takes from May's personal archives (rumoured to be around 110 tracks), though there was nothing that matched the innovation of his best work nor did the album include any of the unique mixes of his own work that he uses in his DJ sets.

In 1997 May again plundered the archives for a new version of 1991's **Innovator**, this time combining his classics with material from **Relics** and "To Be or Not to Be", a track commissioned by Sony for use in a PlayStation game. The collection appeared in several different forms around the world, some adding and subtracting tracks, others simply altering titles. A mix album, **The Mayday Mix** (1997), also emerged, providing those who had never experienced his considerable talents behind the decks with an idea of what May can sound like at his best. Combining House favourites such as Lil' Louis' "French Kiss" with Techno by Jeff Mills, Stacey Pullen and Aubrey, **The Mayday Mix** was as mercurial as its creator.

The lack of new releases has, of course, added to the mythology that surrounds May and perversely elevated his status on the dance scene. From Detroit, there is news from those who have been helping May with setting up a new studio. But the same story emerges periodically and, as has been the case since the early '90s, no new material appears. Instead he has devoted his energies towards a rejuvenated Transmat, with a number of extraordinary new signings and a major project already commissioned from Kevin Saunderson.

⊙ **Innovator**   Transmat, 1997

Not as concise as the previous but now unavailable **Innovator** album on
Network, but nevertheless, an extensive introduction to May's
extraordinary talent.

Woody McBride

G rowing up in the relatively conservative environs of Bismarck,
North Dakota, Woody McBride's first love was film and experimental art. Musically, however, Bismarck was a backwater which even
alternative rock didn't penetrate. In 1988, McBride moved to Minneapolis where he discovered an emerging dance scene at nights like Club
Degenerate and House Nation Under a Groove. Behind the turntables
at those nights was Kevin Cole whose performances inspired McBride
to take up DJing for himself. It was at Cole's subsequent Depth Probe
nights that McBride honed his deck skills and began charting a dual
career as DJ and promoter around Minneapolis and St. Paul.

McBride's first productions, including the "Psychapocalypse" single with Freddie Fresh and a series of 12"s for the Drop Bass Network
label, mapped out a terrain distinguished by super-hard velocities,
snaking Acid and dark, sometimes oppressive, moods. "Rattlesnake",
a track he recorded for Dave Clarke's Magnetic North, was a characteristic fusion of Chicago's bleaker side (drawing at least some inspiration from tracks like "No Way Back" by Adonis and Sleazy D's "I've
Lost Control") hard-wired to the kind of stripped, straight-ahead Techno that connected with Adam X, Frankie Bones and the harder
precincts of the European scene.

Oscillating between his own name and the alias DJ ESP, McBride hooked up with Alan Oldham's Generator Records for the less bruising "Mind Behind Nature". McBride's trademark "wall of bass" – arena-sized sound systems in colossal 20-foot-high, 100-foot-long arrangements – became a particular feature of his parties, with flyers repeating an especially favoured line: "300,000 watts of true rave power." Initially modelled on European raves, the Midwest events evolved a peculiarly distinctive personality of their own and McBride's music and a growing network of local DJs and producers orbiting the hub of his Communique Records were a crucial element in developing that identity.

Furiously prolific, McBride has preferred to concentrate on singles rather than albums. Forged in the cauldron of the Midwestern rave scene, the results aren't always subtle, shot through with a rigidity which betrays a significant debt to the European hard Techno scene of the early to mid-'90s, but McBride is nevertheless a more significant producer than his relatively low profile outside America suggests.

⊙ **Neighbors**   Communique, 1995

A compilation that provides an accurate and intriguing document of McBride's abilities as producer, promoter and mentor.

Jeff Mills

A one-time architecture student, Jeff Mills made his first influential record during the late 1980s as part of the three-piece Final Cut. Fusing relentlessly heavy industrial textures with Techno and raw, street-based Electro, the band's first and only LP, **Deep Into the Cut** (1989), drew the blueprint for what would eventually become the sound of European Hardcore.

But it was as The Wizard, the alter ego he used for his nightly radio shows on Detroit's WJLB station, that Mills had his first significant impact on the course of Techno. At a time of intense competition on the airwaves, Mills developed a furiously fast and astonishingly skilled turntable technique in order to keep listeners tuned into his show, playing only a record's strongest section before mixing into the next with often breathtaking displays of technical virtuosity aimed at packing the maximum impact into his brief 45-minute shows. The intensity of these

broadcasts soon saw off the competition and left Mills dominating the airwaves as the most revered DJ in the city. His influence was such that, ten years later, the type of mixing he developed is now the one identifiable factor among a whole generation of Detroit DJs and much of the music coming from the city is now tailored specifically for the technical demands of that style.

It was during this period that Mills first met up with Mike Banks who had dropped a tape of "Share My Life" by his group, Members of the House, at WJLB with a view to persuading The Wizard to remix it. Following the break-up of Final Cut, Mills and Banks eventually embarked on one of the most radical and creative partnerships in the history of Techno as Underground Resistance. In 1992, however, Mills decided to accept the offer of a residency at Peter Gatien's Limelight club in New York, effectively ending the duo's collaborative efforts and leaving Banks to continue under the UR banner alone.

Mills' experience at The Limelight eventually manifested itself in his first solo album, **Waveform Transmission Vol. 1** (1992). It was an extraordinarily ambitious debut, coupling relentless, pulsing rhythms with harsh, often abrasive, synthetic textures. It was also shockingly minimal; a legacy of Mill's fondness for the stripped-down, hard-jacking sound of Chicago producers such as K. Alexi. Having relocated to Chicago himself, Mills began concentrating on his own Axis label, recruiting Robert Hood to furnish the second part of the **Waveform Transmission** series in 1993. For the most part, however, Axis has remained a vehicle for Mills' own releases, notably the heavily experimental **Atlantis** album (released under the name X-102) and a series of critically acclaimed 12"s such as 1993's **Mecca** EP, the **Growth** EP and 1995's **Humana** EP.

By the time of **Waveform Transmission Vol. 3** (1994), Mills was becoming increasingly popular on the European Techno circuit. His incendiary DJ sets made him one of the star attractions at major events. Dividing his time between Chicago and Berlin, Mills continued to combine his commitments as a DJ with productions which focused more and more on hermetic concepts and minimal structures. However, in 1995, he completed a series of tracks, originally designed as "links" for use in his own DJ sets, which were eventually released as the **Purpose Maker** EP. Less abstract than previous releases, **Purpose Maker** was enormously popular and gained Mills access to a wider audience. The success of this release prompted him to set up the Purpose Maker label for similarly DJ-oriented releases.

Mills' popularity in Japan led to a deal with Sony and the subsequent release of his first mix album, **Live at the Liquid Room – Tokyo** (1996). Despite being a critical and commercial success, however, the album did scant justice to Mills' superlative technical abilities and, at times, the sound quality was barely higher than that of a bootleg.

By the time Mills released his first compilation of Axis material, **The Other Day** (1997), the level of his influence as a producer was apparent in the huge numbers of hard, minimally abstract 12" records that were flooding into record shops every week. Though the majority of these releases were poorly disguised and badly executed pastiches of the Mills sound, it was evident that there were a growing number of talented producers who were becoming uncannily adept at replicating the hard-as-nails, stripped-down funk which separated authentic Mills releases from the legion of copyists.

Mills renewed his commitment to minimalism with another collection, **Purpose Maker** (1998), which brought together tracks from the original **Purpose Maker** release on Axis and some of the best moments from the recently established label of the same name with a quartet of unreleased gems. But while some sections of the Techno community have already begun expressing discontent over minimalism's inherently spartan sense of musicality, Mills' enthusiasm for the genre remains undimmed.

⊙ **Waveform Transmission Vol. 1**   Axis/Tresor, 1992

Shockingly new, determinedly abrasive, this was the album that redrew the parameters of Techno in the early '90s.

⊙ **The Other Day**   Axis/React/Sony, 1997

The best of the Axis material collected together in one essential package.

Miss Djax

S askia Slegers, otherwise known as Miss Djax, has played a significant role in European Techno through her Djax Upbeats label, providing a platform for artists such as Stefan Robbers, Claude Young and Luke Slater's Clementine project. She has also released a number of her own smouldering dancefloor tracks such as 1994's "X-Factor" and 1998's "303" (in conjunction with Acid Junkies) and continues to be one of the scene's most in-demand DJs, spinning a fusion of hard, jacking House (Djax played a crucial role in supporting Chicago's House renaissance during the early '90s) and deep, muscular Techno.

During the early '80s, Slegers had played bass in a Dutch new wave group. A day-job in a record shop eventually led to a burgeoning DJ career (spinning rap, funk and the beginnings of House) and a growing desire to launch her own project. Djax, she claims, could have been either a record label or a music magazine. In the end, she says, she chose the label because it was "more interesting".

She originally set up Djax Records as a hip-hop imprint, launching the label in 1989 with 24K's **No Enemies** album. Within a few months of the 24K release, however, she'd tapped into Holland's emerging Techno scene and set up a subsidiary label, Djax Upbeats, to provide a platform for the new sound. Early releases, such as Terrace's "916 Buena Avenue" and Trance Induction's "Mindflower", forged a funkily experimental groove that quickly established Djax as a cult label for fans of deeper, more underground moods.

The typical Djax record was a raw, sometimes inchoate fission of motoring bass and beats that eschewed the then fashionable multi-layering of Trance in favour of a direct, low frequency punch that drew on classic moments from both Chicago and Detroit to create a near-perfect DJ tool. By 1994, when Slegers finally released her own debut (the adamantine, UR-styled "X-Factor"), Djax Upbeats had established itself alongside Renaat Vandepapeliere's R&S as one of Europe's most influential labels.

The day-to-day requirements of running a prolific label in conjuction with an exhaustive series of DJ commitments on the European circuit have prevented Slegers from enjoying anything more than an intermittent career as a producer. 1995's "Miss Djax Versus The World" or the "Spin Machine" 12" which emerged a year later, however, proved that her talent in the studio was considerable. Other singles, including 1997's "Spiderwoman" and 1998's "Moon-ranger", were equally solid, though the 1999 release of "The Analog Sessions of Darkness" was accompanied by rumours of a full-length release which might yet see Slegers achieve the kind of reputation as a producer that she has already gained as the sole driving force behind one of Europe's most prestigious and revered dance labels.

⊙ "X-Factor"   Djax, 1994

Fierce, funky and blisteringly direct, Miss Djax's debut still stands as one of her most compelling moments to date.

Mixmaster Morris /
The Irresistible Force

Mixmaster Morris or The Irresistible Force (the name he uses for recording) is one of Techno's major cult figures. He's famous for promoting chill-out music and has spent the past decade making well-received records and DJing around the world. As an artist he has a distinctive and original style – gently psychedelic, faintly experimental, bubblebath-soft and flower-pretty.

He first entered the music scene in 1985 as a pirate broadcaster working alongside Coldcut. Influenced by avant garde music, Krautrock and hip-hop culture, Morris' first public incarnation was as a wildstyle, collage DJ – fusing long-lost German synthesiser music with African rhythms. In one early interview he floated the idea that he wanted to become the "Jimi Hendrix of the sampler." In other interviews he discussed how psychedelics and LSD were essential influences on his artistic make-up. Interested in technology, sampling, drugs, computers and electronic music, it's clear he was more than ready for Acid House and Techno when these cultures finally arrived.

Between 1989 and 1991, Morris emerged as an Ambient House DJ. He found his own way through the rave scene, often playing illegal parties, squats and outlaw festivals. He gigged with Psychic TV, joined The Shamen on their Synergy tour and worked with CND to compile their "Give Peace a Dance" records. His debut LP, **Flying High** (1992), seemed like a snapshot or soundtrack to his Ambient DJing experiences. The album flowed and seemed designed for a fractured or post-drug consciousness. It sounded so warm, passive and enveloping that critic Simon Reynolds related it to womb-music. It was hailed as a classic, sat happily inside the indie Top 10 and cemented Morris' growing following. He played Glastonbury for the first time the same year both officially, in between bands, and unofficially on various sound systems. By this time, his DJ style had developed into something unique that mixed avant garde electronics, ambient Detroit b-sides and environmental sounds into a healing, psychedelic soundtrack.

His increasing reputation earned Morris gigs all over the world. He became one of the first English DJs to achieve significant success on

the German Techno scene, leading to a collaboration with Frankfurt ambient/trance producer Pete Namlook on two acclaimed Dreamfish albums. Always pursuing the cutting edge of psychedelic (as opposed to dance, Ecstasy or Techno) cultures, he was closely identified with the Zippy movement (techno-literate hippies) and was invited to celebrate the 50th anniversary of LSD at a gig in Basle, home of the Sandoz Factory where the drug was first synthesised. Similarly pursuing his "techno" (in the broadest sense of the word) interests, Morris was perhaps the first well-known artist not only to have a Web site but to have authored and designed it himself.

The second Irresistible Force album, **Global Chillage** (1994), was well received by both the critics and the public. Soon after its release, a marijuana coffee-shop opened in Amsterdam and called itself Global Chillage – a tribute that's been bestowed on no other contemporary musician. *Mixmag* offered him a monthly column and over the next four years he used it, along with his Web site, to promote new talent – including Pork, Jimpster and Squarepusher – and to attack the UK's burgeoning corporate dance industry.

When the Rising High label folded in the mid-'90s, Morris signed to Ninja Tune and began recording and touring with Matt Black and his Ninja posse. As a DJ his style moved closer towards hip-hop and jazz – fitting into the new eclecticism also explored by Kirk Degiorgio, Carl Craig and Ninja themselves. His open-minded chill-out sets were a vital influence on the emergent freestyle, post-Ecstasy club aesthetic, although **It's Tomorrow Already** (1998) remained as far out, hallucinogenic and whisperingly beautiful as its predecessors.

⊙ **Flying High**   Rising High, 1992

An Ambient Techno landmark, full of sighing synthetics and inspired psychedelia: soft, perfectly shaped music for hard dreaming.

⊙ **It's Tomorrow Already**   Ninja Tune, 1998

With a wide-eyed optimism that recalled post-rave summer mornings, the third instalment of the Irresistible Force manifesto is perhaps the most beautiful so far.

Tony Marcus

David Morley

David Morley is something of an enigma. As one-time house engineer for Belgium's R&S label (alongside CJ Bolland and The Advent's Cisco Ferreira) he played a crucial role in shaping the sound of European Techno. He was also responsible for some of the earliest and most influential releases on the label's Ambient offshoot, Apollo. Yet his reputation has never really kept pace with his achievements and, these days at least, he prefers to pursue a relatively secluded existence in the small south German town of Regensburg rather than participate in the frenzied club culture of London, Munich or Frankfurt.

His involvement with R&S dates back to 1987, when R&S was still known as Ferrari Records. After moving from England to Belgium with his parents, Morley picked up a job in a local studio and began working on his own tracks. A chance encounter with Renaat Vandepapeliere led to various collaborations, first on a number of New Beat records (inspired by Ghent's main club, Boccaccio) and, eventually, on embryonic Techno under the name Spectrum. When Vandepapeliere converted Ferrari into R&S, Morley – by now a combination of in-house engineer and producer – was a key component in developing the new label's sound.

After being diagnosed as suffering from diabetes, Morley found himself unable to sustain the heavy schedule of recording and clubbing which characterised the early days of R&S. Instead, he concentrated on building his own studio and recording a number of tracks for the label's cult subsidiary TZ. The relative calm of his new circumstances eventually filtered into his music, resulting in the Ambient classics "Evolution" and – under the name Atlantis – "Paradise" on the new

R&S offshoot Apollo (originally set up by Vandepapeliere as an outlet for Morley's beatless excursions). Morley's relaxed attitude to his output – he released no more than a handful of records during the mid-'90s – meant that the momentum built up by the success of "Evolution" and "Paradise" was quickly dissipated.

A chance meeting between Vandepapeliere and long-term Morley fan Andrea Parker (she was DJing with Morley's "Evolution" at the time) led to a long-standing collaborative venture which has sustained over a number of years. She and Morley discovered a shared passion for vintage synths and an oblique take on club culture that first surfaced on "Too Good to Be Strange" under the tongue-in-cheek pseudonym of Two Sandwiches Short of a Lunchbox (though they reverted to David Morley and Andrea Parker for the subsequent **Angular Art** EP on Infonet).

The pair have continued to record together, though Morley did eventually find time to issue a solo album, **Tilted** (1998). The album signalled a move towards a more eclectic and wilfully unpredictable sound that oscillated between the determinedly lo-fi shapes of "Heading South" and the exquisitely sculpted shapes of tracks like "Being There" or "Symmetry". This direction was subsequently developed on Morley's work with Andrea Parker for her album, **Kiss My Arp** (1999), later described by *The Face* as "the coolest kind of uneasy listening".

⊙ **Tilted**   R&S, 1998

Weaving distortion, deep bass and muscular drums through a series of broad filmic soundscapes (somewhere between Dimitri Tiomkin and – ulp! – Vangelis), this is a solid introduction to Morley's idiosyncratic vision of Techno, though purists may prefer to search out his anonymous contributions to the hard-to-find but seminal TZ series.

Mouse On Mars

As Mouse On Mars, Andi Toma and Jan St. Werner have carved an intriguing path through Techno, drawing as much on post-rock experimentalism as the shapes of Motor City electronica. Their first album, **Vulvaland** (1994), inhabited the lo-tech spaces somewhere between Can, Neu! and Cluster, updated for the Acid House generation, but subsequent releases – including their 1997 collaboration with former Kraftwerk member Wolfgang Flür as Yamo – have demonstrated an eclectic and often vividly compelling quality that suggests the kind of restless creativity which could make them a major force.

When the duo first met in 1991 – on the Cologne–Düsseldorf–Dortmund studio circuit (Werner was a rock musician, Toma a studio engineer who'd also dabbled in hip-hop production) – the German Techno scene was developing the embryonic Trance sound which would eventually infiltrate the national pop charts. Typically, that particular formula didn't appeal, so the pair's first musical endeavours together sidestepped the underground white label scene in favour of contract work for German satellite station Vox.

While television work paid the bills, Werner and Toma used their spare time to evolve the weird, recombinant voodoo that eventually became the Mouse On Mars sound. Sensing a kindred spirit, they sent a cassette of their tracks to Seefeel, who promptly passed the tape to their record label, Too Pure. The result was 1994's "Frosch" which, although not fully formed, signalled Mouse On Mars' distinctive mix of odd, lo-fi experimentalism and tangled melodics.

Vulvaland offered a warm, densely layered joyride through studio trickery and warped harmonics. Tracks such as "Future Dub" or

the strange sampladelia of "Die Seele von Brian Wilson" were fantasy excursions through lush textures and improbable sonic landscapes. **Iaora Tahiti** (1995) refined the process, though it sounded
more like Techno filtered through David Lynch's *Eraserhead* than
anything else. Wolfgang Flür guested on drums, although the
album's lineage was more accurately hinted at on a live tour with
Stereolab – short-wave radio, fractured sequences and found
sounds suggested more of a kinship with Can than with Kraftwerk.
Werner's interest in the perimeters of electronic avant-gardism was
further explored in a collaboration with Oval's Markus Popp, resulting in an album as Microstoria.

Werner and Toma were behind the mixing desk again on Wolfgang
Flür's **Time Pie** (1997). The product of an intensive four-month collaboration in Toma's Düsseldorf studio, the album was a remarkable mix of
lush syncopations, playful psychedelia and, on "Guiding Ray" at least,
a shared passion for the throbbing riffology of Neu!.

The third Mouse On Mars album, **Autoditacker** (1997), was dreamily experimental – less a refinement of what had gone before and more
a blurring of boundaries, shapes and ideas. Tracks such as "Juju" and
"Scat" were stoner symphonies, designed, it seemed, for hard-tripping
and dizzy, sonic head games. Elsewhere, the album flirted with quirky
beauty and the same fascination with texture which had been apparent
on **Iaora Tahiti**.

⊙ **Vulvaland**   Too Pure, 1994

Idiosyncratic, ambitious and experimental – this stunning debut is still
the key release in the Mouse On Mars back catalogue.

Move D

D avid Moufang grew up in Heidelberg listening to his parents' collection of early Pink Floyd and Kraftwerk records, but the most overwhelming influence on his childhood was outer space, the result of a trip to the cinema with his father to see *2001: A Space Odyssey*. By the age of 12, he had taken up drums (he eventually went on to study classical percussion) and took up the guitar a few years later, this time taking lessons from two separate jazz guitar teachers. He played guitar in a band called Rivers & Trains well into the '90s. Occasionally he even plied his trade as a DJ, spinning Electro, funk and jazz.

It wasn't until 1989 that he discovered Techno when a friend of his, D-Man, invited him to a club he was running in the industrial suburb of Mannheim. When Moufang walked into the Milk Club that night – like so many others before and after him – he discovered a scene that changed his life. Discovering Detroit, 808 State, Nexus 21 and the first stirrings of Ambient Techno, Moufang became a committed clubber. Through D-Man, he met Peter Wiederroth (Redagain P) who converted Moufang's nickname "Mufti" into the more kinetic Move D.

Moufang's first records were made with Jonas Grossmann as Deep Space Network. Their first two albums, **Earth to Infinity** (1992) and **Big Rooms** (1993), suggested a significant, unpredictable and innovative talent which was confirmed by the release of **Homeworks** (1993), a Source Records compilation that included solo tracks such as "Pulsar" and "I've Been On Drugs" alongside collaborations with D-Man. Ranging from subtle, Detroit-inflected grooves to wired electronic jazz, Moufang's music seemed to operate on ambience, slow motion and subdued rhythm.

Reagenz (1994), a collaboration with Space Time Continuum's Jonah Sharp, was an astonishing fusion of beautiful, experimental electronics that reached out to a point that even Detroit's most visionary producers hadn't yet achieved. Recorded between Heidelberg and San Francisco, it sounded like pianist Bill Evans might have if he'd grown up surrounded by *Star Trek* instead of modal jazz.

Moufang's debut album, **Kunststoff** (1995), was equally remarkable. Tracks such as "Soap Bubbles" and "In/Out" oscillated between soft, dreamlike textures and the spiked electronics that Detroit was beginning to explore. The glittering production surfaces were a legacy of Moufang's days as a student at the School of Audio Engineering, but the music they encompassed was equally compelling. It was an album full of contrasts between the jagged drugfloor grooves of, say, "Nimm 2" and the gentle, synthetic lullaby of "Beyond the Machine". Amazingly pretty and wildly innovative, **Kunststoff** remains one of the most accomplished Techno albums to emerge from Europe so far.

The collaborative ventures that followed – including **Exploring the Psychedelic Landscape** (1996) and **A Day In the Live** (1997) with Pete Namlook – preceded an experimental single for Sheffield's Warp label. Moufang had been a big fan of the label's "bleep Techno" output in the early '90s and "Cymbelin" was, in some ways, a homage to that sound, twisting beats and synths into a bass-heavy groove. But the producer's ability to soften almost any structure with aching prettiness transformed the record into a unique fusion.

Another unique fusion was suggested by the release of **Conjoint** (1997). A collaboration between Moufang, jazz veteran Karl Berger, Jamie Hodge (of Born Under a Rhyming Planet) and Gunter "Ruit" Kraus, it was Moufang's most overtly jazzed outing so far, but provided spectacular evidence of his growing abilities as a producer and composer.

⊙ **Reagenz – Reagenz**   Source Records, 1994

Move D and Jonah Sharp surfing far out on Techno's perimeters with a
combination of Detroit ambience, dusted jazz and pure inspiration.

⊙ **Move D – Kunststoff**   Source Records, 1995

Soft electronic lullabies, super-funk grooves and wired experimentation
add up to sheer brilliance on this official solo debut.

Pete Namlook

I f the Ambient Techno scene can be said to have both a spiritual
leader and a guiding force, then that role falls without question to
Pete Namlook, whose prolific output (rumours that he makes an
album per day are only slightly exaggerated) and quietly understated
experimentalism have dominated the entire movement since the
release of "True Colours" in 1992.

Born Peter Kuhlmann – the adopted surname is simply a phonetic
reversal of his original – Namlook began his career as a guitar player,
studying music at Frankfurt's Goethe University before going on to
make several albums with his band Romantic Warrior. His first ventures
into Techno were with a local DJ, Criss, who persuaded him to use
some of his unreleased solo endeavours as chill-out tracks on the flipside of their early singles together. Introduced to the burgeoning Frankfurt dance scene, Namlook began working with a number of other
producers including Non Eric and Pascal FEOS. (with whom he recorded "True Colours"), but it was with Dr. Atmo that he produced his first
significant Ambient classic, **Silence**, early in 1992.

Silence confirmed Namlook's Fax label as a key component of the evolving Ambient scene (though Namlook prefers to describe his music as "environmental"). By 1994, the label had released a dizzying number of albums, many of them collaborations involving Namlook and like-minded artists such as Mixmaster Morris, Tetsu Inoue, Dr. Atmo and Biosphere's Geir Jenssen. It had also spawned two sub-labels, Ambient World and Yesterday Tomorrow, spitting out limited edition releases on an almost weekly basis.

1995's **Koolfang**, recorded with David Moufang, charted a languid course through Techno, Ambient and jazz, though, by this time, he had already essayed Trance, oblique experimentalism, wired synth-pop and ethnic currents on the 150 or so Fax projects he'd completed, either solo or in collaborative mode.

A meeting with veteran electronic music pioneer Oskar Sala led to Namlook's exploration of subharmonic scales and much of his subsequent experimental output has attempted to alchemise a synthesis between traditional, harmonic structures and the more avant garde modes suggested by Sala.

Since the mid-'90s, Namlook's output has slowed to more manageable proportions (in 1997, Fax released just fourteen albums), focusing on series such as his Jet Chamber collaborative venture with

Atom Heart and his own self-titled output, including **Namlook XIV** (1999) and **Air IV** (1999). But he continues to play a crucial role in the Ambient Techno scene, both in providing a platform for the circle of experimental producers who orbit the Fax label and in terms of creative leadership.

⊙ **Silence**   Fax, 1992

Narrowing down the best of Namlook's extensive releases (numbering hundreds so far) is a mammoth task, but this collaboration with Dr. Atmo was the first in a series of truly ground-breaking works.

⊙ **Namlook III**   Fax, 1994

Glittering electronics, spaced-out experimentalism and edgy atmospherics combine to make this one of the most compelling of Namlook's mid-'90s releases.

Neuropolitique

The tale of how "a middle class Sussex kid fucked on drugs" appeared on Derrick May's doorstep in Detroit at the fading end of 1989 (just a couple of months after meeting him for the first time in a London club) is one of dance music's favourite insider anecdotes. "At that time I had been shovelling Ecstasy down my throat for 18 months," Matt Cogger later told Joost de Lyser of *Surreal Sound*. "I wanted to go somewhere, calm down, get better." Cogger began working for Transmat, spending his nights learning studio craft from the likes of Juan Atkins and Kevin Saunderson. His first tracks, including "Mind You Don't Trip" for Metroplex and his classic ART outing "Artemis", were done with Inner City/Reese Project engineer Marty

Bonds. By the time he returned to England in 1991, he had already perfected the sharp, multi-layered sound which would become his trademark.

Cogger spent the next few years shifting around London, recording in various locations – Forest Hill, Bow, Camden and Soho – "begging, borrowing and stealing" equipment and studio time to work on his music. "Bananagate", the track he contributed to the ground-breaking **Virtual Sex** (1993) compilation, was typical of his sound at the time – a dense tangle of distorted beats, melodies and counterpoints wired to a bass rhythm that was pure Detroit. **Menage à Trois** (1994) was the result of a deal with Akin Fernandez's Irdial Records which allowed Cogger to pool equipment and recording space with one-time schoolfriend Lee Purkis of In-Sync. Having a firmly established base to work from didn't, however, seem to impact on Cogger's capricious – sometimes anarchic – production style.

A move to the Beechwood subsidiary New Electronica followed, resulting in the assured **Are You Now or Have You Ever Been?** (1995). Tracks such as "Now the Screens Were" or the bittersweet tone poem "This Gnome Came Up to Me…" were introspective and dreamily abstract, but Cogger maintained a distinctly low profile, either too reluctant or, as he jokingly suggests, too apathetic to capitalise on the opportunity. A comprehensive collection of tracks recorded in various locations over the preceding years, **Nomenclature** (1996) traced the development of Cogger's individual take on Techno.

Beyond the Pinch (1997) was the final Neuropolitique album (Cogger announced his "retirement" from the music scene soon after its release), this time adopting a more eclectic, sample-based approach. Though the sound of tracks such as "Naughty Sisters In Rio" and "The Importance of Selling Pins" seemed far removed from his earlier, Detroit-influenced work, they retained the same adventurous, distinctively volatile spirit which has threaded through Cogger's career.

⊙ **Nomenclature**   Axis/Tresor, 1992

Shockingly new, determinedly abrasive, this was the album that redrew the parameters of Techno in the early '90s.

Nu-Era

In September 1994 one of the most intriguing indicators of the UK's Detroit fixation emerged from a small attic studio in London's Dollis Hill. The press release which accompanied **Beyond Gravity** provided few clues beyond a description of the lush, melancholic grooves of tracks such as "Mono Concentrate" or the gorgeous "Blackhole In the Sun" and the declaration that "Nu-Era are London duo Mark and Dennis…"

In fact, Nu-Era had made only one previous appearance, along with Underground Resistance, Dan Curtin and Octave One, on a stunning compilation, **The Deepest Shade of Techno**, released earlier that same year by the Reflective label. Sandwiched between contributions from Eddie "Flashin'" Fowlkes and Josh Wink, Nu-Era's "Cost of Livin'" was an exquisitely tripped-out articulation of Detroit's deepest, late-nite listening moods built from weightless vocals, fluttering TR-808 rhythm patterns and gently ethereal piano. Anticipating the spirit of Strictly Rhythm's ground-breaking **The Deep and Slow** collection later that year (also featuring Dan Curtin and Josh Wink), **The Deepest Shade of Techno** signalled a move away from the bruising tropes of the dancefloor towards calmer, more introspective waters. At a time when Techno was struggling to shrug off an almost synonymous association with Hardcore, it was an incredibly significant release along the lines of Buzz's seminal **Virtual Sex** (1993).

Beyond Gravity offered the duo room to stretch out. From the wild, unruly shapes of "Mirror Images" to the cooler, jazz-textured outlook of "Mono Concentrate" (a dreamier cousin to Underground Resistance's stellar jazz excursions) it was an impressively crafted album that hinted at a significant talent and an intuitive, almost umbilical connection with Detroit's most inspired producers.

It was an achievement made all the more astonishing when it was revealed that Nu-Era was the Techno sideline of drum 'n' bass pioneers 4 Hero who had already launched breakbeat into the stratosphere with the influential **Parallel Universe** album earlier that year. Both **The Deepest Shade of Techno** and **Beyond Gravity** were the results of Dego McFarlane and Mark Clair's long-held passion for Motor City Techno. The music had such a hold on them that in 1993 they had travelled to Detroit to meet up with their production heroes. As it turned out, 4 Hero already had a number of other admirers in Detroit's music community and the links they forged during that trip have sustained over a number of years. Following the release of 1995's "Stars" single, however, the Nu-Era project has mainly been confined to remix work, while the main thrust of McFarlane and Clair's Detroit preoccupation has been translated into the Jacob's Optical Stairway project which also featured contributions from Juan Atkins.

◉ Beyond Gravity   Reflective, 1994

One of the highpoints of the UK's fascination with Detroit Techno, Nu-Era's debut is a stunning mix of syncopated grooves, lush synthetic backdrops and, in "Blackhole In the Sun", a romantic classic to rival even As One's "Amalia".

A Number of Names

O ne of the most obscure and enigmatic of Detroit Techno legends is that of A Number of Names (Paul Lesley Sterling Jones and Roderick Simpson). Their discography spans only two songs, but the group remains an important and "missing" link between the legacy of disco and the revolution of Techno.

In Detroit Techno's pre-history (1978–1981) there were several important subcultures at work, not the least of which was that of the high school party scene – an amazing network of teenage promoters, DJs and audiences that gathered in clubs and halls all over the city. One of the most legendary of cliques was that of Charivari, named after a hip clothier chain in New York City (the name itself is French for "hullabaloo"). At the peak of Charivari's success, they would pull in as many as 1,200 kids a night.

Leslie, Simpson and Jones were at the centre of an as yet unnamed group of young musicians. They composed a tribute to Charivari – their version called "Sharevari" (changing the spelling to avoid any future conflicts with the party club or the clothing store chain). The song was an instant success when the group brought it down to a Charivari party for the resident DJ to test out. "Sharevari" capitalised on the funky, sparse beginnings of Italo-disco, namely Kano's "Holly Dolly" – imagine the chorus of that song doubled-up through two turntables set to a basic electronic clap-driven beat and you have the blueprint for "Sharevari". However, what made the song so memorable wasn't so much the distillation of Italo-disco, but the over-the-top mock-European vocal, extolling the virtues of Porsche 928s, bread, cheese and "fine white wine".

Released on the local Capriccio imprint and later on Canada's

Quality/RFC, "Sharevari" was seminal in the evolution of Techno. Even before Cybotron's "Alleys of Your Mind" brought futuristic funk to its logical conclusion (though "Sharevari" and "Alleys Of Your Mind" were both released in 1981, there is still some debate over which one was in stores first), Detroiters had picked up on the electronic and quasi-sophisticated aesthetics of Italo-disco and new wave. As much as the "Kraftwerk + P-Funk" equation, these components were equally important in the birth of Techno.

⊙ **"Sharevari"**   Capriccio, 1981

Sounding like the bastard offspring of Telex and Rhythim Is Rhythim, Detroit Techno's missing link is loaded with weird, Europhile synth-lines, motorik beats and a "once heard, never forgotten" vocal hook. Possibly the most influential "unknown" record ever made.

Dan Sicko

Nüw Idol

Michel Spiegel grew up in the small French town of Mulhouse, near the border of Germany and Switzerland. These days, he claims his musical influences are drawn from what he calls "the sound-track of life" but, as a teenager, he was fascinated by the music emerging from English groups like Death In June, Sisters of Mercy and March Violets. He learnt to play guitar, eventually joining a local metal-goth band and making a pilgrimage to the London club The Batcave, which was a focal point of the English goth scene. His experiences on that visit sparked a desire to move to England, though initially he moved to Paris instead to work in studios there as a Fairlight programmer.

By 1986 the lure of London proved too strong and Spiegel relocated, ending up on the squat scene for a few years before discovering Techno. A self-financed single led him to the Plink Plonk label where he became in-house engineer, working on a number of the label's highest-profile projects (including the spectacular series of singles which made Plink Plonk one of the most respected London Techno labels during the mid-'90s). Spiegel's first release for the label, under his preferred alias of Nüw Idol, was 1994's "Wü Maze" which took the fundamental Frankfurt Trance blueprint of racing sequences, stomping kick drums and machine gun hi-hats and then twisted it out of control, accelerating it up to around 180 bpm and appending the kind of Acid riff that suggested long nights spent in the dark, saucer-eyed mayhem of London's Clink Street. It was a sound that keyed perfectly with the amphetaminised edges of the city's free party scene – Techno designed with a utilitarian single-mindedness to crank the drugfloor up to max and beyond.

Units of Potential Injury (1995), however, displayed some prettier edges. The influence of the German scene was still evident in most of the ten tracks on offer, though there were hints that Spiegel could touch the wayward, abstract genius of Thomas Heckmann at times rather than the more pedestrian purveyors of identikit Trance. Unfortunately, the album was caught up in Plink Plonk's untimely demise and relatively few copies still exist.

Though Spiegel admits that Dave Clarke's "Red 2" made a difference to his production outlook, it was perhaps inevitable that he would find himself drawn to the emergent Goa Trance scene. Still working as an engineer in the state-of-the-art studio which Plink Plonk had created for its acts to work in, he began exploring a more mainstream Trance sound, releasing a number of singles on Dave Wesson's Zoom Records and on his own self-financed Well Wicked Records. An album for Zoom, **Thunder and Lightning** (1999), was still-born when contractual and financial difficulties set in. Despite the setback, Spiegel remains determined to continue, unconcerned by the fact that both of the only albums he has recorded to date have been stalled by one mishap or another.

◉ Units of Potential Injury   E.A.R, 1995

Joined at the hip with Frankfurt Trance, Nüw Idol's debut (released on Plink Plonk subsidiary Electro Audio Response) is a perfect indicator of the mid-'90s Euro Techno sound.

Ian O'Brien

Ian O'Brien makes Techno so full of warmth, funk and distant dreams it seems to tap directly into the listener's empathogenic centres, turning synthetic hooks into sinuous skeins and connecting deep, syncopated rhythms to a primal, hip-tugging urgency. However, his version of Techno is also a uniquely private affair, designed not for the dancefloor but for the more abstract climes of late-night home-listening, early morning reveries and fantastic interior voyages.

Though he was born in his grandmother's house in Ireland, O'Brien grew up in Essex, eschewing the more regular soundtrack of teen rebellion in favour of West Coast jazz fusion. Inspired by John McLaughlin and Pat Metheny, he began playing guitar. Eventually, he wound up with his own three-piece jazz fusion outfit, Cat's Club, extrapolating themes from notoriously difficult Mahavishnu Orchestra covers and picking up gigs around the local area.

Then, suddenly, late in 1992 he heard Underground Resistance's "Hi-Tech Jazz" for the first time. "It changed my life," he says simply.

He began devouring Techno mix shows on the radio, searching out records that seemed to connect with the same alchemical intensity as "Hi-Tech Jazz", "Strings of Life" or Black Dog's early output. He took a job in a studio to fund his own recording set-up and started teaching himself to play keyboards and program sequencers, spending night after night dreaming hard and imagining himself into the future.

O'Brien's first release was a collaborative effort which came out under the name Memory Tree in late '95. That was followed by another single on Reverb Records as Wideo Kids. But it was the subsequent trio of astonishing releases on the Ferox and 4th Wave labels during 1996 which began to establish his reputation as "the most significant talent to emerge from the UK techno scene in the last five years." The first of these was the **Intelligent Desert** EP which collided deep syncopations with surprising key changes and lush synthetics. **It's an Everyday World** on 4th Wave shifted towards a House feel, while **Monkey Jazz** layered a wildly swinging jazz groove with warm strings and stunning melodies.

Early the following year, O'Brien's outstanding debut album, **Desert Scores** (1997), emerged. It was a masterpiece full of jazz breaks, pure Techno and assured combinations of melody and counterpoint. Soon after the album's arrival, O'Brien found himself the focus of hyperbolic media attention which placed him alongside some of Techno's most revered producers. A number of exceptional remixes for artists such as Haçienda ("Discoking"), Lisa Stansfield ("The Line") and Russ Gabriel ("Cube of the Blues") did little to dampen the media's ardour. O'Brien's response was to retreat into his studio and submerge himself in a wealth of new material.

If, as *Muzik* magazine's Dave Mothersole suggested, O'Brien's debut album sounded like "a space-age Herbie Hancock", then the projected follow-up, **Gigantic Days**, skirted close to being Stevie Wonder on MDMA. An even more innovative and compelling record than its predecessor, the album was sadly stalled by the closure of Clear Records, who had signed O'Brien after his departure from Ferox. It remains one of Techno's great lost classics, packed with thrilling, inspired moments and a visionary interpretation of Techno as future jazz fusion.

In 1998 he signed a one-album deal with Peacefrog for what would be, technically at least, his third album. The album was eventually renamed after the still-born second album and released as **Gigantic Days** (1999). This release marked a further development in O'Brien's astounding trajectory as one of Techno's most accomplished and persuasive *auteurs*, capable of spaced-out brilliance, gentle precision and breathtaking innovation all at the same time.

⊙ **Desert Scores**   **Ferox, 1997**

With cadences, textures and structures pulled from jazz and then fused with the seductive contours of Black Dog/UR/Red Planet-style Techno, this is one of the most assured debuts you're ever likely to hear.

⊙ **Gigantic Days**   Peacefrog, 1999

Sky-kissing melodics, fluttering syncopative beats and deep, sub-oceanic funk meet in one achingly romantic, essential release.

Octave One

It's more than a decade since Lawrence Burden, along with his brothers Lenny and Lynell, set out on their collision course with dance music. As Octave One, the trio have produced classics like 1989's "I Believe" and pushed the frontiers of Techno to embrace both funk and soul on a clutch of near-perfect releases for their own 430 West label. Although their output is relatively small, Octave One's influence on the dancefloor has been significant and they're particular favourites with some of the world's best DJs.

The Burden brothers grew up on Detroit's West Side. It was while the Burdens were providing the lighting and effects for the legendary Music Institute that they found themselves in the centre of the Techno scene. Listening to DJs like Darryl Wynn, Derrick May and Kevin Saunderson playing sets full of Techo classics like "Strings Of Life", "No UFOs" and "Sharevari" inspired them to begin making their own music. With the proceeds from their day-jobs, they began investing in recording gear. "We had very little input from other musicians back then," remembers Lenny. "We had no idea about what other people were using." However, they struck lucky when Fade II Black's Jay Denham sold them a TR-909 drum machine – a Techno standard – just before they were due to go into Juan Atkins' Metroplex Studio to record their first single.

With its warm strings and distinctive rhythm programming, "I Believe" became an instant dancefloor classic. Virgin Records chose the track for their follow-up to the ground-breaking **Techno! – The New Dance Sound of Detroit** compilation and provided a budget for some more recording. The Burdens began working on a series of exceptional tracks including "The Journey" (which came out under the name Never On Sunday), "Falling In Dub" (under the name Random Noise Generation) and "Octivate" which eventually became the first release on 430 West.

Subsequent releases like the **Foundation** and **Conquered Nation** EPs confirmed Octave One's unique ability to combine the hard futuristic elements of Techno with the warmth and emotionalism of Detroit's musical roots. Tracks such as "Empower" (from the **Foundation** EP), with its tribal drum rhythms and distinctive sonic palette, somehow manage to fuse the forward-thinking innovation of, say, Jeff Mills or Basic Channel with a deeply soulful edge.

Octave One's long-awaited debut album, **The Living Key (To the Images From Above)** (1997), stretched Octave One's unique tribal grooves into a polyrhythmic haze that was part Detroit street style, part Kraftwerk and part outer-space ritual. Tracks like "The Living Key" and "Divisions" turned the usual dancefloor formula upside down, modulating drums and twisting synths into percussives with subtle rhythmic shifts and careful edits.

The album was the end result of a decade spent at the front-end of Detroit Techno. With an influence which belies their modest output, Octave One's impact on the course of modern dance music cannot be underestimated – a fact that was underlined with the release of **The Collective** (1998), a compilation of some of the group's classic releases.

⊙ **The Collective**   Direct Beat/430 West, 1998

All the classics in one definitive package. Simply essential.

Alan Oldham /
DJ T-1000

Alan Oldham is the exception that proves the rule. Instead of the usual Kraftwerk and George Clinton influences, he grew up listening to a mix of heavy metal and indie rock, name-checking My Bloody Valentine and Joy Division as particular influences. But Oldham was equally at home in the rareified climes of jazz – he'll happily chat about Wes Montgomery or Cannonball Adderley with knowledgeable enthusiasm – and maintains a consuming passion for the early Chicago jack sound of House.

As a college student in the mid-'80s, Oldham was offered an internship with a local radio station, WDT. When the station needed a host for its late-night *Fast Forward* show, the kid who'd been filing records and processing new releases seemed to be the perfect choice. Thus Oldham – who had known Derrick May since childhood and so had impeccable links with the embryonic Techno scene – became a crucial link, alongside Electrifying Mojo and Jeff Mills, in the network of influences that took the new sound onto the airwaves and helped propel its development.

Oldham was also a gifted graphic artist. In 1986, he published the first in a series of *Johnny Gambit* stories for his own Hot Comics imprint. He has continued to work on comics ever since, including three volumes of *Gambit & Associates* for Eclectic Press and a monthly serial, *Danger Girl*, for the UK dance magazine *Muzik*. It was this talent which led to him working on the label art for the original release of Rhythim Is Rhythim's "Nude Photo" in 1987 and a subsequent long-running association with the Netherlands-based Djax Records providing graphics for many of the label's best-known releases.

In 1989, Oldham set up the Technika label, but aborted the project after what he describes as "some really bad experiences". He then began working with Underground Resistance. Along with Robert Hood, Oldham was responsible for helping with the group's various administrative activities, but when Jeff Mills left the group, Oldham was co-opted as the official Underground Resistance DJ and was one of the main features on their 1992 Australian tour.

Following that trip, and encouraged by Mike Banks, Oldham established the Generator label which opened for business with the **TXC1** EP. Over the next four years, Generator provided a platform for producers such as Italy's Passarani & Monteduro, Woody McBride and the Japanese duo Mind Design alongside Oldham's own excursions under the name DJ T-1000.

Generator's forward-thinking approach, combining the fractured electronic jazz of tracks such as Passarani & Monteduro's "Dreaming Detroit" with the bruisingly funky, hard Techno of DJ T-1000's "Liquid Metal Meltdown", was captured on the exceptional label compilation **World Sonik Domination** (1994). But Oldham began to consider the label's eclectic outlook as a drawback in the increasingly separatist Techno scene and grudgingly closed the label in 1996 with the experimental **Enginefloatreactor** double-pack. In its place, he set up Pure Sonik as an exclusive outlet for his own material.

Pure Sonik debuted with the hard, uncompromising shapes of "Pure Sonik Manifesto" and has since continued to chart Oldham's tough, individual trajectory through Techno with releases such as "Downshifter" and the **Signals and Minimalism** EP. Some of these outings were brought together for **A Pure Sonik Evening** (1998), an intriguingly minimal set which, technically at least, constituted Oldham's debut album. A follow-up for Berlin's Tresor label, **Progress**

(1999), built on the success of his **Jetset Lovelife** EP which combined the hard-as-nails aesthetic with a quieter and more reflective strain of experimentalism. The Tresor material is probably the closest he has come to defining his original and compelling vision of Techno.

As his T-1000 alter ego suggests, Oldham has also become one of the most exciting DJs on the circuit. It's worth tracking down either of his superb mix albums, **Supercollider** (1997) and **Live Sabotage** (1998), for further evidence of his incendiary deck skills.

⊙ **Supercollider**   Generator/Pure Sonik, 1997

Oldham cuts loose on this essential mix outing, shifting beats and breaks across locked grooves to create a wild symphony where hard means hard and the funk is delivered through an all-out assault of accelerating bpms. Pure Techno.

Neil Ollivierra

As a teenager in Detroit during the mid-'80s, Neil Ollivierra found himself swept up in the vortex of Techno's second wave, when a confluence of elite club kids, a vibrant house party scene and increasing access to the airwaves took the new music into downtown clubs such as The Leidernacht and The Music Institute. Ollivierra made connections quickly, thanks to his friendship with Derrick May. But as Detroit's hometown scene foundered during the late '80s, Ollivierra withdrew to concentrate on a number of activities.

Among the projects he worked on during the subsequent wilderness years was *Reality Slap*, a novel set around the Eastern Market district of Detroit where part of Techno's initial creative surge had

taken place. Though it has yet to be published, Ollivierra revisited at least some of the book's themes on his debut album, the sensual and evocative **Soundtrack 313** (1996). Prompted by a series of recordings made with a portable DAT recorder as he cycled around the downtown area – the bars and cafés of Greektown, the muffled beats leaking from 4x4s and the gentle lap of the waves at the edge of the Detroit River where the Renaissance Centre beams over to Canada – the album attempted to capture at least some of Detroit's unique character in sound. The result, like the city itself, was a compelling combination of warm beauty and desolate force. On tracks such as "Gratiot" (named after one of the city's main thoroughfares) or the swooning abstraction of "Tai Chi and Traffic Lights", Ollivierra delineated an almost note-perfect vision of late-night Detroit that was suffused with both the romance of the city's French past and the bittersweet ache of its contemporary urban environment.

After the release of **Soundtrack 313**, Ollivierra went to work for Derrick May at Transmat. His involvement helped to ignite the label's creative renaissance. Ollivierra also contributed the languidly seductive "Plumb" to the Transmat compilation, **Time:Space** (1999). The track was one of a number of unreleased gems which had been recorded during the years since his debut album and which were originally planned for single release under the name of The Detroit Escalator Company, the name he uses for all his recorded work.

Ollivierra's forthcoming second album, **Black Buildings**, is part of a larger project which initially began as a series of paintings (Ollivierra is also a graphic artist). As with the relationship between the *Reality Slap* novel and the **Soundtrack 313** album, the new material offers further evidence of a fascinating cross-pollination between each of Ollivierra's distinct talents.

⊙ **Soundtrack 313**   Ferox, 1996

A sonic document of a late night in downtown Detroit, loaded with beauty and exquisite cadences, this is one of Techno's most overlooked classics.

Omegaman

B oomer Reynolds began his career as a DJ in 1983, just as Electro moved into its upswing. As tracks like Warp 9's "Light Years Ahead" and The Jonzun Crew's "Pack Jam" spun dance music into the nexus of computer games, galactic futurism and weird cyber-pop, the sixteen-year-old Reynolds began hustling for gigs around the Norfolk, Virginia area where he grew up. Within a few years, Reynolds succumbed to the lure of Detroit Techno and began producing his own tracks at the beginning of the '90s. Detached from the music industry's central currents, it was 1994 before the first Omegaman single, "2 Saxy", found its way into the world courtesy of John Acquaviva's Definitive label.

"2 Saxy" was a promising beginning, but the track Reynolds chose to follow up with was the one which will forever justify his place in any history of Techno. "72 Nova" occupied the mid-point between the elastic minimalism of Richie Hawtin and the dreamily romantic inclinations of Detroit's new digital era, but in truth its spirit was closer to the drugged-out astral travelling of, say, David Moufang and Jonas Grossmann's Source Records. Locking together a simple, minimal groove, a deep, grittily syncopated bassline and what sounded like a series of hallucinatory reverbs, Reynolds shot the track through with a bittersweet melody line that seemed to tell of floating freefall in outer space, heartbreak and Zen-like calm. It seemed designed neither for passive chill-out nor the full-on, wired-up hedonism of the dancefloor, instead opting for the trippier, prettier environs suggested by tracks such as Carl Craig's "Microlovr" or Move D's "Beyond the Machine". As DJs began to cross-pollinate House and Techno once again, "72 Nova" became the record everyone seemed to want in their box.

As a result, Reynolds found himself playing DJ gigs across the Midwest with Derrick May, Kevin Saunderson, 808 State and Richie Hawtin, but the Omegaman tracks which followed – including "Home-bass" and the self-explanatory "Guitar Groove" – reined back from the spaced-out explorations of "72 Nova" in favour of a more ascertainably down-to-earth mood. He eventually settled on a kind of discoid House hybrid which he has explored on his subsequent releases for Definitive (including the well-rated "Dolas Track") and on "Everybody Loves", the inaugural single on the Out the Box label which he set up with partner Tim Price early in 1999.

⊙ "72 Nova" Definitive, 1994

Although this single went on to achieve classic status on the Techno scene, Reynolds has since pursued a more House-oriented direction.

The Orb

Formed in the heat of the UK Acid House explosion in 1988 by Alex Paterson and Jimmy Cauty, The Orb began by hosting the VIP room at Paul Oakenfold's now legendary Land of Oz club where they created beatless soundtracks with the aid of a sampler and as many turntables and tape decks as they could blag. These experiences lent themselves to their early studio escapades. "Tripping On Sunshine" became the first Orb track to be commercially released in November 1988 when long-time friend Youth included it on a compilation entitled **Eternity Project One**.

The first Orb record proper was the limited **Kiss** EP in early 1989, made up of samples from New York's Kiss FM radio shows and issued on Wau! Mr Modo, the label formed by Alex and Youth. In the spring of that year Paterson and Cauty recorded their first masterpiece, "A Huge Ever-Growing Pulsating Brain That Rules From the Centre of the Ultraworld/Loving You" – a colossal fusion of ambience, dub effects, wave sounds, sequences and choral voices, over which Minnie Riperton's '70s hit "Loving You" was floated. Initial reaction was slow during that furiously hedonistic summer, but the track began to build when John Peel became one of the few DJs to give it radio airtime and subsequently offered them a session for which they dispensed another mutated version of this ever-evolving epic.

In early 1990, Cauty left The Orb to pursue his musical interests with Bill Drummond as Justified Ancients of Mu Mu (later KLF). Undeterred, Paterson recorded "Little Fluffy Clouds" with Youth. It was during these sessions that they befriended an 18-year-old engineer called Thrash (Kris Weston) who later replaced Cauty for The Orb's first live performances. That summer, whilst still holding down an A&R position at Brian Eno's EG label, Alex began recording the first Orb album with the aid of various friends and collaborators.

Adventures Beyond the Ultraworld (1991) captured the blissed-out mood of contemporary clubland, with a fluid blend of House, dub, ambience and classical and swiftly became a seminal chill-out album. Later that year saw the release and deletion (on the same day) of **Aubrey Mixes: The Ultraworld Excursions** – an album of remixes that would have made The Orb's debut album a triple if the manufacturing costs hadn't proved so prohibitive.

During the summer of '91, The Orb produced Primal Scream's free-spirit anthem, "Higher Than the Sun", while Paterson also spent time collaborating with Steve Hillage and Miquette Giraudy (both former members of '70s space-rock band Gong) on their System 7 (Paterson was almost single-handedly responsible for the rehabilitation of Hillage's 1977 album, **Rainbow Dome Musick**, as an Ambient classic).

In early 1992, The Orb recorded their third Peel session, serving up a remodelling of "Oobe" (later to materialise on that year's **UFOrb**) and a cover of The Stooges' "No Fun". Their next release, "Blue Room", became the longest-ever single, clocking in at just a second under the 40-minute guideline laid down by the British Phonographic Industry, and breached the UK Top Ten. **UFOrb** reached #1 almost instantaneously. It was already light years on from **Adventures...** and revealed more of the band's dub influences. The album concept was based around the UFO phenomenon, in particular the supposed existence of The Blue Room at Wright Patterson Airbase in the American desert, where aliens and working flying saucers are rumoured to be held.

After resolving long-standing legal situations involving management and previous label Big Life, Island released **Pomme Fritz – The Orb's Little Album** (1994). Its content was far removed from the sublime Ambient Techno of **UFOrb**; instead the hyper-complex rhythms they'd been experimenting with had evolved into profound, landscaped electronica.

When **Orbus Terrarum** arrived in 1995, it also signalled the departure of Thrash. His replacement was Andy Hughes (who had already been The Orb's engineer for six years), but the pressures of recording an album in the middle of a line-up change weren't visible on the surface. **Orbus Terrarum** was a spacious album full of fresh electronical dimensions: the dreamlike "Plateau", which had been a feature of the live set for the past two years, the dramatic atmosphere of "Montagne d'Or" and the serene electronic waves of "Oxbow Lakes". Like its predecessor, **Orbus Terrarum** was greeted with muted enthusiasm by large sections of the British press, but it opened up America for the group.

Orblivion (1997) began life at the Berlin home of long-time Orb collaborator Thomas Fehlman. It brought with it further mood changes and a distinct drum 'n' bass flavour. While "S.A.L.T." (featuring David Thewlis' turbulent "666" rant from Mike Leigh's film *Naked*) was probably one of the most chilling pieces to come out of the Orb camp, the chart hit "Toxygene" was a nod back to their "Perpetual Dawn" days. The rest of the album focused on six-minute strikes as opposed to their usual extended excursions.

The beginning of 1998 found the group performing low-key gigs as Le Petit Orb to test out new material and, in October, **UF Off – The Best of the Orb** attempted to put their first decade into perspective.

⊙ **Adventures Beyond the Ultraworld**   Wau! Mr Modo/Big Life, 1991

One of Ambient Techno's most comprehensive classics, this is still an astonishing testimony of Alex Paterson's restlessly eclectic musical vision.

⊙ **UF Off: The Best of the Orb**   Island, 1998

The story so far. Bringing together the finest moments from The Orb's inimitable oeuvre, this is a fine introduction to the group for those who have yet to investigate their capricious, unruly and indefinable sound.

Sherman

Orbital

Named after London's M25 orbital motorway – a potent symbol for both ravers and police during the 1988 and '89 Summers of Love – Orbital have spent the last decade as one of dance music's most enduring and best-loved acts. They've pioneered a multimedia approach to live dance music, become one of Techno's first true album acts, headlined Glastonbury, remixed Madonna, and imbued the hedonism of the British dance scene with a political dignity and artistic sensitivity previously unseen.

Formed in 1989 by brothers Paul and Phil Hartnoll in Sevenoaks, Kent, and influenced by second generation punk, On-U Sound's mili-

tant dub, and hip-hop, Orbital heralded their arrival with an original single called "Chime". London DJ Jazzy M pressed up just 1,000 copies of "Chime" on his Oh-Zone label, but the single, riven with classical-sounding, instant melodies and a cautious optimism, instantly caught the imagination of ravers nationwide and the initial pressing rapidly sold out. DJs around the country were paying up to

£40 a copy until London Records subsidiary ffrr signed both single and band. Within weeks, the Hartnoll brothers found themselves performing on *Top of the Pops*, wearing "No Poll Tax" t-shirts while their record rocketed to #17 in the national charts.

With their background in indie and punk, Orbital had been playing rough shows even before the instant success of their first single and wanted – much to the consternation of their record company – to develop a full live show rather than the fifteen-minute, mimed "live PA" that most dance acts of the time preferred. The pair also wanted to record proper artist albums, in stark contrast to the club hit compilations and illegal mix tapes that dominated the early '90s dance scene.

Their first, untitled, album, the so-called Green Album, was released in 1991 and critically acclaimed for the diversity of its approach. It broke the mould for dance albums. This and its, again, untitled follow-up (the Brown Album) were clear signals that electronic music had progressed far beyond the dancefloor. Classical sensibilities, harsh Acid noises and beautiful synthesised melodies all fed into a river of sound, at once futuristic, emotional, rhythmic, and highly melodic. Tracks like "Belfast" (from the Green Album) and the Brown Album's "Halcyon + On + On" – written about their mother's addiction to tranquillisers – demonstrated a unique musical awareness and a deft sensitivity that previously only Detroit Techno artists had achieved.

In 1993 Orbital helped compile and headlined a unique dance music concert tour: the Midi-Circus, alongside the Drum Club and Aphex Twin. By this time, their live shows had developed into a an event that melded elements of sound system, DJ set, and live performance while the brothers stripped their tracks back to the bone, then rebuilt them. This was a whole new agenda for dance music which was welcomed not just by ravers disaffected by the cartoon excesses of their own scene, but by indie fans unable to handle the disco hedonism of mainstream House clubs.

In the wake of the Conservative government's Criminal Justice Act, Orbital returned to the political arena. Their third album was the first with a title, **Snivilisation** (1994), and was backed up with sneering interviews about the state of society. **Snivilisation** entered the album charts at #4, followed by the single "Are We Here?" which played with the kind of breakbeat rhythms that characterised Jungle, 1994's other big music event.

By the summer of 1995, Orbital were headlining Glastonbury again, remixing Madonna's "Bedtime Stories" and contributing to the soundtrack of the PlayStation game WipeOut. **In Sides** (1996) was Orbital's fourth album and moved into more sombre territory as the brothers swapped club influences for film soundtrack atmospheres. With its dulcimer melodies, "The Box" had an almost baroque feel and brushed the Top Ten. The album reached #5 in the album charts and was followed by the release of a fierce, 27-minute, live version of "Satan" which entered the charts at #3. Conclusive evidence that Orbital were as much a live act as they were an album band.

The cinematic influences of **In Sides** were further explored in 1997 when Orbital released a version of the theme to '60s cult TV show *The Saint*, to accompany the Hollywood remake. Again, the single reached #3. 1998 was spent recording another ambitious and yet more difficult album, **The Middle of Nowhere**, released in 1999, preceded by the bizarre single, "Style". By this point, the Hartnoll brothers were as far from dance music as they could possibly get, with tracks like "Nothing Left" layering folk influences and female vocals over a mish-mash of backing tracks that included rock, breakbeats and pure noise.

⊙ **Untitled ("The Brown Album")**   Internal, 1993

A landmark dance album. Includes the emotive "Halcyon + On + On".

⊙ **Snivilisation**   Internal, 1994

Their finest album played with breakbeats (on "Are We Here?"), worked
lush melodies into taught grooves, and hummed with a political intensity.

Dom Phillips

Oval

F ew artists have emphasised the links between the avant garde
and Techno quite as much as Oval. The trio of Markus Popp,
Sebastian Oschatz and Frank Metzger first emerged with **Systemisch** (1993) on the Mille Plateaux label. Employing musical methods of deconstruction involving distressing CDs, dismantling
technological hardware and then digitally reconstructing the resulting
chaos, **Systemisch** was surprisingly easy to listen to. Subtle, discor-
dant textures played counterpoint with complex rhythmical interplay
and simplistic harmonic refrains to create a manifesto of stark, edgy
dissonance.

It was an approach which they continued to explore to occasionally unlistenable extremes with **94 Diskont** (1994) which revolved
around the 24-minute epic "Do While" – a single looped refrain, slipping in and out of sync originally written for their 128-speaker mobile
sound installation. **94 Diskont** was also accompanied by a remix version on vinyl which included interpretations of "Do While" by Mouse
on Mars, Scanner, Cristian Vogel, Jim O'Rourke and Mike Ink.

In 1995 Markus Popp teamed up with Jan St. Werner of Mouse On Mars for the Microstoria project, releasing two albums: _snd (1995) and the remix collection **Reprovisors** (1997). With the exception of the poorly received and musically less inspired **Dok** (1995) on Thrill Jockey, Oval however have remained quiet, apparently disengaged from the process of music-making.

⊙ **Systemisch**   Mille Plateaux, 1993

An album of textural diversity which found impenetrable frequency snatches intermingled with soothing refrains. Very much from the school of endless repetition, **Systemisch** is in fact an album of strangely hypnotic beauty.

Martin James

Panasonic

Their music has been compared to the pulsing, abstract expressionism of Mark Rothko and derided as the last word in self-indulgent, electronic flatulence. The truth about Finland's Panasonic – as they'd probably be the first to concede – lies somewhere in the middle.

Based in a converted sauna on the eastern outskirts of Turku, the trio of Mika Vainio, Ilpo Väisänen and Sami Salo cultivated an intriguing image for themselves by borrowing liberally from post-modern art theory and existing pop mythology (in particular, their emphasis on self-built sonic devices veered eerily close to a line already well-used by both Aphex Twin and Kraftwerk). Their output, however, was more obviously involved with a stubborn attempt to dissolve the structures of Techno into extreme ambience, machine noise and unsettling distortion.

This wasn't particularly new territory for Vainio and Väisänen. In the late '80s, they'd been members of a Helsinki performance art group, Ultra 3, experimenting with sensory deprivation/overload and sub-bass frequencies. As a founder member of Corporate 09 with Pertti Grönholm, Vainio had appeared to mellow, recording what was reputed to be Finland's first Techno album and tracing an icily refined route through abstract melodies which keyed into the tastes of the rapidly maturing Ambient scene. After splitting with Grönholm, he'd explored more extreme excursions under the name Ø, contributing tracks to the then in-vogue Sähkö label, which combined fractured rhythms with test tones and spaces pregnant with possibility. To the untutored ear, it hardly sounded like music at all, just empty clouds of electronic noise and irritatingly repetitive drones. To the converted, it was a brave new world that revolutionised music by freeing it from the constraints of melody, rhythm and – best of all for the elitists – accessibility.

Panasonic took this all one step further. Their debut album, **Vakio** (1995), was a curiously uncertain offering which vacillated between turgid unlistenability and moments when the theories threatened to produce something much more imaginative. By the time **Kulma** (1997) rolled around, Salo had left – to join the army – and the similarly named Japanese electronics giant was breathing down their necks, forcing a belated change of name to Pan Sonic. Now based in Barcelona, Pan Sonic have increasingly identified themselves more with the art world than the music world, crafting sound installations for galleries in New York, Paris and Minneapolis – though a third album, **A** (1999), suggested that they haven't quite abandoned the record industry just yet.

⊙ **Vakio**   Blast First, 1995

It's music, Jim . . . but not as we know it. Shrill, dislocated textures, atonal rumbles and an approach to composition which makes the listening experience resemble a feat of endurance, this is not for the faint-hearted.

Percy X

A t the beginning of 1995, Glasgow's Soma Records released "X-Traks", a tough, minimal groove that went on to become a substantial underground hit. The identity of its mysterious creator, Percy X, was the subject of much debate. A number of producers, ranging from Detroit's Claude Young to Chicago's Harrison Crump, were suggested as likely candidates.

Percy X's second single, "Odyssey", arrived five months later and, by then, there were already a few people who had guessed that the answer lay closer to home. But the mystery producer's identity remained a closely guarded secret until the release of "Percy X versus Bloodsugar" – a soundclash with Andrew Weatherall – when it was officially revealed that Percy X was, in fact, Havana's Tony Scott.

Since his partnership with Richard Miller in Havana had disintegrated by this time and his contractual ties to Limbo had expired, Scott was now free to capitalise on the huge European success of his Percy X alter ego. He continued to mine a similar vein of hard, dub-inflected Techno to the one which had made Havana's final releases so compelling, but this time added hip-hop, German electronica and sparse experimentalism to the blend.

The release of **Spyx** (1996) confirmed Scott's eclectic fusion of a number of different dancefloor genres. Tracks such as "Loner" and "Subloop" operated in paralllel territory to Jeff Mills, while Scott's gift for narcotic melody was still evident on "Faint". At times, the production values of **Spyx** moved close to the brilliant patina of Havana's **Hitch**, a fact that was underlined by the presence of engineer Chris Cowie who has provided an important key in helping both Scott and Miller unlock the best of their creative work, both during Havana's final recordings and in their subsequent solo careers. Cowie remains one of Techno's most unsung studio wizards and his contribution to **Spyx** (he co-wrote and co-produced many of the album tracks) should not be disregarded.

Subsequent releases – such as the **Day Three** EP (1996), "New Ground" (1998) and "User Friendly" (1999) – emerged at lengthy intervals. A second Percy X album is planned, but Scott has a relaxed attitude to his studio forays and seems content for now to release occasional singles for Soma alongside his more DJ-oriented work for R&S and Music Man (as Mion).

⊙ **Spyx**   Soma, 1996

Deep, dark and dubby Techno that's purpose-built for the dancefloor at 4am but still sounds great at home too.

Plaid

I n 1989, Ed Handley and Andy Turner, two East Anglian teenagers looking to broaden their interest in computers, hip-hop and Electro, answered an ad in a music technology magazine, placed by Ken

Downie, ex-sailor turned electronic musician. The three got together, got on and got themselves a name: The Black Dog. The rest, as they say, is history.

Black Dog Productions, however, was a hermetic environment. Downie was content to closet himself in Black Dog Towers, their studio in the East End of London, actively constructing a cloak of anonymity for the group. Perhaps reflecting the disparity in age between them, however, Handley and Turner were more outgoing in their approach, and were keen to translate the music they were making on their own Black Dog Productions label into a live setting. Not only that; they were also beginning to make music as a self-contained unit, free of Downie's influence. As an outlet for this creativity, they released **Mbuki Mvuki** (1991), a lively melting pot of electronics, Calypso, Latin and alien radio frequencies. Keen to set the project apart from Black Dog itself, the duo named themselves Plaid. Released in an ultra-limited run of 1,000 copies, the album has become one of the most sought-after Techno LPs – and a pension plan for anyone who actually owns a copy.

It also signalled the long-drawn-out beginning of the end for The Black Dog. The acrimony generated by **Mbuki Mvuki**'s release was further aggravated by their decision to perform live, a situation that lingered on until early 1995 when, following the release of **Spanners** (1994), the trio called time on things.

The same year, Plaid released an EP an the then-fledgling Clear label and were invited to support Björk on a tour of the Far East. The duo had already performed both remix and songwriting duties for her, so when her regular keyboard player left the band as the tour was about to begin, she asked them to fill in. For the next year, they toured the world, as both support act and main band.

After producing Nicolette's **Let No One Live Rent-Free Inside Your Head** (1996), they released **Not for Threes** (1997), an arresting mixture of fuzzy/fizzy Electro, quirky electronic sketches and digital torch songs, voiced by, amongst others, Björk and Nicolette. Most recently, the duo have been involved in production work for Kushti's **Secret Handshakes** (1998), an album of samba-tinged instrumental hip-hop, which may or may not actually be them.

⊙ **Not For Threes**   Warp, 1997

From the Calypso-Electro squelch of "Ladyburst" to the devotional beauty of "Rakimou", this features every type of electronic music you could imagine on one disc – and some you couldn't even dream of.

Peter McIntyre

Pluto

When Techno reached the UK and merged with Acid House to propel modern dance culture into existence, the story of Rolo McGinty – one-time indie hero with the Woodentops who succumbed to this new subculture and retrained himself as a Techno producer – became emblematic of the time and a narrative which was destined to repeat itself again and again over the coming years.

But close observers might have noted that, after all, the Woodentops' frontman wasn't such an unlikely candidate for conversion. "The band was influenced, to a degree, by artists such as Suicide, Kraftwerk, Can and Yello," noted McGinty. "We were heavily into electronic recording methods such as sampling and drum programming."

By the time the Woodentops' single "Why, Why, Why" was adopted as a Balearic anthem, McGinty had already discovered House and Techno during one of the group's final US tours. By 1989, he was collaborating with Bang the Party on "Tainted World" – a favourite with DJs such as Tony Humphries and Todd Terry – and planning to dissolve the group in favour of a dance-oriented solo project.

McGinty went on to work with a number of artists in the fast-developing scene, including Orbital, Robert Owens, Mr C, Farley "Jackmaster" Funk and Armando, and built up a considerable cult following with his own project under the name Pluto. Singles such as 1992's "Free to Run" and "Pluto Beat" outlined the territory: a fluid mix of freaked-out Detroit Techno and exuberant funk that was stretched, twisted and filtered through the prism of the British Acid House experience.

Pluto Rising (1994) was an accomplished debut which hovered somewhere between the uplifting positivity of "Someday" and the darker, more abstract terrain of "Nude Photo". Tracks such as "Diablo" or "Indian Runner" were ecstatic distillations of dance culture's twin origins, though it was obvious from "Mach 3" and "Let Me Lie" that developments in Europe hadn't been entirely ignored. There was even a reworking of "Sueño Latino" (as "Sueño Plutino") that was emblematic of McGinty's curious mix of devotion and iconoclasm.

There was a lengthy hiatus before the arrival of **Demolition Plates** (1997) which built on the success of **Pluto Rising,** but the advent of drum 'n' bass had made a predictable impact on McGinty. As Dogs Deluxe, he began experimenting with breakbeats and released an eponymous album in 1998. McGinty re-emerged in 1999 with the "Sno Queen" single and the promise of a third album of deliciously celebratory techno.

⊙ **Pluto Rising**   ITP, 1994

The sum of six years on the dancefloor getting wild to "Strings of Life", "Wiggin" and "Can You Feel It", Pluto's debut still sounds as fresh and celebratory as it did when it was first released. A gem.

Ian Pooley

A t the age of 12, Ian Pooley was at home in Germany making tapes of classic Detroit Techno and Chicago House. A mere five years later, in 1991, he was DJing and producing alongside his peers and by 1998, with the release of his **Meridian** album, even eclipsing them.

Hailing from Mainz, Pooley was born of dual nationality. His mother is Welsh but moved to Germany in the late '60s. He grew up, like his future Detroit heroes, listening to the electronic pop of Kraftwerk. His father got so annoyed with his obsession that – when Ian was six – he broke all his Kraftwerk records. Collecting the seminal Detroit/Chicago tunes was a difficult hobby in Techno-starved Mainz in 1987, but Pooley found a friend who shared his musical aspirations. Thomas Gerhard (later known as DJ Tonka) and Pooley began producing under the aliases Spacecube and T'N'I, eschewing the Teutonic Techno sounds associated with Sven Vath and Hardfloor for melodic Detroit-style Techno on Germany's Force Inc. imprint.

Pooley and Tonka split in 1994 leaving Ian to explore his own sound. Tonka was a classically trained pianist responsible for the more harmonic sounds in T'N'I. Pooley, who cannot play any instruments, had to suffice with fewer tools. The results were the bone-shaking **Twin Gods** EP and the **Celtic Cross** EP. One DJ legend who met Pooley around this time was Plus 8 boss John Acquaviva who immediately signed him to his Definitive label. During 1995, Pooley made his mark on the underground with "Rollerskate Disco", "Relations Do" and the classic "Chord Memory". His Definitive releases captured the mood of a time when Chicago was undergoing a renaissance with artists like Glenn Underground and Boo Williams capturing both the soulful funk of House and disco and the harder-edged alien aspects of Techno.

In 1996, he released his first album, **The Times**, more like a double-pack release of club tracks than a listening album. DJ offers around the globe flooded in. Pooley's ability to play sublime House, banging Techno – or both – earned him regular appearances at Manchester's Bugged Out!, London's The End and Slam in Glasgow. The remix offers also flooded in from such luminaries as Dave Angel, Green Velvet, Ken Ishii, Yello and The Cardigans. Working with rock acts is something Pooley admits he is not averse to. In fact he records unreleased guitar music despite the obvious limitation of not being able to play the instrument! Influenced by Bristol's Flying Saucer Attack, Pooley samples guitar sounds and uses numerous delay pedals like the Superfuzz Big Muff to achieve "a specific feedback sound" to which he adds breakbeats and occasionally sequencers to make soundtracks.

His 1998 album release, **Meridian**, won Pooley further critical acclaim. It was a triumph of his eclectic tastes. More for sofa surfers than his club-oriented debut – the beats were more delicate and the production more elaborate – **Meridian** was full of blissed-out grooves.

◉ The Times   Force Inc., 1996

Though "Celtic Cross" is sadly absent, the classic "Chord Memory" and another dozen of Pooley's rough-house club cuts make this a fine introduction to his sound.

John Burgess

Darren Price

For a brief spell in the early '80s Darren Price was heavily into the Electro boom. After Electro, he developed a taste for reggae and began hanging out at the Dub Vendor record shop in Clapham. Initially at least, he wasn't convinced by House music. That view altered considerably when, towards the end of 1988, he discovered Shoom. Price was particularly fascinated by Andy Weatherall's occasional sets at the club and at the legendary Boys Own parties. He'd already begun DJing tentatively during the Electro years, but after hearing Weatherall he was inspired to return to the decks and started buying records more seriously. He played slots for some of Phil Perry's nights and also played at the equally influential Clink Street Studios where Kid Batchelor and

PETER WALSH

Eddie Richards provided a darker, more experimental alternative to the Balearic sound of Shoom.

His fledgling career as a DJ was put on hold, however, in 1989 when he was arrested and jailed for three years. Following his parole, he got a job in the same office as the Junior Boys Own label and, championed this time by Weatherall, began making his mark on the scene as a DJ. With Gary Lindop and Eric Chiverton, Price also started recording for Junior Boys Own as Centuras. Following several well-received singles, the trio recorded an album but Price was unsure about the results and, despite the label's enthusiasm, the project was shelved and the group went their separate ways.

A residency at The Havana in Middlesbrough and frequent appearances at London clubs like Full Circle bolstered Price's reputation as a DJ, but he has become best known for his association with Underworld. It was after playing a set alongside Darren Emerson at Full Circle that he was invited to become the group's "official" DJ and he has been a permanent fixture with them ever since.

Price's career as a producer stalled temporarily after the break-up of Centuras, but he re-emerged in 1995 with the well-rated **Attic** EP. This was followed by 1996's **Blueprints** EP for Novamute which was successful enough for the label to invest in an album. **Under the Flightpath** (1997) was a solidly workmanlike debut which blended muscular dancefloor Techno with sometimes unsettling Progressive House overtones. Since then – aside from a project for Darren Emerson's Underwater label – Price has been quiet, though he is expected to return with a follow-up in the near future.

⊙ **Under The Flightpath**   Novamute, 1997

The title was inspired by the fact that the album was recorded in Craig Walsh's studio near Heathrow airport, but tracks such as "Airspace" and "Long Haul 747" didn't quite hit the heights that many expected of Price.

The Prodigy

O f all of the acts to have emerged from the UK rave explosion of the early '90s none can claim to have achieved greater success than The Prodigy. The Prodigy story begins with a teenage Liam Howlett. Turned on to the hip-hop old skool by "The Adventures of Grandmaster Flash on the Wheels of Steel", Howlett was quick to embrace the b-boy lifestyle which has continued to inform The Prodigy's work ever since. A few weeks after buying his first pair of decks he approached local hip-hop outfit Cut to Kill – with whom he recorded an unreleased album – and gained an impressive reputation for his mixing skills, subsequently winning a DJ competition run by London's Capital Radio hip-hop show.

Increasingly excited by the emerging breakbeat House sound, Howlett soon became a part of the quiet revolution which was going on behind the closed curtains of Britain's bedrooms where kids were knocking out tunes on basic set-ups of samplers and Atari computers. At a free party where Howlett was DJing, Keith Flint approached him for a mix tape which he promptly delivered. On one side of the tape, however, were a few of the tracks which he'd been experimenting with in his minimal bedroom studio. Suitably impressed, Keith and a friend called Leeroy Thornhill decided to approach the young programmer to become his dancers. With a gig set up at Dalston's infamous Labyrinth, Howlett decided the fledgling group also needed an MC. A friend suggested Keeti Palmer aka Maxim Reality (later shortened to Maxim) who had been recording Go-Go-style material with Nottingham producer Sheik Yan Groove.

In the interim, Howlett had given a cassette of his music to XL Records who offered a record deal immediately. Released in February

1991, The Prodigy's first single, "What Evil Lurks", was lifted directly from the original tape. It proved to be an underground success selling 5,000 copies in a few short weeks. Following six months of performing at every rave that would have them, The Prodigy made their first big breakthrough with their second single. Released in August 1991, "Charly" became a runaway success in the mainstream, thanks partly to its sampling of a well-remembered public information film. Ironically

STEVE GULLICK

it was the b-side, "Your Love", that had been played constantly at the raves. The cartoonish nature of "Charly" may have opened the doors for a series of infantile rave tracks – resulting in a damning attack from dance magazine *Mixmag* – but The Prodigy continued through the next twelve months releasing a series of singles which had as much impact on the underground as they did on the mainstream. "Everybody in the Place" (December 1991), "Fire" (September 1992) and "Out of

Space" (November 1992) – featuring a Max Romeo vocal sample from "Chase the Devil" – all helped to opened up new horizons for the band.

With the release of the debut album, **Experience** (1992), Howlett showed his true potential. Featuring versions of all of the singles alongside the standout psychedelic ambience of "Weather Experience", it was the best artist album to emerge from the rave scene. **Experience** spawned one more single in the shape of "Wind it Up".

With its Trance groove, Arabic refrains and heavy percussion, the next single, "One Love", was The Prodigy's first non-breakbeat track. The subsequent release of "(No Good) Start the Dance" and the chart-topping second album, **Music for the Jilted Generation** (1994), marked further creative departures for The Prodigy. Born from Howlett's experience of playing the festival circuit and coming face to face with rock music, the album was aimed at a much broader constituency, a fact further underlined by the Nirvana-sampling "Voodoo People" and the downtempo, grungy hip-hop of "Poison".

In the worldwide live shows that followed the album's release which featured live guitars, Keith Flint rolling around in a hamster ball and Maxim resplendent in metal gauntlet and mirror contact lenses, only the old skool dance style of Leeroy and Howlett's synapse-snapping beats acted as a reminder of The Prodigy's roots. The press described them as the greatest rock 'n' roll show on earth and the scene was set for the worldwide domination that was to follow.

It was with the release of "Firestarter" in February 1996 that Flint came to the fore. His snarling vocals and increasingly punky appearance gave the band a natural frontman. The Walter Stern-directed monochrome video was so striking that it became an instant MTV favourite. **The Fat of the Land** (1997) arrived amid a flurry of frenzied hyperbole. Featuring the singles "Firestarter", "Breathe" and "Mind-fields", the album was divided between live favourites like the controversial "Smack My Bitch Up" and collaborations with other vocalists. The release of "Smack My Bitch Up" as a single saw the controversy surrounding the band reach a peak. In hip-hop slang the single's title meant "handle my business", but the mainstream focused on what they assumed were misogynistic connotations. Questions were asked in the House of Commons, radio refused it airplay and the accompanying X-rated video proved too racy for broadcasters. In spite of it all, the single still landed in the upper reaches of the charts.

During their first break from touring for four years, Maxim continued work on his long-term solo project featuring Guru (Gang Starr) and a collaboration with indie band Six by Seven. Leeroy returned to the studio to work on his Electro-House project The Longman – he'd already released a white label under the name in 1997 – while Keith Flint indulged his love of motorbikes and tried out a spot of acting.

⊙ Experience   XL, 1992

Something of a rave concept album, **Experience** harnessed the power of the free party and placed it into a cauldron of rapid-fire samples and manic breakbeats. The album also features radical reworkings of their previous singles – including a version of "Charly" sub-titled "Trip Into Drum and Bass" which all but eliminated the cartoon cat.

⊙ Music for the Jilted Generation   XL, 1994

Enter the guitars on this varied album which arguably marks the band's finest moment. From the thrash Techno of "Their Law" to the electric intensity of "The Narcotic Suite" this was the sound of a band taking the underground to the world.

Martin James

Psychick Warriors Ov Gaia

Alternately revered and reviled, Psychick Warriors Ov Gaia are one of Techno's weirder manifestations, exploring a sound which has its origins in the more experimental fringes of Belgian New Beat, psychedelia and Ambient Techno.

Psychick Warriors evolved from a mid-'80s industrial outfit known variously as The Infants or The Infantiles with a two-year incarnation as Sluagh Ghairm before settling on the name by which they are currently known. But the group's shifting line-up – Robert Heynen, Bobby Reiner, Joris Hilckman, Reinier Brekelmans and soundman Tim Freeman have all been members at one time or another – has ultimately mattered less than the Psychick's overt entanglement with the currents of ritual and magic which intersect in the work. For some – suspicious of the Temple Ov Psychick Youth (with which the Warriors are associated) or any attempts to rationalise the mechanics of the dancefloor in terms of mysticism – this has proved a particularly hard pill to swallow.

Signed to Belgium's Kk Records, the first Psychick Warriors release, "Exit 23: Ritual Dance Music", was a tremulous, pulsing affair. However, it was their second single, "Ov the Maenads", with its drifting, Eastern ambience and dense electronic atmospheres, that provided the template for much of what was to follow. **Ov Biospheres & Sacred Grooves** (1992) was a lengthy, sprawling affair that combined tribal percussion, warm ambience and ethnic cadences with bleaker, industrial textures and proto-Trance. The album was relatively successful, though two subsequent releases, the dancefloor-friendly **Obsidian**

EP and 1993's Drum Club remixes of "Exit 23" keyed in to a prevailing mood that was more sympathetic to their sound. Partly this was due to the increasing impact of Frankfurt Trance on the European dance scene and the significant success of Aphex Twin's experimental take on the structures of dance music.

By 1995, Heynen – the Psychick's chief writer – had left the group. Heynen was the force behind much of the group's melodic drive, though the remaining members claimed that Heynen's contribution had been overstated and that the fact that he had been solely credited with many of the group's compostions was because he was the only one of the Warriors registered with the Writer's Guild. Heynen's departure had an immediate effect on the group, however, resulting in a darker, bleaker sound.

Record of Breaks (1997) was PWOG's official second album, but it had little to recommend it. The relentlessly dark, formless nature of many tracks suggested a group desperately searching for a decent idea and accordingly the release was panned by critics. A subsequent single, "Kraak", featuring remixes from Richie Hawtin and Mark Broom, fared little better. Since then, the group have been relatively inactive, drifting inexorably towards the fringes of Techno though they retain a sizeable cult following.

⊙ **Ov Biospheres & Sacred Grooves**   Kk, 1992

Though it hasn't dated well, the Psychick's debut still has some intriguing moments, such as "The Challenge" and "The Tides (They Turn)", but from here on in it was downhill all the way.

Stacey Pullen

B uilt on structures and rhythms drawn from traditional African music, Stacey Pullen's version of Techno is a back-to-the-future amalgam of spaced-out electronics and tribal roots. A member of Detroit Techno's so-called "second generation" (along with Carl Craig and Kenny Larkin), Pullen's music at its best can sound like a less abstract, more spiritual variation on the themes explored by Derrick May on "Nude Photo" or "It Is What it Is", though the glittering surfaces and pristine sheen of his productions suggest a closer affinity with Larkin than with anyone else.

A mix of influences – ranging from Model 500 and Mr. Fingers to jazz icons such as John Coltrane and Herbie Hancock – inspired Pullen to begin a career as a DJ in the mid-'80s. His first release was the "Ritual Beating System" single for Transmat subsidiary Fragile under the name Bango. Pullen also articulated the Detroit scene's loathing of European Hardcore with his first Silent Phase track, "Wave the Rave Goodbye". However, it was his "Mystical Adventures" contribution to the seminal Buzz compilation, **Virtual Sex** (1993), which brought him to wider attention. A lush, dreamily romantic confection of warm strings and electronic counterpoints, "Mystical Adventures" was a key indicator of Detroit's resurgence as Techno's creative centre and marked an emotive peak for electronic music which has rarely been surpassed.

As Kosmic Messenger he recorded the "Eye to Eye" single for Paul Rip's fiercely underground, London-based label Plink Plonk. After the beautifully pristine moods of "Mystical Adventures", "Eye to Eye" was a solid return to the dancefloor, a rambunctious groove harnessed to sombre atmospherics that proved Pullen could deliver

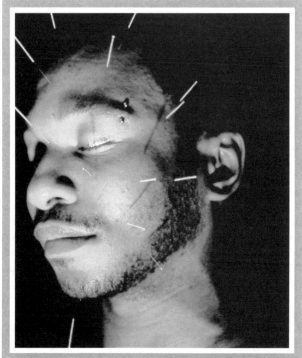

power as well as prettiness. **The Theory of Silent Phase** (1995) followed soon after. The bulk of the album had been recorded in Kenny Larkin's studio over the preceding two years and the same loving attention to sonic detail apparent in Larkin's work manifested itself in tracks such as "Spiritual Journey" or the luxurious "Forbidden

Dance" – acutely sculpted bass patterns from the Yamaha DX100 surrounded by gorgeously expensive sounds from the Kurzweil K2000 which was, at the time, a particular favourite of many Detroit producers. One track, "Air Puzzle", offered a brilliant display of polyrhythmic virtuosity which had its roots in the percussive exercises Pullen had done while playing drums in a marching band at high school, while others bore the influence of May who fulfilled the role of executive producer during the album's protracted gestation. The result was an outstanding record which was hailed as one of the best Techno releases in a year that was notable for a number of the genre's landmark albums.

Behind the decks, Pullen's sets are more House-oriented, pulling in a broad range of diverse strands (including both Techno and African music) to deliver an intriguing and distinctive blend. Legal practicalities prevented any of his wilder forays from making it onto his first mix album, **DJ Kicks: Stacey Pullen** (1996), though the result was still a worthwhile gauge of his talents.

The Collected Works of Kosmic Messenger (1997) brought Pullen's singles for Plink Plonk together with a handful of unreleased cuts. The collection worked remarkably well as a cohesive album though critical response was relatively muted compared to the overwhelming salutations which had greeted his debut album. Nevertheless, the album was successful enough to garner major label interest in Pullen (who had, by now, set up his own imprint, Black Flag Recordings, a highly conceptual enterprise aimed at combining music and art in the grand tradition of ambitious art-house labels) and he signed to the Virgin subsidiary Science in 1998.

⊙ **The Theory of Silent Phase**   Transmat/R&S, 1995

An astonishing debut that combined sharp, digital romance and deep, tribal-influenced, polyrhythmic grooves.

Q-Moog

O ne of the more mysterious entities in Techno, few facts are known
about Q-Moog. Early singles such as "Lire" and "Bloom" (both
on Rhythm Tech) were brooding affairs, layered with a sense of unease
and troubled funk that was both unsettling and compelling. Brussels-
based DJ and writer Joost de Lyser was intrigued enough to track down
the producer responsible. The details that de Lyser uncovered suggested elements from pulp, cyber and detective fiction. Q-Moog, it turned
out, was the alias of Green, a one-time jazz experimentalist who, following the death of his mother, had moved from New York to Detroit at the
age of 12. Hooked in with other Motor City producers such as Drivetrain
and D-Knox, he began converting his jazz training into Techno. Green
revealed that Kenny Larkin had been one of the people who got him further into the Techno scene, mentioning influences such as Kraftwerk,
808 State and Juan Atkins. But he didn't give much else away.

When **The Arc of Blueness** (1997) materialised on SSR/Crammed,
it seemed that even the record company had been unable to penetrate the veil of mystery surrounding Q-Moog other than that Green's
real name was Roy Parker. Like Green, the music itself defied convention. The tracks on **The Arc of Blueness** oscillated between unsettling weirdness ("Mirabella") and aching beauty ("Angela") touching
base with jazz, Electro, rave and noisecore. Two tracks – the sharp,
jit-friendly, street Techno of "Swingin'" and "Forbidden State" –
sounded as though they'd been crafted especially for the raw adrenaline rush of Detroit downtown clubs like Legends or the State Theatre,
while elsewhere Green seemed to plug in to Techno's warmest, most
romantic recesses. The overwhelming mood of the album was, however, a bittersweet sadness: vulnerable music for vulnerable times.

⊙ **The Arc of Blueness**   SSR, 1997

Expect the unexpected. Q-Moog's debut is a deep rewiring of dance music, locked to a baseline grid that's pure Detroit Techno but encompassing jazz, soul, UK rave and Electro.

Quazar

A long with Eddy de Clercq and Corné Bos, Gert van Veen was involved in Holland's first House release, a single called "Dance to the Music" back in 1989. A year later he and de Clercq teamed up with producer Eric Cycle to form House of Venus (responsible for a Europe-wide club hit with "Dish 'n' Tell"). However, it was his fledgling side-project Quazar which eventually blossomed into van Veen's full-time enterprise.

Quazar's debut single, "Seven Stars", began initially as an experiment with the harder Techno sound which was beginning to emerge in Amsterdam's clubs. Its subsequent success across Europe led to **Seven Stars** (1991) and two promotional tours which ignited van Veen's interest in live performance – Quazar have toured consistently since then, rotating personnel for each tour. A second album, **Here and Now** (1993), was commercially successful, yielding a Top 40 hit with "Unity", but signs of creative tension between van Veen and the other group members – Eric Cycle and Farida Merville (later of Atlantic Ocean) – were apparent. The more mellow sound of the album, a reaction to the super-hard Gabba sound overtaking Holland at the time, didn't interest him.

Instead van Veen returned to his studio and began recording harder, more experimental tracks. On the dancefloor of Amsterdam's Roxy club, he met Daphne Mollee. Since van Veen was living in his studio at the time, it was perhaps inevitable that, shortly after she moved in with him, Mollee began working on the Quazar material alongside him. The singles which followed – "Deeper & Higher" and "North Star" – signalled a more intriguing sound.

Featuring guest vocals from Underworld's Karl Hyde, "Sunflower" was the opening track on Quazar's third album, **Zodiac Trax** (1995). Recorded in their new Lighthouse studio, **Flight Recorder** (1997) was Quazar's most cohesive outing to date. Ranging from the gorgeous Tech-House thump of "Future Glide" to the spiked abstraction of "Confusing the Sun" (featuring another appearance by Karl Hyde on vocals), the album was a lush confection of expert programming, synaptic grooves and experimental modes. At times, **Flight Recorder** sounded as if van Veen was somehow uncannily anticipating the shapes and textures of Underworld's **Beaucoup Fish** (1999).

⊙ **Flight Recorder**   Seven Stars/Superstition, 1997

From the punching off-kilter groove of "Electric" to the dreamy "Future Glide", this is an album full of intriguing sounds, twists and moments of brilliance.

Steve Rachmad

During the early '80s, Steve Rachmad was a fan of Minneapolis producers Jimmy Jam and Terry Lewis. Their meticulously-produced creations inspired his own R&B-tinged ballads and some rudimentary experiments with remixing and editing. But it was a stint working behind the counter in an Amsterdam record store that provided Rachmad with his first introduction to the new dance sound spilling out of Chicago and Detroit.

Rachmad was particularly intrigued by the records of Larry Heard and Derrick May. Armed with a Roland TR-808 drum machine, he began devising his own version of their spaced-out, deeply abstract sound. It wasn't until 1993, however, when a deal with the Amsterdam-based ESP label gave Rachmad an outlet for his music, that he began

building a reputation for himself as a producer. Released under the name Black Scorpion, his debut single, "Phenomenon", was a characteristic fusion of taut, electronic funk and other-worldly atmospherics, while "Sitting on Clouds", his first release as Sterac – the alter ego he uses for his most abstract, Detroit-edged material – placed him firmly

MICHEL MEES

alongside the new wave of European acts such as Black Dog, Stefan Robbers and Kirk Degiorgio who were by then exploring a quieter, more reflective strain of experimental Techno.

Rachmad's delicately crafted releases as Sterac were counterpointed by the records he began making as Tons of Tones for the Urban Sound Of Amsterdam label. Fusing his talent for creating dancefloor grooves with a more accessible melodic sensibility, Tons of Tones offerings such as "Teardrops" or the funkily warped "Smooth Touches" demonstrated Rachmad's versatility and underlined his growing confidence in exploring the breadth of his talents. A meeting with Derrick May at the time of the latter's self-imposed exile in Amsterdam during the early '90s led to Rachmad recording the "Aquadance" single for the Transmat subsidiary Fragile.

Sterac's **The Secret Life of Machines** (1995) was largely ignored by the dance scene, but its seductive combination of rippling grooves and gently under-stated melodies made it something of an underground classic. This was followed by **Tons of Tones** (1997), which provided a solid introduction to his more dancefloor-oriented material.

A series of variable releases on Amsterdam's Outland label did little to dent Rachmad's growing fan base in the underground scene. Remixes for Acid Junkies, Phuture 303 and Jamie Anderson were well-received both on the dancefloor and by the critics. But when the second Sterac album, **Thera** (1998), appeared, it was again overlooked in favour of more mainstream offerings. Yet, while many of his contemporaries were retrenching, the album demonstrated that Rachmad was continuing to refine and evolve his sound.

A solid mix album, **Emerging** (1998), gave Rachmad the chance to show off his considerable skills behind the decks. Containing tracks by Jeff Mills, Robert Hood and Adam Beyer, it confirmed his fascination with the harder, more abstract end of Techno. In fact, soon after its release Rachmad announced that – in between working on an all-new album for Belgium's Music Man imprint – he would be recording for Hood's highly rated M-Plant label, one of the cornerstones of Techno's tough, minimalist aesthetic.

⊙ **Sterac – The Secret Life of Machines**   100% Pure, 1995

Classic Rachmad in every sense. Spaced-out dancefloor symphonies nestle side-by-side with exquisite flurries of digital romance.

Radioactive Lamb

J oe Cicero, Paul Cutler and Robert Murray had known each other since the early '80s when they'd gone to school together. Tyrone Reece was an older friend who'd already experimented with music and shared a passion for the most forward-thinking strands of pop culture. By the time Acid House arrived, they had already surfed the cusp of Electro, jazz and rare groove, but the new sounds issuing from Chicago and Detroit were what prompted them to begin making their own music.

In 1990, the quartet set up their own Radioactive Lamb label. Their first release was a sample-oriented, intriguing 12" containing tracks such as "The Dream" and "Muhammed's Mind" which hinted at what was to come. "Visions of Paradise", released later the same year, was a better indicator of the group's emerging talent. Concentrating more on programming than sampling, the release gave free rein to an eclectic and diverse sound which touched on a number of disparate influences. Partly this was the result of their collective approach which gave Radioactive Lamb a distinctive, multiple personality that sent their releases skidding across a spectrum that ranged from electronic jazz to straight Techno.

By 1993, however, Cutler, Cicero and Reece each had their own studios, and the collaborative process which had helped form exceptional releases such as 1991's **Beyond the Limits** EP was beginning to feature less and less. In 1995, an exceptional EP as Vango Noir for the Fifth Freedom label helped raise Radioactive Lamb's profile to the extent that some were optimistic that they could fill the space recently vacated by Black Dog. Ironically, the group signed later that year to Freedag Nouveaux, a subsidiary of the GPR label which had issued some of Black Dog's finest moments. The deal, however, turned out to be problematic. A completed album, **The Memoirs of Reverend Cowhead and Sheriff Lamb Boy**, was supposed to be released in 1996, but was stalled when the relationship between group and label disintegrated. A small number of copies did reach the warehouses of export distributors, but not enough to prevent Radioactive Lamb from slipping almost completely out of sight. These days, the individual members – including Joe Cicero and Tyrone Reece (now based in New York) – produce music on their own, though most of their material remains unreleased.

⊙ **The Memoirs of Reverend Cowhead**
   and Sheriff Lamb Boy   GPR, 1996

One of the great "lost" albums of the '90s. Copies are hard to find, but the wild sonic games on offer make this well worth searching the secondhand stores for.

Redagain P

Peter Wiederroth learned to play keyboards as a kid, yet the music he makes as Redagain P seems more in tune with spaces, atmospheric flickers and dreamscapes than with conventional techniques. Like his Source Records label-mates Deep Space Network, Elfish Echo and My Little Yoni, his interests seem to lie in disconnecting Techno from its fundamental dancefloor structures, projecting it instead into an experimental landscape of internalised spaces, fractured grooves and dense, barely mobile ambience.

"Not the average four-on-the floor Techno," is how Wiederroth describes his music. Outings such as 1992's One From The Posse EP, **Milk**, on Force Inc. underlined the point. On the follow-up to that release – More From The Posse's **Milk Vol. 2** – the 160 bpm "Scandis In The House" or his less frenetic 145 bpm collaboration with David Moufang on "A Kind of Mother" hinted at a producer surfing the perimeters of Techno, pushing velocities, modes and structures in a starburst of different directions. His debut album, **Electronic Congress** (1993), anticipated the rapid-fire technoid groove of drum 'n' bass, though overall it was a record that suggested late nights spent in his bedroom studio dreaming hard into the future rather than an attempt at electronic prescience. **Electronic Congress** sewed abstract ambience ("Cybernaut"), Electro lullabies ("America's Problems"), proto-breakbeat Techno ("Selector") and fractured Acid ("Therapeutics Of Joy") into a compellingly strange and intriguing whole.

Though located in similarly hypnotic territory, **Gigantochelonia** (1995) pushed the boundaries even further. An increasingly abstract taste in track titles (the album boasted cuts such as "Troitanica", "Aclipted Inquestings" and "X-clewats") seemed to suggest that – like Aphex Twin and Autechre – Wiederroth now preferred to invent and distort language to fit his increasingly complex sound rather than tether it to predetermined concepts.

A collaboration with Berlin House producer Smash J resulted in **Deep Blue** (1996) under the name Aurora. The mix of Acid, Ambient and breakbeat made obvious connections with Wiederroth's previous releases. A more dancefloor-oriented single, "Divine Dive", was released simultaneously. Since then Wiederroth has been content to focus on singles such as "Bee Tee Rock" (in conjunction with Keen K) rather than full-length offerings.

⊙ **Electronic Congress**   Source Records, 1993

Intriguing, seductive and disturbing in equal parts, Redagain P's debut album traverses Techno's more experimental frontiers.

Regis

The style of Regis, real name Karl O'Connor, could be construed as the Birmingham sound: minimal Techno underpinned by more complex layers of texture and hard-edged tones and loops. Based on the city's outskirts in Halesowen, his Downwards label was launched in 1995 with the scything, metallic rush of Surgeon's debut releases, "Manganese" and "Electronically Tested". Regis soon followed with the ferocious, sonic roar of **Montreal** whose insistent loops on "Speak to Me" thundered with hellish funk. Although embryonic, the sound was startlingly fresh and dynamic. Most importantly, it was unmistakable. With further releases from Surgeon ("Pet 2000" and "Communications"), Female and Portion Reform, the label's identity began to develop and solidify. In 1996, Regis' own sound showed considerable signs of maturity with the release of "Application of Language" which smoothed the rough edges and raw urgency of the label's infancy.

The sounding board for these early releases was Chris Wishart's House Of God club where Surgeon was already one of the resident

DJs with O'Connor (as Regis) occasionally playing live. The club's burgeoning reputation and the fact that the Birmingham sound was fast becoming an identifiable commodity on the Techno underground helped to provide O'Connor with a warm reception for his first album, **Gymnastics** (1996). Based around volcanic, textured loops and industrial bass, the album was a wall of sound.

In an extension of the label's independence, O'Connor – in conjunction with Anthony Vieira and Female's Peter Sutton – set up the Integrale Muzique distribution company in 1996, from little more than a shed in a Halesowen industrial estate. Whilst Surgeon hooked up with Berlin label Tresor, O'Connor developed the label through further album releases by Female and Portion Reform and continued to play live predominantly throughout Europe and America. His second album, **Delivered Into the Hands of Indifference** (1998) – the title was a jibe at unscrupulous club promoters – displayed more subtle uses of tones and textures within his still uncompromising and individual production style.

⊙ Gymnastics   Downwards, 1996

The album's harsh loops and industrial bass minimalism represented a turning point for both artist and label identity.

Jonas Stone

Rejuvination

Jim Muotune and Glenn Gibbons met when they both worked part-time in a Glasgow diner called Chimmy Chungas. It was there that they sat down to formulate – with their friends Stuart

BRIAN SWEENEY

McMillan, Orde Meikle and Dave Clarke – plans for their own label to release the kind of music which had already begun overtaking the city's clubs. It took a while but, in essence, that was how Soma Records came into being, after long nights of clubbing, talking and dreaming.

In the beginning, Muotune and Gibbons were the musical directors of the operation. They worked on Slam's first tracks, engineered and played on most of the label's early output. And, as Rejuvination, they furnished one side of the label's first single (along with Slam's "Eterna"). "Ibo", named after the Nigerian tribe to which Muotune's family belonged, was a solid debut, but the releases that followed, 1992's **Work In Progress** EP and 1993's "Requiem", charted an individual take on House and Techno. Gibbons and Muotune shaped a sound that referenced classical music, jazz, hard Techno and their unquenchable passion for The Clash.

1994's "Sycophantasy" was a characteristic Rejuvination outing: densely layered, full of spiralling percussives and twisting 303 lines. But it was followed by the ethereal downbeat of "Dr Peter", a tribute to Dr Peter Jepson Young's struggle with AIDS, which fused a plangent piano motif (inspired by Erik Satie) with hip-hop drums and Moroder synths. The track impressed a number of television producers who recognised the cinematic qualities of Rejuvination's music and led to a number of soundtrack commissions.

Introduction (1995) signalled the breadth of Rejuvination's ambitions – sampling Noam Chomsky (on "Subtle Indoctrination"), borrowing from Robert Hood (on "The Conflict") and extrapolating a luscious fusion from the best of Lil' Louis, Model 500 and Kraftwerk – but it was also a brave attempt to create a classic narrative album along the lines of Marvin Gaye's **What's Going On** from the elements of electronic dance music.

Rejuvination's final single, "Don't Forget Who You Are", was Techno stripped to its essential bass riffs and beats methodology. Ironically, Soma's very next release – Daft Punk's "Da Funk" – employed the same riffing technique, reconstituted for mass consumption. It went supernova and led to a major label deal for the French duo while their Glaswegian counterparts eventually drifted apart, Muotune to work on his own drum 'n' bass material and Gibbons to a series of unnamed projects.

⊙ **Introduction**   Soma, 1995

Germanic strings, warbling Acid lines and an eclectic range of influences: the kind of amalgam that should have made Rejuvination sure-fire contenders for major label success.

Resistance D

J ust one of the seemingly endless stream of Frankfurt Trance outfits who dominated the European Techno scene during the early
'90s, Resistance D had their roots in the Belgian New Beat and industrial scenes of the previous decade. Pascal Dardoufas was a maths
student who earned extra cash by working as a DJ in his own club (La
Boom in Giessen) and in Frankfurt's legendary Dorian Gray, spinning a
mix of Nitzer Ebb, Skinny Puppy and Front 242. His eventual partner,
Maik Maurice Diehl, played in a band called Media Docena. The pair
got together after Diehl approached Dardoufas with a demo tape. The
DJ thought the music was awful, but when Diehl approached him subsequently with a view to working on a track together, he agreed and
the first Resistance D release – "Cosmic Love" – emerged.

With a swift name change, Dardoufas quickly became Pascal
F.E.O.S (it stands for "from essence of minimal sound" though the let-
ter "m" was dropped since "it didn't sound good") and together the
pair began forging their characteristic blend of dramatic strings and
racing sequences on singles such as 1992's "Eclipse" and "Emphasis".
A deal with Harthouse followed, resulting in 1993's well-rated **Human**
EP, though it was the release of "Airwalker" the following year which
provided them with their biggest underground hit so far. By this time,
F.E.O.S and Diehl had perfected the Resistance D blueprint with tracks
that hammered along between 145 and 155 bpm, dense layers of
sequences and a selection of portentous melodies that could be
downright offensive depending on your musical sensitivity.

Ztrings of Life (1994) borrowed a title from Derrick May but sadly
little else. In effect it was simply a refinement of the formula although it
was subsequently praised out of all proportion to its actual content.

Although F.E.O.S was listening to Black Dog and Plastikman and organising collaborative sessions with Pete Namlook (as Hearts of Space), the impact on Resistance D was negligible. In a bizarre twist, Diehl also began collaborating with Namlook on a Trance project under the name Pulsation which jettisoned Namlook's usual subtleties in favour of the Resistance D prototype.

Inexhaustibility (1994) arrived just months after Resistance D's debut, but already there were signs that the duo were beginning to drain the scant formula they'd created for themselves. Perhaps jumping the gun slightly, Harthouse released **Best of Resistance D** the following year, though unkinder critics suggested that the title was something of an oxymoron.

F.E.O.S and Diehl parted company just before Harthouse's closure in 1997, though they reformed Resistance D for a new single, "Impression", and a new album, **A Modern World of Today** (1998), on the Polydor subsidiary What's Up?

⊙ **The Best of Resistance D**   Harthouse, 1995

Resistance D's clunky Trance formula hasn't aged particularly well, but this has all the relevant tunes for those looking to excavate some of Frankfurt's Trance history.

Stefan Robbers

A s with so many Techno artists, 1988 proved to be Year Zero for Stefan Robbers. Raised on a diet of early House music and the electronic body music of Front 242, DAF and Liaisons Dangereuses, it was in this year that he heard his first Acid House record, "Fantasy

Girl", by Pierre's Fantasy Club. In 1989, however, a different music began into seep into Robbers' psyche. Techno, in the form of Derrick May's Rhythim Is Rhythim releases, had a profound effect on him and he set about fashioning his own version of the sound.

In August, 1990, a demo tape of Robbers' music caught the attention of Saskia Slegers, founder of the rap label Djax. Inspired, she decided to start a new Techno sub-label, Djax Upbeats, and in October of that year, Robbers' first EP was released under the name of Terrace. This was followed in May 1991 by "Straight Trippin", which became something of an albatross around Robbers' neck, labelling Terrace as part of the minimal Euro Techno wave that was popular at the time. Interested in creating a more intelligent type of music, he created an alter ego, R.E.C., as an outlet for his more minimal experiments. There were two R.E.C. EPs, **Lightning Strike** and **Powerplant**.

Frustrated that a number of his more experimental tracks didn't seem to fit with Djax or any other company, Robbers decided to release them himself, and in August 1991, founded Eevo Lute Records with his friend Wladimir Manshanden. Adopting the name Florence for this facet of his musical personality, he released his own **US Heritage** EP and collaborated with Manshanden on his **As the Leaves Fall From the Trees** EP. A record that mixed electronic atmospheres with the spoken word, it typified the Eevo Lute approach. In the intervening years, this approach has introduced the world to the talents of Max 404, David Caron, Ballet Mechanique and many others.

1992 saw the release of **Round-Up** (1992), a compilation of Terrace tracks that revealed Robbers as the architect of some of the most intricate yet achingly beautiful Techno to date. The following year saw the debut Florence LP, **Dominions** (1993). One of the most precisely constructed of all electronic albums, it showed Robbers operating at a level all on his own. Other releases in '93, including the **Afridisiac** EP on 100% Pure and Terrace's **My Mirror Image** EP on GPR, only served to confirm this.

Meanwhile, a new name had begun to crop up in the Robbers canon, The Acid Junkies. A collaboration with Harold de Kinderen, this was Robbers reliving his Acid House days, producing raging Acid music that is best heard in a live context. To date, there have been four Acid Junkies EPs and two albums, including the skull-wrecking **Paranoid Experience** (1995). As far from the complexities of his other personae as possible, this was the sound of a man revelling in his formative influences.

With the exception of the occasional EP and remix, the years between 1994 and 1996 were barren ones for Robbers, as he struggled with a crisis of confidence. 1996, however, saw him return in triumph, first with five new Electro-tinged Florence tracks on **Assembled 019/020** (1996), and then with **Konnekt** (1996), the debut album from Terrace. An album that seemed to distil all of Robbers' musical heritage into one heady blend, it mixed upbeat Techno, trip-hop, Ambient, even vocal numbers into abstract shapes that were instantly recognisable as the work of only one man. It was undoubtedly one of the Techno albums of the year.

Florence's **Occurrences** (1997) continued the momentum. With the gap between his musical personalities seemingly vanishing, this was a logical progression on from **Konnekt**. Music of the utmost complexity, moulding the original Detroit blueprint into new abstract shapes using any tools available, from drum 'n' bass to trip-hop and back.

More recently, Robbers' music has entered a looser phase, with his two most recent EPs, **Interesting Times** and **California**, displaying even more of the Electro influences that first surfaced on the **Assembled** tracks.

⊙ **Terrace – Konnekt**   Eevo Lute, 1996

A record of vaulting ambition, displaying a breadth of imagination, a
gift for melody and a sense of production dynamics rarely equalled.
Ranging from the quasi-classical wordless drama of "Life In 6.45" to the
Latin-tinged Deep House groove of "Downtown" and the abrasive
dancefloor muscle of "Moonbeam".

Peter McIntyre

Ross 154

Growing up in the suburban environment of Haarlem in Holland,
the arrival of House music at the end of the 1980s had the same
seismic effect on Joachem Peteri as it did on a million other teenagers.
Prior to this, he had been a big hip-hop fan, but hip-hop was a group
thing. In the DIY ethic of House he saw that anyone could make music –
and they could do it on their own, pleasing only themselves.

So Peteri took advantage and began making his own music. His
first efforts were club-oriented, heavily influenced by the type of music
he was hearing on the dancefloors. Under the name of Pallas, he
released the **Horizons** EP on Lower East Side Records in 1992. It was
a group of narrowly focused tracks, suitable only for the situation that
provided their inspiration. Around this time, however, he moved to
Amsterdam, and became exposed to Techno. With this strange new
music, it seemed possible to go anywhere. As with Detroit, the influence of the urban proved decisive. As Peteri himself said, "inner city
life corrupted Pallas and made schizophrenic music possible".

For his new schizophrenic music, Peteri chose the name of Ross 154,
a reference to a star constellation he had read about in a secondary school

science book. Hooking up with Stefan Robbers' Eevo Lute Records, he released the **Fragments** EP in 1993. As far from the Pallas material as Ross 154 is from Earth, the EP moved from the classic, austere melancholia of "Mayflower" to the hydraulic throb of the title track and the twilight hip-hop groove of "Within You". Schizophrenic *in extremis*, it was hard to take in the distance Peteri had travelled in just a single year.

Two tracks from the EP were featured on the Eevo Lute compilation LP **Agenda 22** (1994), along with "Living the Love of the Afterlife", a new track that saw Peteri moving into darker, beatless ambience. It revealed another, equally adventurous side to his newly discovered sonic schizophrenia, and promised much. Yet with the exception of the mildly disappointing **Dusk** EP, released on 100% Pure in 1996, he has failed to find an outlet for the rich, deep seams of his musical mind. New recordings on the Nu Dawn and Rush Hour labels are promised, but for now, Peteri's contribution to music is, in his own words, "selling other people's records". Which is a real waste of talent.

⊙ Fragments   Eevo Lute, 1993

If ever a record typified Stefan Robbers' description of Eevo Lute as an outlet for challenging, experimental electronica, this is it. Four faces of Techno's potential, ranging from the heartbreaking "Mayflower" – one of the purest Techno tracks never to come from the Motor City – to the deeply unsettling "Remembrance".

James Ruskin

Alongside fellow DJ/producers such as Steve Bicknell and Birmingham's Surgeon (Tony Child), Blueprint Records co-founder

James Ruskin has
become an integral
part of the UK's cur-
rent Techno sound: a
style based around
loops, rhythm and
abstraction, fused with
a distinctively British
edge that nestles
somewhere between
Detroit's pristine angu-
larity and Berlin's dirti-
er, rounder approach.

Previously based in
New Milton, Hamp-
shire, Ruskin allied
with Richard Polson in
the late '80s through a
combined love of
House, funk, soul and
hip-hop. It was, how-
ever, the new sound of
Techno that was to
unite the two in their
early musical sketch-
ings. Feeling increas-
ingly isolated from
their South Coast envi-
ronment, the pair relo-
cated to North London

DINAH ALUM

in 1994 to begin building a new studio and seriously define their own style.

The first fruits of this new approach eventually surfaced in 1995 on Josh Brent's Not Guilty label. Although Void's "Shock Treatment" sold out its initial pressing, they soon realised the need to produce and release independently. The duo worked on new material that was to form the backbone of their debut release the following April on their own label, Blueprint. Using machine-based, symmetrical, mechanical designs and a blue dyeline print, their debut release as Outline ("First Contact") looked as distinctive as it sounded. The follow-up, "Examined Life", confirmed their forward-thinking maxim. Ealing's Oliver Ho soon joined the label with the individualistic releases "Gathering", "Cosmetics" and "Duality". Maintaining this nucleus (with additional collaborations from Surgeon), they continued to define the label's sound which made significant developments with Ruskin's first solo production – the aptly titled "Transition" – in the autumn of 1997.

Polson has since established the Surface label (again with Ho and Ruskin), whilst Ruskin's ferocious, three-deck DJ style has taken him the world over. Moreover, Ruskin has developed an increasingly individual sound that resulted in the critically acclaimed debut album, **Further Design** (1998). Exploring both dancefloor and listening atmospheres (elements of Krautrock's disregard of pop music's structural rigidity combined with the raw looped funk of Mills and co.), Ruskin has refined his style into a mature perspective on modern electronics that currently sits at the cusp of cutting edge Techno.

⊙ **Further Design**   Blueprint, 1998

Ruskin's design is one of dark cyclical atmospheres, truncated tribal rhythms and muted bass distortion fused by futuristic blood-pumping beats.

Jonas Stone

Kevin Saunderson

I n the mid-'80s, Kevin Saunderson was an undergraduate student studying telecommunications at Eastern Michigan University. The youngest son in a family of nine, he grew up in Brooklyn before relocating to the Detroit suburb of Belleville when he was 12 years old. It was at Belleville High School that he first met Derrick May and Juan Atkins (the elder brother of one of their classmates, Juan had already made a considerable impact on the local music scene as a member of the ground-breaking Cybotron). Together, they invented a whole new music. It was Saunderson's Inner City project which launched Techno into the charts, first with "Big Fun" and "Good Life" in 1988 and then with a string of compelling hits like "Ain't Nobody Better" and "Watcha Gonna Do With My Lovin'" which established Detroit alongside Chicago in Europe's dancefloor mainstream.

In the beginning, Kevin Saunderson's introduction to dance music came, not from Detroit, but from New York and Chicago. It's not difficult to trace the impact of Garage and House music on his own material; his work with Inner City embraces a unique fusion of all three cities which, perhaps, only Terrence Parker has come close to emulating. His early success, first with Kreem's "Triangle of Love" and then with deep underground dance missives like "The Groove That Won't Stop" and "Bounce Your Body to the Box", demonstrated a diverse talent that could switch between a warmly soulful, anthemic style and dark, uncompromising sonic futurism – sometimes within the space of a single track.

Saunderson's extensive catalogue of early underground hits – including Reese & Santonio's "The Sound", "Bounce Your Body to the Box" and the essential E-Dancer cut, "Feel the Mood" – was re-released as

Faces & Phases (1997) by Planet E. It was an exhaustive archive of his most influential dancefloor material, and includes many of the hard-to-find and much-sought-after tracks which British producers like Dave Clarke consider seminal in the development of today's Techno sound. Many of his most influential moments have been reworked and revised or used as source material by other dance producers. Most famously there's Clarke's "Red" series of singles which are directly related to the darker currents of Saunderson's work, but there has been a similar development amongst drum 'n' bass producers who've begun using the raw, low-frequency edge of his Reese material to fuel their own dark-side adventures.

Saunderson's consistent emphasis on an intuitive, feel-oriented style of composition (he describes it as "vibing…" or "tripping out")

was best realised on one of his most successful underground tracks, "Ahnongay", which, ironically was recorded in London during some downtime following an Inner City studio session. **Heavenly**, a collection of Saunderson's work since 1989 as E-Dancer, was another sparkling retrospective that once again showed the debt that dance music owes to Saunderson's "computer soul".

⊙ **Faces & Phases**   Network/Planet E, 1997

All the hits and more in one essential package.

⊙ **E-Dancer – Heavenly**   KMS, 1998

A return to an early alter ego and to the raw underground feel that Saunderson originally trail-blazed.

Scan 7

In the early years of Detroit Techno's pre-history, Lou Robinson found himself in a local group called The Preps. Singles such as "Hotbox" and "Prep it Up" (co-written by Robinson and Was Not Was's Dave McMurray) sold well around the local area, promoted tirelessly by Express Records MD and Buy Rite record shop owner Cliff Thomas, whose distribution business later became an important conduit for the emerging techno scene. The Preps, however, eventually disbanded as the city's new dance sound began to coalesce.

In 1988, Robinson set up another group, recruiting a local DJ, Terrence Parker, and an unpromising alternative musician, Marc Kinchen, to form the soon-to-be semi-legendary but ultimately short-lived Separate Minds. Record company problems and Kinchen's subsequent departure for New York brought the group's career to an abrupt end, though they did contribute "First Bass" to the seminal KMS compilation **Techno 1** (1988). Robinson continued Separate Minds as a sporadic collaborative venture with Vernell Shelton, most notably on the House-tinged **Trouble World** EP released on the self-financed Direct Hit label and "Scattered Thoughts" which appeared some years later on **New Electronica: Global Technological Innovations Vol. 1** (1993).

Robinson discovered a spiritual and creative home with Underground Resistance, though characteristically his first contribution was to the label's limited edition series sold only in Detroit. His next releases for UR, "Scan 7" and "Undetectable", marked a creative watershed and predicated the warm shapes and compellingly tough grooves which have become his trademark. **Hidden Territory** (1996) was a powerful debut. Named after his secluded studio, the album delivered an expansive and ambitious vision of Robinson's production powers. Much of the record's drive was inspired by nights spent on the dancefloor of legendary Detroit club the Music Institute. His production technique, he insists, centres on investing his own music with "the same sense of excitement" he once felt when the air raid siren announced Derrick May's imminent appearance behind the decks at the MI.

Though he has released singles as Unknown Force, The Shadow and The Specialist, Scan 7 remains the main focus of Robinson's creative output. A well-received collaborative project with Detroit's DJ Reggie under the name Allergy emerged on Glasgow's Soma label in 1997, but the release of a second Scan 7 LP, **Resurfaced** (1999), eclipsed even the best of his previous work. Tracks such as "Invisible Invasion" and "Random Soul" were broodingly funky affairs, easily matching up to Robinson's previous highlights, while "Black Wall" and "Mind Trap" explored a melodic seam that suggested a broadening of Scan 7's musical scope. The album was a *tour de force*, one of the best dancefloor albums to emerge from Detroit in some time and proof that, after all this time, Trackmaster Lou still has what it takes.

⊙ **Resurfaced**   Tresor, 1999

Trackmaster Lou's masterpiece is broader and wider in scope than its predecessor and may prove hard to beat.

Anthony "Shake" Shakir

One of Detroit Techno's great unsung heroes, Anthony "Shake" Shakir has been a talent integral to the genre since its formative years. Like many producers, Shake started out as a DJ while at Cooley High School (also the *alma mater* of Carl Craig), though he spun Electro, R&B and funk rather than House. He was introduced to Derrick May and Juan Atkins (and subsequently the nascent Techno subculture in Detroit) through DJs Mike Huckaby and Eric Sims. Shake had been experimenting with keyboards around the same time, and gave some of his tracks to May on tape. By his own admission, those early songs were "pretty terrible", but one track that mimicked Fingers Inc.'s "Mystery of Love" caught May's attention and he recognised Shake's potential.

Before long, he found himself contributing to the seminal 1988 compilation **Techno! – The New Dance Sound Of Detroit** on 10/Virgin. Shake recalls recording his contribution, "Sequence 10", while compiler Neil Rushton was in Detroit finalising the album's running order. But while other artists rode the waves of attention that the compilation attracted, Shake remained behind the scenes for several years after, preferring the roles of producer, A&R and remixer instead. Many have benefited from Shake's talents and connection to May, Atkins and Saunderson – most notably Octave One, whose surprise anthem "I Believe" he co-produced, co-wrote and mixed.

Shake re-emerged as a solo Techno artist on Metroplex with 1992's **5% Solution** EP and continued to find outlets in labels such as KMS, Trancefusion and Peacefrog. In the following years he founded two labels: Frictional Recordings with Claude Young in 1995 and Puzzle-box with Keith Tucker in 1996. While Puzzlebox is now Tucker's responsibility, Shake continues to run Frictional on his own and the label has provided a home for a brilliant and diverse series of releases, including "Mood Music for the Moody", "Club Scam II" and "The Revisionist's Theory".

In addition to his Techno productions, Shake has also been involved with local hip-hop artists like Scarelly Moe. He has also remixed many artists, including Inner City and the Belgian Techno-pop band Telex, but one of his finest moments remains his co-production of Urban Tribe's exceptional album for Mo' Wax, **The Collapse of Modern Culture** (1998).

◉ Schematics – Toyland   KMS, 1993

Tough percussives, pure Detroit sounds and the kind of raw but soulful feel that Shake is best known for.

⊙ "You"   SSR, 1998

Shake's contribution to SSR's **Freezone 5** is one of his best moments so far. Track it down.

Dan Sicko

The Shamen

Now caught in limbo between the mainstream, where they once held sway, and the underground, where their sympathies so obviously lie, The Shamen have found themselves marginalised by the fast-moving currents of the dance scene. Their role as crucial evangelists for the emerging culture has been long since forgotten.

With their roots in '60s psychedelia, The Shamen's original incarnation was as an indie-based guitar band. Their debut, **Drop** (1987), appeared just as House and Techno were beginning to leak out of Chicago and Detroit. The following years saw a steady reinvention as the group began to metamorphose. Keyboard player Colin Angus and bassist Will Sinott soon jettisoned life in Aberdeen and relocated to London, recording with Acid House legend Chris "Bam Bam" West-brook and transforming into the indie-dance proposition that was unveiled on **In Gorbachev We Trust** (1989).

By 1990's **En-Tact**, the transformation was complete. Preceded by the group's most compelling single so far, "Progen (Move Any Mountain)", the album delivered The Shamen's new manifesto: motoring machine rhythms, driving sequences and an enviable knack for hooklines. It was followed by their decision to tour their Synergy night which provided the first taste of a realistic Acid House experience for many of those in the provinces. The combination proved irresistible, with the album and tour doing much to proselytise on dance culture's behalf.

The tragic drowning of Sinott during a video shoot in the Canary Islands in 1991 seemed to signal the end for The Shamen just as their career had begun to pay dividends. Faced with the decision to quit and see all Sinott's hard work come to nothing, Angus chose to carry on, recruiting Clink Street regular Richard West (aka Mr C) and vocalist Jhelisa Anderson to work on **Boss Drum** (1992).

Two singles emerged before the album, "LSI" and the manic "Ebe-neezer Goode", which provided The Shamen with a UK #1 and listen-ers all over the country with the dubious thrill of Mr C chanting what sounded like "E's are good, E's are good" all over mainstream televi-sion and radio. When he wasn't on *Top Of The Pops*, however, Mr C was to be found working as a DJ at underground Techno nights, often refusing payment from promoters as the royalties began to pour in.

Within a year of **Boss Drum**, it was clear that The Shamen's trajec-tory was in danger of stalling. Almost every track from the album had been lifted as a single, with little or no new material forthcoming. In addition, Colin Angus had adopted a strangely reclusive existence, emerging only to utter mystical and baffling pronouncements which confused the group's hard-won audience no end. West meanwhile helped set up a highly regarded Techno label, Plink Plonk, which focused on broodingly dark, experimental and inventive releases from a collective of largely unknown and mysterious producers. For the brief period of its operation, Plink Plonk enjoyed a reputation as an assured, deeply intriguing and very hip label which made West's involvement in the next Shamen album hard to fathom.

Axis Mutatis (1995) was a sprawling, odd and unsatisfying affair. Indistinguishable from the flood of third-rate Trance efforts which record-buyers were forced to wade through that year, the album was devoid of the witty hooks and clever constructions which had made **Boss Drum** a huge success. Even worse, claimed some critics, was the psychobabble which surrounded the project as Angus seemed to retreat even further from reality. The album was released simultaneous-ly with the Ambient **Arbor Bona, Arbor Mala** which possessed the kind of recondite underground charms unlikely to appeal to those who had bought **Boss Drum**.

In the wake of Plink Plonk's untimely demise, West found himself with a nightclub, The End, and a matching record label, also called The End, through which he has released a number of his own singles. Apart from a series of sought-after Shamen remixes by a number of drum 'n' bass luminaries, however, his partnership with Colin Angus has produced little of note since **Boss Drum** and it now seems unlikely that the group will ever repeat the critical and creative success of their best work.

⊙ **En-tact**   One Little Indian, 1991

Pounding kick drums, raging sequences and a clutch of great tunes made this The Shamen's finest hour.

Slam

Slam emerged from Glasgow's vibrant Acid House scene which, in common with other northern cities in the UK, had gravitated towards a deeper, more Techno-oriented sound than its southern counterparts. Stuart McMillan and Orde Meikle had played a key role in converting the city's club culture to the new sound with nights such as Black Market and, most famously, Atlantis at the Sub Club. By 1991, along with a number of friends, they were already talking about setting up a record label to provide a platform for the city's growing pool of artists and producers. Inspired by Aldous Huxley's *Brave New World*, they named their new label Soma and debuted with the crossover shapes of "Eterna".

1993's "Positive Education", a single partly inspired by the throbbing rhythm section of The Clash, owed a sizeable debt to Terrace's mix of the Ron Trent classic "Altered States", but it provided Slam with their first full-scale underground hit. Remixes for Kym Sims, House of Virginism, Sunscreem and even Jean Michel Jarre followed, as the pair found themselves increasingly celebrated both by major labels in search of underground credibility and by the newly influential dance

BRIAN SWEENEY / SOMA RECORDS

media. Behind the decks, McMillan and Meikle were equally busy, adding an exhausting list of international DJ commitments to their already established hometown residencies at the Sub Club and the Arches.

In 1995 they emerged from the studio with **Snapshots**, an extend-ed double-pack which explored a deeper, more experimental amalgam than anything they'd previously essayed. Meanwhile, Slam at the Arches was rapidly becoming one of the UK's most celebrated underground club nights, merging hard, dancefloor Techno with deep and deliriously funky House — a fusion that was later celebrated on the duo's first mix album, **Psychotrance 4** (1996).

Headstates (1996) was a distillation of McMillan and Meikle's prime influences — the immersive, tribal percussives of Octave One, the lush, plaintive orchestrations of Underground Resistance's jazz excursions and the gentle, emotive languour of Mr. Fingers — enveloped in a sparkling counter-cultural sheen that threaded each of these disparate but related strands into a single, expertly articulated celebration of their career to date. On "White Shadows" the pair layered weightless synths and hazy, narcotic atmospheres over tough but seductive grooves. Elsewhere, they adopted a more visceral, immediately physical approach that seemed to have drawn inspiration directly from the Dionysian fervour of the Arches' dancefloor at peak-time.

A lengthy hiatus was only punctuated by the release of **Twisted Funk** (1999), a McMillan/Meikle side-project under the name Pressure Funk that focused exclusively on harder, dancefloor tracks. Largely overlooked in a climate that was cycling through a fascination with the more commercial end of dance music, **Twisted Funk** was nevertheless a classic in the making, aligning itself with the Hood/Mills/Surgeon school of tough minimalism shot through with deep exploratory subtleties.

McMillan also began a loose collaboration with Glenn Gibbons and Nick Peacock under the name Universal Principles, resulting in an LP later the same year. A second Slam album, meanwhile, gestates slowly (Meikle and McMillan are notorious perfectionists) with a release date scheduled early in the new millennium.

⊙ **Headstates**   Soma, 1996

A luscious and compelling travelogue that maps Techno's altered states and interior landscapes.

Luke Slater

ike a number of other influential Techno DJs and producers, Luke Slater's entry into dance music came through the Electro of Cybotron, Hashim and Warp 9. Originally a drummer (he joined his first band when he was just thirteen years old), the early '80s Electro boom inspired him to swap his drum kit for a set of decks and he began playing at parties. Then he discovered House music.

A residency at legendary Acid House club Troll followed, as well as stints behind the counter at My Price Records in Croydon and, most famously, his hugely influential Jelly Jam store in Brighton (Slater's early singles, under the name Translucent, were released on the shop's short-lived Jelly Jam label). During the early '90s, with production partner Alan Sage, he crafted a number of well-received singles, beginning with Morganistic's "In the Shadow" for Irdial, Clementine's "Silent Voices", "Approaching" and "Cosmopolitan for the Cosmos" on Djax and the **Maiden Voyage** EP on Loaded. However, his most consistent and enduring work during the early years of his career emerged from his long-standing relationships with two small UK independent labels, GPR and Peacefrog.

Slater's first EP for Peacefrog, **X-Tront Vol.1**, was a compelling fusion of both Detroit and Europe that confirmed a rare talent for combining wired dancefloor dynamics and menacingly abstract experimentation. It was followed soon after by his debut album, **X-Tront Vol. 2** (1993), a masterpiece of weirdly looping, grainy Techno which sounded like little else around at the time.

Around the same time, Slater began a parallel career on GPR with his 7th Plain project. Early singles for the label such as "To Be Surreal" suggested a more accessible, Detroit-oriented direction. This was confirmed on **The Four Cornered Room** (1994), a masterpiece of subtle shapes and seductive grooves that underlined Slater's ability to explore several directions almost simultaneously. A second 7th Plain album, **My Yellow Wise Rug** (1994), developed similar themes, but pursued a more distinctly experimental approach. It was a radical update of the sound previewed on the first GPR album, but the fact that the two releases were just months apart signalled just how fast Slater was travelling.

Perhaps his best-known alias, Planetary Assault Systems, debuted on Peacefrog with the superb "Planetary Funk". Years after their release, demand for the early singles was still high enough to necessitate the release of **Archives** (1996), a retrospective of some of the most revered Planetary Assault Systems material, which had, by

SPIROS POLITIS / NOVAMUTE

that stage, been burning up dancefloors for the best part of three years. A purpose-built Planetary Assault Systems album was eventually delivered with the masterful **Electric Funk Machine** (1997).

Archives proved that interest in Slater's earlier, now deleted, releases was continuing to grow. In part, that was assuaged by the release of **Luke Slater 92–94** (1997) which brought together the best of his early work on Peacefrog. But by far his most visible success, however, was a new album for the London-based NovaMute label. **Freek Funk** (1997) was universally acclaimed as Slater's best work to date, combining the hard shapes of his Planetary Assault Systems material with the dreamier, atmospheric experimentalism of his 7th Plain output. Ranging from raw Electro workouts like "Are You There?" to expansive symphonic Techno cuts such as "Time Dancer", **Freek Funk** measured itself with ease against some of the best Techno albums of the '90s.

A third Planetary Assault Systems long-player, **Drone Sector** (1998), marked the furthest outposts of Slater's exploratory instincts, but in comparison to **Freek Funk** was accorded only low-key coverage in the music press. Yet the album offered the best indications yet of a talent in the process of going supernova, pushing dancefloor Techno towards previously unexplored terrain with both wit and subtlety. Instead, most of those who had been introduced to Slater's work by the astonishing critical acclaim meted out to the previous NovaMute album found themselves directed towards **Wireless** (1999), a more Electro-based outing than its predecessor that engaged with a more rock-centric dynamic than anything with which Slater had been previously involved.

⊙ **Planetary Assault Systems – Archives**   Peacefrog, 1996

A crucial retrospective of the much-sought-after, but hard-to-find, early Planetary Assault Systems releases.

⊙ **Freek Funk** NovaMute, 1997

Slater's most critically acclaimed album to date, full of biting, dancefloor
shapes and the occasional nod towards romance, particularly on the
single "Love, Love".

Jonah Sharp /
Spacetime Continuum

I t's been a long, strange trip for Jonah Sharp. Growing up in Edinburgh during the '70s, his musical interests were a million miles
away from the output of local groups like the Bay City Rollers. Instead
the young Sharp developed a precocious interest in jazz, eventually
moving south to London to study music full-time and spend his nights
on the jazz club circuit. By 1989, he was working as a session drummer for the Acid Jazz label, but found himself increasingly attracted by
the twin lure of electronics and turntables. He began playing in underground clubs and became involved in running some of London's first
chill-out rooms. Sharp's Space Time parties in East London – where
artists such as Björk rubbed shoulders with KLF and The Shamen –
were landmarks in the evolution of the capital's dance culture and have
since become an essential part of UK club mythology. But, as the Pay
Party Unit moved into full swing and existence became progressively
more fraught for the organisers of underground parties, Sharp decided
to leave London, finally relocating to San Francisco in 1991.

Once established on the West Coast, Sharp set up his own Reflective imprint. The label's first release, in August 1993, was the **Flures-**

ence EP, a solo effort by Sharp under the name Spacetime Continuum. The next Spacetime Continuum release, **Alien Dreamtime** (1993), was a live album featuring Terence McKenna, a one-time disciple of Timothy Leary and, by this time, something of an anti-establishment guru himself, promoting a complex system of values which rotated around a central notion of "consciousness expansion".

The Spacetime Continuum sound existed somewhere in the space between Ambient and the new romanticism drifting out of Detroit which had coalesced on the hugely influential Buzz compilation, **Virtual Sex** (1993). But it also keyed in with the work of a number of maverick, though highly respected, producers on the burgeoning Ambient/experimental scene, among them Pete Namlook, Material's Bill Laswell and David Moufang, each of whom Sharp would collaborate with over the next few years.

A collection of inspired hallucinatory excursions, **Sea Biscuit** (1994) was Spacetime Continuum's "official" debut album. Shot through with evanescent, pastel-shaded melodies, it became a milestone in the developing US Ambient scene, but poor distribution prevented the album from making the wider impact it deserved. Collaborations with both Pete Namlook and Tetsu Inoue followed, though it was a trip to Heidelberg to record with David Moufang which resulted in his finest hour to date. **Reagenz** (1994) was an astonishing record, outstripping even the wildest innovations of Detroit or the revered cadre of European experimentalists led by Aphex Twin. Filled with moments of spiralling abstraction, fractured beauty and hauntingly dislocated atmospherics, the album captured two producers at the peak of their powers, surfing a strain of pure electronic jazz that sounded like Detroit Techno on DMT. It was, unequivocally, one of the most inspired records ever to emerge from Techno. Shockingly new, filled with the kind of alien longing that had fuelled the original Metroplex and Transmat records, **Reagenz** was to Techno what **Bitches Brew** had been to jazz – a revolutionary creative step which seemed to have arrived fully formed from some time far in the future.

In comparison to the huge creative surges of 1994, the following year was relatively quiet for Sharp. He collaborated with Plaid's Ed Hanley and Andy Turner on the critically acclaimed **South of Market** EP and released two exceptional 12"s, Spacetime Continuum's "Freelon" and the **Kairo** EP, but spent most of the year focusing on Reflective's new signings such as Jake Smith's Subtropic project.

Emit Ecaps (1996) was a solid follow-up to **Sea Biscuit**. Less unrelentingly strange than **Reagenz**, it nevertheless boasted some startlingly original moments. While tracks such as "Iform" were compelling, but relatively straight, extrapolations of the Midwest Techno blueprint, others – like "Simm City" or the gorgeous "Movement #2" – sounded like peak-era Derrick May vibing out on ambience. Sharp continued his involvement in a series of creatively successful collaborations – notably with Mixmaster Morris and former Yellow Magic Orchestra star Haruomi Hosono on **Quiet Logic** (1998) and with Tetsu Inoue on **Instant Replay** (1997) – but despite having created a significant and critically acclaimed body of work, his profile has never really kept pace with the considerable size of his talents. A third Spacetime Continuum album, **Double Fine Zone** (1999), may finally alter that, though Sharp is clearly more interested in artistic satisfaction than commercial success.

⊙ **Reagenz**   Source/Reflective, 1994

One of Techno's absolute creative highpoints. Jonah Sharp and David Moufang's classic is an essential purchase for anyone interested in the furthest outreaches of the genre's fertile imagination – an album so exquisitely spaced-out it could have been designed by NASA.

Speedy J

L ike many of Techno's maverick figures, Rotterdam's Speedy J
(aka Jochem Paap) developed a simultaneous interest in electronic music and the art of DJing in his early teens. It was from his
uncanny ability to mix at high speed that Jochem gained the moniker
Speedy J; however, it was these early lo-fi experiments in sound which
were to continually inform his musical output. Following these tentative
tape loop voyages, Paap recorded a series of stripped-down Trance
adventures, typified by their non-symmetrical beats and dissonant
ambience. By 1991 these tracks had come to the attention of Ritchie
Hawtin and John Acquaviva. Paap signed to their Plus 8 label and
released a series of critically acclaimed singles, including the stunning
"Pullover".

Speedy J unleashed his first album, **Ginger** (1993), on Warp
Records. An amalgamation of rapid-fire beats and other-worldly ambience, the album represented a landmark in European Techno, predict-
ing the move towards the "artificial intelligence" style of lush, layered
textures and brittle four-to-the-floor beats.

Two years later Jochem released the **G-Spot** (1885) album which
further refined the ideas on **Ginger**, taking the atmosphere into ever
more contemplative depths. No doubt this was as a direct result of the
album being recorded following a serious dose of glandular fever and a
number of months recuperating in the idyllic surroundings of Lan-
zarote. Fully recovered by the time of his third album, **Public Energy
No. 1** (1996), Paap could be found in much darker terrain, exploring
the psychotic cut-ups normally associated with the idiosyncratic
experimentalism of μ-ziq and Aphex Twin.

Paap's obvious admiration for the work of μ-ziq's Mike Paradinas

in particular led to a collaboration between the two in 1998. Under the bizarre alias of Slang Boon Van Loom, they delivered an eponymous album full of stunning soundscapes that ranged between classical *noir* sketches and obtuse, industrial jazz workouts. A further shift from the sound Paap had defined with his early Speedy J material was signalled by the release of **VRS-MBNT-PCS 9598** (1999) on Pete Namlook's Fax Records. A collection of abstract soundscapes and beatless atmospherics recorded between 1995 and 1998, it marked his most radical departure yet from the releases which made him a significant player on the European Techno scene during the early to mid-'90s and suggested that Paap had come full circle by returning to the sonic experimentation of his earliest musical endeavours.

⊙ **Public Energy No.1**   NovaMute, 1996

A melting pot of deconstructed frequency snatches, disquieting ambience and fractured beats, this album echoed the works of artists as disparate as Stockhausen, Faust and Throbbing Gristle as much as it was inspired by Jungle and the likes of Aphex Twin or µ-ziq.

Stasis

G rowing up as a teenager in East London, breakdancing and writing graffiti with B12's Mike Golding, Steve Pickton's musical education moved along a familiar path, from hip-hop to Electro and onto Techno. Schooling himself in music theory, and getting a sampler, Pickton set about making his own music. At the time (1991–92), he was working in London's Time Is Right Records. The shop also ran a small label, and when they heard some of his material, they decided to release it.

Kirk Degiorgio's seminal ART imprint released Pickton's first full-length album. By this time, his music had begun to reach a wider audience and he had signed a record contract with Peacefrog Records, under the name of Stasis, releasing **Circuit Funk**, an EP of lush Detroit melodics in 1993. But the music that appeared on **Unexplained Phenomyna** (1994) was of a darker, more pensive type. A different facet of his musical personality, Pickton chose to release this aspect of his vision under the name of Phenomyna.

Kapellmeister, a collaboration with Mark Broom, released the debut EP on Otherworld Recordings, Pickton's own label, which started in 1994. To date, there have been only four releases on the label – all of them are worth tracking down. In 1995, the debut Stasis album was released. **Inspiration** (1995) was full of Detroit trademarks – deep, melancholy synths, skittering drum patterns, tubular bass runs – but there were also the hip-hop beats of "Inside" and the syncopated jazz breaks of "Pork Chop Hill". It was the sound of Pickton attempting to move beyond the traditional blueprint, to synthesise elements of his musical heritage into something new. These fledgling experiments reached maturity on the follow-up, **From the Old to the New** (1996), which fused Techno, funk, hip-hop, dub, blues and jazz into a sound so dense, it seemed ready to collapse under its own weight.

He contributed an EP to the Mo' Wax Excursions series, and, on the back of this, signed to produce a full-length album for the label. Sadly, this fell victim to the closure of Mo' Wax's parent company A&M in 1998. On a happier note, he hooked up again with Kirk Degiorgio and released the **Nova** EP on the re-named Op-Art label as Paul W. Teebrooke, the name he had used before on his own label productions. Both this and the ensuing LP, **Connections** (1997), saw Pickton experimenting even further with his sound, twisting breaks into strange new shapes and producing a sound as sparse as **From the Old** was dense. Techno was now just another piece of an increasingly complex puzzle, as Pickton proceeded to join the dots between many musics to produce something that sounded like none of them.

Such open-mindedness, however, had no place in Techno's increasingly narrow vision, and Pickton retreated from the music he'd once loved. His last appearance on record came on the Ferox compilation, **Further Adventures in Techno Soul** (1998).

⊙ **Stasis – From the Old to the New**   Peacefrog, 1996

The album where Pickton began to slip his Techno shackles and head
for uncharted waters. The echo chamber dramatics of "Gun" and
wayward lurch of "Ale House Blues" were a long way from Detroit,
while few tracks have demonstrated the sheer breadth of electronica
more dramatically than "Utopia Planetia".

Peter McIntyre

Steve Stoll

ife in Midtown Manhattan may sometimes feel like being in the
middle of a Scorsese movie, but for Steve Stoll it's home. It's an
environment, he claims, that's helped to shape his distinctively muscular, stripped-down approach to Techno. Although Stoll's music has
often been compared to the output of other New York producers such
as Joey Beltram and Damon Wild, there's a compulsive funkiness in his
work which locates him further west, alongside the minimalist auteurs
of Detroit and Chicago.

Initially Stoll's career seemed likely to follow an entirely different
course. After enlisting in the US army, he worked with satellite tracking
systems and saw active service during the Gulf War interpreting satellite imagery for the allied forces. Outside the army, however, his passion was music. He spent time working as the in-house percussionist
for Chicago-based industrial label Wax Trax. His first release, an EP
under the name Data Cloud, appeared on Richie Hawtin's Probe label,
though tracks such as "Birth of Gaspra" and "Dreaming of Phobos"
hinted at an uncharacteristic mysticism which has rarely appeared in

his work since. This was followed by several releases on Damon Wild's fledgling Synewave label, including 1994's "Wires" under the name Ausgang and his subsequent collaborative ventures with Wild as Voyager 8 on "We Left the Planet" and "La Troisième Planete du Soleil".

JOSEPH COLTICE

Wild's success with Synewave encouraged Stoll to set up his own imprint, Proper NYC, which was launched with the solid Techno of "The Infinity Circuit" and quickly earned itself a reputation as one of New York's most consistent underground labels. Released on Sm:)e, **Pacemaker** (1995) was a compelling debut, loaded with tensile, stripped-down moments such as "French Kill" and "Floor Control". Despite its obvious quality, the release was overshadowed by the creative successes of drum 'n' bass and Stoll's brand of hyper-kinetic, dancefloor Techno seemed unfashionably direct. Largely ignored by the media, **Pacemaker** did, however, gain the producer a growing cult following.

Although he produces on a collection of vintage analogue synths and drum machines, Stoll's music has a curiously warm and elegant feel. His tracks are full of carefully crafted shapes, neat percussives and the kind of controlled energy that suggests more than a passing acquaintanceship with the work of Robert Hood and Jeff Mills. But as his prolific output on Proper during 1996 and 1997 proved, Stoll's sound has a distinctive quality that marks him out as "a producer's producer". This was confirmed with the release of **The Blunted Boy Wonder** (1998), his most accomplished offering to date. If anything, Stoll had refined his music for this release, making it both harder and funkier, but the result was an album that sounded like it was running on hi-octane adrenaline. Tracks such as "Model T" and "Falling Down" twisted rolling, tribal rhythms together with abstract, but instantly compelling, melodies, while the vivid electro-boogie of "Mosquito" – all bass rumbles and super-funk riffing – sounded as unstoppable as a runaway freight train.

Stoll began 1999 with two exceptional releases on Proper, "The Observer" and the **Il Mostro** EP which was dedicated to his obsession with Ducati motorcycles and apparently "inspired" by the sound of his own M7 machine.

⊙ **The Blunted Boy Wonder**   NovaMute, 1998

Beautifully shaped minimalism that meets somewhere between Joey Beltram and Jeff Mills. Possibly Stoll's finest hour.

Suburban Knight

Better known as Suburban Knight, James Pennington was the youngest member of the celebrated group of Detroit Techno pioneers who attended Belleville High School. It was with Kevin Saunderson that he formed the closest links. The pair were room-mates for almost three years and they made their first, tentative experiments at making music together. Pennington was one of the original members of Inner City, though his first solo release, "The Groove" on Transmat, quickly established itself as an early Techno classic. After recording Inner City's "Big Fun" with Saunderson and Art Forest, Pennington was approached by Paragon Records and signed an ill-fated deal with the label which prevented him from capitalising on the upsurge in Techno's fortunes.

Pennington did help out on tracks like Santonio's "It's Not Over" and Art Forest's "Vehicle", but his profile was negligible until 1990 when the long-delayed release of the second Suburban Knight single, "The Art of Stalking", imprinted his classically angular style back onto the scene. Cutting loose across frequency-shifting beats and an elegant, low-slung rhythm, "The Art of Stalking" was one of Transmat's most inspired releases, pushing Techno into a darker, more claustrophobic vein. With its weird, altered perspectives and thick textures it sounded like nothing so much as Cubism translated onto record.

Pennington continued to work a day-job caring for the developmentally disadvantaged, but he returned to his Suburban Knight alter ego for "Nocturbulous Behaviour", this time on Underground Resistance. 1995's "Dark Energy" and the subsequent "By Night" developed a sound which Pennington designated "minimal darkness" — a strategy he intended to explore on his long-awaited debut album. However, despite a higher profile during the mid-'90s, Pennington has elected to spend much of the time since then undercover at his base in Inkster, just outside Detroit, and there seems to be no prospect of a long-player.

◉ "The Art of Stalking"   Transmat, 1990

One of Detroit's all-time classics. "In my mind, I was thinking about the African plains, at night-time, and all those nocturnal animals searching for food, stalking their prey," remembers Pennington. What he hunted down, of course, was an unforgettable groove.

Sun Electric

A few brief months before the dismantling of the Berlin Wall began, a local Electro outfit called Fischerman's Friend released a self-titled album and then promptly split up. Two of the group's members, Tom Thiel and Max Loderbauer, were often to be found hanging out in West Berlin's clubs. Neither of them looked like archetypal ravers (in fact, as has been frequently pointed out, they could have been mistaken for architects or bank clerks), but they were to have a significant impact on the development of European Techno.

Thiel had grown up in Erlangen in southern Germany, but eventually picked up work in a studio near Nuremberg, going on to engineer for both Palais Schaumburg and Yello. It was while he was working on Yello's classic "Stella" that he met Loderbauer who, at the time, maintained and serviced the studio's CMI Fairlight sampler. Together they relocated to Berlin and quickly found themselves drawn to the city's vibrant club scene. Within months they were working on the Fischerman's Friend album under the guidance of the group's manager Thomas Fehlmann. One of the tracks they contributed was "O'Locco", a drifting collage of chilled samples and weightless synths.

When Fischerman's Friend disintegrated, Thiel and Loderbauer used "O'Locco" as a template for the musical excursions they embarked upon as Sun Electric. Holed up in their studio, hunched over a mixing desk that had – significantly enough – once belonged to Tangerine Dream, the pair crafted a sound that touched base with avant garde electronics, sampladelica and the dreamy abstraction of Detroit Techno. "O'Locco" came to the attention of The Orb's Alex Paterson who secured its release on Wau! Mr Modo late in 1990. The track became one of the key reference points for the developing Ambient scene, with remixes by Paterson, The KLF's Jimmy Cauty and Youth supporting Sun Electric's blissful sonic washes.

An ill-fated deal with Trevor Horn's ZTT label followed, but the resulting album was never released and the duo moved to R&S in 1992. Their official debut album, **Kitchen** (1993), was an intriguing, often hypnotic, weave of delicately spun Ambient textures, imperceptible shifts and dislocated atmospherics. By November 1993, when Sun Electric accompanied The Orb on tour, their sound had morphed towards a looser, more live-oriented sense of improvisation and jamming. Another LP, **Aaah!** (1994), this time with Fehlmann moving from the role of executive producer to co-producer, documented the change.

Their new-found confidence onstage led to a live album, **30.7.94 Live** (1995). Containing just three tracks that had been specially written for their performance, the album twisted on an axis of gently refracting jazz electronics, pulled, stretched and manipulated across the borders of Techno. Unfairly overlooked at the time and now deleted, **30.7.94 Live** remains one of the better releases from an era when the concept

of live Techno betrayed a curious impulse to drag the genre back towards the accepted conventions of the traditional music industry.

There was a lengthy silence until the arrival of **Present** (1996), although Thiel and Loderbauer had continued their activities with The Orb. But the pair were becoming gradually disconnected from the club culture mainstream, preferring to work instead on more ambitious projects such as their soundtrack for Bobby Roth's *Looosers!* and their *Mindrevolution* CD-ROM. By 1998, they were admitting to journalist Tony Marcus that the music they'd been listening to veered from Miles Davis and Weather Report to the post-rock of Tortoise.

An album scheduled for release early in 1998 was postponed when

Thiel and Loderbauer developed a new working method which they described as "like playing a video game – we would both sit in front of the computer and take different bits of the music to work on at the same time." Fascinated by the free-form potential of the process, the pair scrapped the ten tracks they'd recorded for their new album and spent the next six months evolving the loose, organic structures of **Via Nostra** (1998). Acclaimed by critics as the duo's best release so far, the album signalled yet another creative high from one of Berlin's most intriguing acts.

⊙ **Via Nostra**   R&S, 1998

Sun Electric tapped into the prevailing mood that Techno's emphasis on repetition had turned into a dead end. The result was this masterpiece of constantly evolving structures and tones.

Surgeon

T ony Child adopted his alternate identity as Surgeon back in 1991 before his first gig in the backroom of a Birmingham pub. As a kid growing up in the village of Kislingbury near Northampton, he'd play with the family record deck, deliberately putting records on at the wrong speed, messing around with tape recorders or the rhythm unit on a home organ. He'd listen to records by the Japanese electronic musician Isao Tomita, fascinated by the sounds he used, or dream aloud to the *Empire Strikes Back* soundtrack. At school, on a borrowed four-track, he composed weird sonic missives with a couple of microphones and some effects units. In 1989, he moved to Birmingham to study Audio Visual Design and began playing tape loops and a battered Arp synth in a jazz/rock/fusion band called Blim.

It was Paul Damage, a self-taught hip-hop DJ, who taught Surgeon how to DJ. "That's where I got the aggressive mixing and cutting style from," he explains. Another friend, Nathan Gregory (who later went on to work at Ideal Trax), introduced him to all the House music that he'd missed in one way or another. Eventually, Surgeon was introduced to former Napalm Death drummer Mick Harris. "He's well into Faust and all that stuff," says Tony, who's also a fan of the experimental work Harris does under the name Scorn. The story that he told journalist Nik Cohn was that Harris had locked him in his makeshift studio, saying, "Go mad. Don't stop to think, just do it. Whatever's in you, get it out." The resulting recordings became the **Surgeon** EP on Downwards.

The fierce sounds of "Badger Bite" (from the **Pet 2000** EP on Downwards) and "Action" (from the **Dynamic Tension** EP on Ideal Trax) followed out of Surgeon's impossibly minimal studio set-up. A cheap, second-hand synth, a budget drum machine and some borrowed bits'n'pieces were twisted into a sonic laboratory, pushing textures and noise and surfaces into increasingly experimental planes. The influence of his surroundings also had an impact on Surgeon's music. Around the time of **Pet 2000** and **Dynamic Tension** he was living on the border between the red light district of Balsal Heath and the more bohemian/student climate of Moseley. The music became darker, more intense and more bruising. A graffito, painted on a wall at the end of Kingswood Road, seemed to sum up the the exhausted and angry mood of the time. "Muggerscum Out" became the title of a ferocious and excoriating workout for Glasgow's Soma label.

1996's **Communications** double-pack on Downwards "hovers around in the area of being an album," he says. But his debut album proper was the stunning **Basic Tonal Vocabulary** (1997) on Tresor. Loaded with fierce rhythms and shifting sequences, tracks like "Nine

Hours Into the Future" and "First" locked onto your synapses. At times mad and calm, aggressive and fragile, it was possible to hear traces of Faust or Coil or even Kraftwerk drift through the stark electronic funk onboard.

⊙ **Basic Tonal Vocabulary**   Tresor, 1997

Brutal, weird and minimal, this was the debut which shaped the so-called Black Country Techno sound. It's since been imitated by producers internationally but none have come close to Surgeon's original blueprint.

System 7

Author and cyber-theorist Douglas Rushkoff has drawn parallels between the astonishing web of coincidence and synchronicity which manifested itself during the UK's conversion to House and Techno and Aleister Crowley's notion of "the chapel perilous". Perhaps one of the instances he was thinking about was the night when hippie avant-gardist Steve Hillage walked into Land of Oz's Ambient room to hear his long-forgotten **Rainbow Dome Music** (1977) playing over the sound system.

The DJ was Alex Paterson and Hillage went on to work with his group The Orb before setting up the flexible, collaborative venture of System 7 with his partner Miquette Giraudy. The duo's first album, **System 7** (1991), featured contributions from Derrick May, Paterson and The Orb's Thrash along with a floating ensemble of musicians, backing vocalists and sessioneers then orbiting Youth and his pop/dance productions. **System 7** fired the first warning shots of Progressive

House and its lush, multi-faceted production (courtesy of Hillage) was endlessly copied over the following years. Hillage and Giraudy, however, moved swiftly on.

777 (1992) delivered a major dancefloor hit with "7:7 Expansion" and retained the group's intriguing digressions into ethnic music while beefing up the bottom end. "A Cool Dry Place" was typical of their evolving sound: percussive sequences, weightless atmospherics and hard machine drums framing tunes which occupied the cusp between melody and abstraction.

It was the perfect fusion between the dreamy world music which had featured in Hillage and Giraudy's earlier career and their growing interest in Deep House and Detroit Techno.

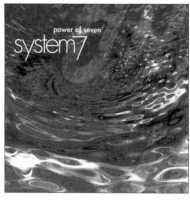

1994's **Point 3**, however, marked a radical shift. With Derrick May, Laurent Garnier and The Orb's Lewis Keogh onboard as collaborators, the album was released in two versions: **Fire** contained tracks tailored for the dancefloor, while **Water** delivered experimental, Ambient versions of the tracks. Both were exceptional with "Sirénes", in particular, demonstrating a clear debt to the cyclical rhythmic patterns of Robert Hood and, another Hillage favourite, Jeff Mills. A successful series of live shows served to underline how thoroughly Hillage had assimilated Techno. More than their album releases, the live performances demonstrated the growing influence of a strain of tough minimalism underpinning Hillage and Giraudy's compelling and subtle sense of melodics.

Power of Seven (1995) featured contributions from both Carl Craig ("Civilization") and Derrick May ("Big Sky City"), yet it was a surprisingly lacklustre effort. A general sense of foreboding wasn't helped by **System Express** (1996), a greatest hits-type round-up of remixes and alternate versions. Despite some inspired moments, **The Golden Section** (1997) seemed worryingly unfocused. A new album is scheduled soon, though it's obvious that Hillage and Giraudy will have to come up with something special to recapture the glory days of the early '90s.

⊙ **Point 3 – Fire**   Big Life, 1994

Brimming with originality, Hillage and Giraudy embraced the front-end of Techno and threw in some new shapes of their own.

⊙ **Point 3 – Water**   Big Life, 1994

Chill-out versions of the same tracks, acutely rendered and draped in System 7's distinctive melodic sensibilities.

Fumiya Tanaka

A s minimal Techno moved into its upswing in the early part of 1994, news began to filter through from Japan about a DJ who could cut fire like The Advent. Within twelve months, though, Fumiya Tanaka was more frequently being described as "Japan's answer to Jeff Mills". When he finally arrived in Europe to promote his major label mix album, the incendiary **I Am Not a DJ** (1995), it was evident that such comparisons weren't too far off the mark. He revealed a similar sense of alchemy behind the decks, fusing Basic Channel, Axis and the super-stripped, hard Techno on his own Torema label into a dizzying rage of clustered beats and white-hot funk.

Tanaka's earliest musical endeavours had been as a guitarist and drummer in a Kyoto punk band, inspired by The Clash and Sex Pistols. He didn't connect with dance music until 1990 and though he subsequently organised a number of parties around the Osaka region, he didn't begin to DJ regularly until a few years later when he set up his own night in Nanba's Club Rockets. Spending his weekends behind the decks, Tanaka began working on his own studio experiments in spare time, eventually setting up Torema Records as a vehicle for the hard, brutally minimal Techno best articulated by later releases such as the **Micro** EP and "Speaker". After a move to Tokyo in 1994 to take up residency at Distortion, he began making contacts among the increasing number of US and European DJs beginning to play in the city, leading to his first gigs outside Japan.

Early in 1996, Tanaka issued "Karafuto" on his new Untitled label, a languid, jazz-House outing that marked his first step away from the abrasive, piledriver minimalism of his earlier releases. A collaboration with Akio Milan Paak under the name Hoodrum resulted in **Business Card**, an ambitious, if not entirely convincing, amalgam of breakbeat ambience. A second mix album, **Mix Up Volume 4** (1996), confirmed the fact that, behind the decks at least, Tanaka had lost none of his fire.

Unknown Possibility Vol. 1 (1997) revealed obvious stylistic links with Jeff Mills (particularly his **Waveform Transmission** series), though there was still enough originality on board to make it a debut that entirely justified the hyperbole surrounding Tanaka's obvious talents. Combining the taut, unrelenting angles of his best work with a more carefully produced sheen, the album confirmed Tanaka's status as one of minimal Techno's most intriguing exponents.

⊙ **I Am Not A DJ**   Sony, 1995

There may be a better mix album that skirts the outermost boundaries of minimal Techno but, confronted by Tanaka's startling performance on this outing, it's hard to imagine.

Tanith

As one of Berlin's most influential DJs during the early '90s, Tanith's impact on the European Techno scene was considerable. Though Sven Vath and Westbam subsequently gained a higher profile, Tanith was the first German DJ ever to play at a UK rave (Universe in 1992) and was to remain a major force until the popularity of German Techno began to wane in the middle of the decade.

As resident at Berlin's legendary Tresor club, Tanith was at the heart of the city's revival as a major musical centre at the beginning of the '90s, though his roots were in punk and, subsequently, in Industrial outfits such as Einstürzende Neubaten, Throbbing Gristle and Nitzer Ebb when he first began DJing at Dschungel in Wiesbaden in 1984. Tanith moved to Berlin in 1987 and within a year had discovered Acid House. He played his first Acid House sets at UFO, a small illegal club in a cellar in Kreuzberg, setting up his own clubnight, Cyberspace, in 1989. Following the city's reunification, he began playing at the popular Tekknozid raves in east Berlin, dividing his time between his DJ activities and music journalism for German Techno 'zine *Front Page*. Along with *Front Page* owner Jürgen Laarman, he also launched Bash Records and began collaborating in the studio with Mijk van Dijk, leading to his first release – the **What Is Noise** EP – for the label.

When Dimitri Hegemann launched Tresor in a former department store vault on the eastern side of the city, he invited Tanith to become the resident DJ (a function he was also to perform for Mayday), leading to Tresor's rapidly acquired reputation as one of Germany's best clubs. His reputation as one of Berlin's major players was confirmed by a series of singles such as "Robocop" and "T2" which he and van Dijk produced over the ensuing months.

By 1992, Tanith was already investigating the breakbeat-driven Hardcore being forged by DJs in the UK. He began organising his own "breakcore" parties – Germany's first breakbeat events – and playing at harder raves such as Amsterdam's Hellraiser, though he continued to be a major draw at Mayday until 1995 when his disillusionment with the commercialisation of the event led him to quit as resident. Tanith's affinity for breakbeat Hardcore translated eventually into an eclectic fusion of drum 'n' bass, Big Beat and freestyle – he hosted the break-beat club Skull & Crossbones (in Berlin's E-Werk) and founded Timing Recordings as a platform for the sound. **Bronco**, his first EP for the new label, reached the German Top Ten just as he was organising the "breakfest" section of 1998's Love Parade with Fatboy Slim and DJ Punk Roc.

○ **"T2"** Bash, 1992

That's Tanith rather than Terminator though the overall effect is the same.

Tanzmuzik

T anzmuzik (it's both the German word for "dance music" and the title of a seminal Kraftwerk track) were one of Japan's earliest

Techno exports. Formed by Akio Yamamoto and Okihide Sawaki, the duo swiftly began releasing records, beginning with the "Muzikanova" single on Fumiya Tanaka's Torema Records. "Muzikanova" brought them to the attention of Rising High who promptly issued the **Tan**

Tangue EP. Falling somewhere between the label's dancefloor-oriented Trance output and the more experimental strains of signings such as Bedouin Ascent and Wagaon Christ, **Tan Tangue** generated significant interest and was followed by the **Love Light** EP. An album, **Sinsekai** (1995), emerged soon after, but was overlooked as the label entered the period of crisis which led to its eventual closure later that year.

A little-known compilation of their solo efforts, **Akio/Okihide – Scratches** (1995), was issued by Sublime before Yamamoto moved to Tokyo, effectively ending their collaborative ventures. He began making brutally minimal Techno under the name Akio Milanpaak for Torema, while Sawaki went on to issue two solo projects – **The Weather Forecast** (1996) and **A Boy In Picca Season** (1997) – though these releases failed to achieve any significant impact on the scale of their Tanzmuzik material.

Yamamoto also teamed up with Fumiya Tanaka for a successful collaboration as Hoodrum for Sony. But it was clear that he was happiest in his creative relationship with Sawaki and soon began formatting the concept of a second Tanzmuzik album, this time recruiting Sawaki and another friend, Daisha Hisakawa, to realise their distinctive version of a soundtrack to a road movie which didn't yet exist.

When it finally emerged, **Version Citie Hi-Lights** (1998) proved to be their most deliberately experimental and eclectic work so far. Fusing harsh, gritty loops, queasy sub-tones and multiple layers of samples, tracks such as "Weekender" and "Propaganda 8" veered towards downbeat and uneasy listening. Few tracks were straight collaborations, however, with only "Broken Analyzer" featuring both Sawaki and Yamamoto together. Hisakawa contributed the fragile textures of "Soul Slides Away", but his input elsewhere remained unclear.

⊙ **Version Citie Hi-Lights**   Sublime, 1998

Imagine *Eraserhead* meets *Easy Rider* and you're in the ballpark.

Mark Taylor

I n 1988, Mark Taylor was working on a production for RJ's Latest
Arrival, a Detroit R&B group, when his co-producer, Eddie "Flashin'"
Fowlkes, introduced him to Juan Atkins. Soon Taylor was hanging out
at the Metroplex studio, occasionally doing remix work for the label
and experimenting with his own Techno tracks in parallel with his R&B
career. Taylor's R&B talents were strong enough to attract heavyweight
management – at one point he was represented by Barry Hankerson,
the man behind Toni Braxton and R Kelly – but he also continued to
produce Techno, attracted by the lack of formal conventions and its
creative freedom.

In the UK with Kevin Saunderson to record Inner City's "Back
Together Again" during 1995, Taylor heard a cover of one of his songs
on the monitor system at the Sarm West studio where they were working. The song was "I've Got a Little Something for You" which went on
to become a significant hit for MN8 all over Europe (it peaked in the
UK at #2 early in March, 1995), and provided the funding for a number
of Taylor's Techno projects.

A snapshot of Taylor's output in the mid-'90s would have revealed
songwriting and production credits on Mark Morrison's **Return of the
Mack** album alongside remix duties on "The Flow" by Model 500, singles for the Florida bass label Pan Disc and a sensational reworking of
Run DMC's "It's Like That" with teenage prodigy Little Johnny for his
own Greyt label. Under the name Croniktronik, Taylor also recorded
"King of Bass" for the Direct Beat label which went on to become a
major hit on the Detroit bass scene.

Currently working on a variety of projects, it's likely that, sooner or
later, Taylor will finally get around to delivering the Techno album he's

been promising. A clue to the direction that might take was offered by "Anti Matter Premium Unlead", his Vintage Future 12" which was released on Underground Resistance late in 1998.

◉ **Croniktronik – "King of Bass"**   Direct Beat, 1997

Described in *The Face* as "Taylor's Run DMC-sampling bass odyssey", this is the classic sound of Detroit's street scene – Electro beats, floor-shaking low frequency mayhem and enough dancefloor energy to power the General Motors plant.

Titonton

Titonton Duvante – the euphonious moniker is a legacy of family antecedents in French West Africa – has emerged from the college town of Columbus to become one of the producers most hotly tipped to take Techno forward to its next stage. Titonton makes music which flirts with impossibility; his records are muscular but delicate, trippy but firmly focused, hard but somehow gentle too. Listen to tracks like "Viscous & Shadowed" (from his **Embryonic** EP on Metamorphic) or his "Chronologic" contribution to Reflective's **Deepest Shade of Techno II** (1997) and you'll hear music that refracts and dissolves in a starburst of different directions all at once.

Titonton first came to the attention of Dan Curtin's Metamorphic label after one of his tracks appeared on a friend's cassette compilation. Curtin tracked him down and quickly offered him the deal which led to the **Embryonic** EP. It was through Curtin that Duvante met Morgan Geist and the pair embarked on a fruitful working relationship which initially resulted in the exceptional **Titonton & Morgan** EP on Environ.

Though both Chicago and Detroit have had a significant influence on Titonton's music, his records carry a compelling freight of classical timbre and subtle dynamic shifts. He studied classical music and opera performance at Ohio State University and it's possible to trace echoes of that training locked somewhere deep inside the alien synthetics and abstract tones of releases such as the **Endorphin** EP. Inescapably seductive currents flow through his work, subverting raw sine waves with breathtakingly warm strings or floating ethereal choirs on a raft of hard b-lines and syncopated rhythms. On the wildly schizoid "Of the Essence", for example, he combined lighter-than-air dreamscape synths with fat Acid and weird-out sound effects before suddenly reinventing the track halfway through as a radical outer-space symphony – a fucked-up concerto of beautiful synth noises and strange emotional counterpoint.

Having grown up listening to everything from his parents' disco records to works by classic minimalist auteurs Steve Reich and Philip Glass, Titonton's attraction to Techno originally lay in a fascination with sonic exploration, but it has endured and the enchantment with innovation which weaves through his best work easily locates him alongside the most revered of Detroit's sonic astronauts.

This was confirmed by the release of a stunning debut album, **Voyeurism** (1999), which drew on a template initially blueprinted by classic Rhythim Is Rhythim, Carl Craig's material as 69 and the dystopian futurism of Model 500, although titles like "Foreplay", "Boudoir" and "Innuendo" also hinted at more than a passing acquaintanceship with **Controversy**-era Prince and Detroit's would-be love machine, Blake Baxter.

◉ Endorphin EP   Metamorphic, 1997

Closest in attitude to Morgan Geist, Titonton's music on this outstanding release harks back to the days of classic Detroit Techno and forward, far into the future. Abstract, but deeply beautiful.

⊙ **Voyeurism**   Star Baby, 1999

Riddled with floor-shaking funk and brittle futurism, Titonton's remarkable debut sounds like the LP that Derrick May should have made.

Keith Tucker

As a founder member of Aux 88, Keith Tucker's declaration that – alongside Kraftwerk, George Clinton and science fiction – his main source of inspiration came from "the street DJs and dancers" of Detroit helps to explain a lot. Aux 88 went on to become a Motor City phenomenon, their records still outsell most other Techno artists in the metro area and theirs is the sound that is played religiously at full volume every weekend by club and party DJs on both sides of the city. The group were already hugely successful on these terms when Tucker took the decision to strike out on his own.

Under a variety of aliases – Alien FM, KT-19941, K-1 and Optic Nerve – Tucker has continued to mine the seam of hard, Electro-edged Techno which he first explored on Aux 88's early releases. Credited as "Aux 88 meets Alien FM", the album **88 FM** (1995) offered the opportunity for Tucker to cut heads with his old crew but, in effect, it proved that the two units were travelling in opposite directions. While Aux 88 gravitated towards an increasingly direct approach by magnifying beats and basslines to almost cartoon-ish proportions, Tucker's work has become, by degrees, more sophisticated and, in some cases, less immediately accessible.

In 1995, Anthony Shakir and Tucker set up the Puzzlebox label as a platform for their own increasingly distinctive productions with the direct aim, so Shakir tells it, of putting "some guessing back" into the Techno scene. Tucker's releases so far, including his "Dark City" offering as KT-19941, have pursued the trajectory initially begun when, back in the late '80s, he recorded as Frequency for Metroplex. It was Shakir who persuaded Atkins to sign Tucker, inadvertently paving the way for one of the label's biggest home-grown hits with "Television/Frequency Express".

An album deal with the Cosmo label in Germany has yet to bear fruit, though Tucker is something of a Techno star there – his performance at Mayday in 1995 pulled a crowd of over 28,000 – but an increasing number of live performances, ranging from Munich to Barcelona and Zurich, suggests that his first album under his own name is imminent.

⊙ Aux 88 Meets Alien FM – 88FM   430 West, 1995

Still the perfect introduction to both sides of Tucker's work since this is a full-on collaborative venture with his former group. Fierce Electro grooves abound.

Underground Resistance

Perhaps the most influential and compelling Techno outfit of the last decade, Detroit's Underground Resistance occupy a territory that is somewhere between the reclusive mystique of Kraftwerk, the radical politicisation of Public Enemy and their own unique interpretation of Afro-futurist tropes. Releases such as 1990's "Sonic Destroyer" or the classic **Riot** EP are among Techno's most astonishing moments – note-perfect syntheses of form and function, medium and message which served to underscore the group's "hard music from a hard city" aesthetic. Subsequent transmissions, including the **Nation 2 Nation**, **World 2 World** and **Galaxy II Galaxy** EPs and the series of "World Power Alliance" singles, have pioneered equally innovative territory. The group's label (also called Underground Resistance) has provided a conduit for some of Detroit's more covert operators – including Drexciya, Suburban Knight and Scan 7 – and a launchpad for the careers of newer artists such as DJ Rolando, André Holland and Marc Floyd. Yet, beyond this, less is known about Underground Resistance than any other entity in pop culture.

Excavating UR's shadowy pre-history is fraught with problems, not least because the group maintain an almost impenetrable veil of secrecy around their operations. Separating fact from myth is equally difficult, though the basic story revolves around a meeting in 1986 between Mike Banks, then involved with Detroit group Members of the House, and Jeff Mills. Following the disintegration of his Final Cut project, Mills reconnected with Banks and the pair began plotting a new group.

"Before we even started making the music," Mills remembered in a subsequent interview, "Mike and I sat down for months and just formatted the whole Underground Resistance thing. We talked about what the label should stand for, what the logo should look like, where it should be presented, the type of releases, everything. We looked at what Kevin [Saunderson], Juan [Atkins] and Derrick [May] were doing and we used them as a guide – not doing what they did but what they *didn't* do."

Underground Resistance launched their new label with a vocal release, "Your Time Is Up" featuring Yolanda Reynolds, then rapidly followed up with a series of experimental Techno offerings, including "The Final Frontier" and "Waveform", before delivering the ground-breaking Tech-jazz of **Nation 2 Nation**. It was a move calculated to prove both the group's versatility and the difficulty of pinning them down.

Adopting an increasingly militaristic outlook – in terms of both image and approach – UR drafted Alan Oldham and Robert Hood (then known as Rob Noise) to assist with a number of non-musical activities, though Hood did record for the label as The Vision. The records which followed were tougher, more overtly militant than anything which had gone before. The signals were there, for anybody who cared to listen, on the brooding "Elimination", but when the **Riot** EP emerged it was as though the group were announcing an all-out assault on Techno. Impossibly hard and laced with the kind of blistering funk that European Hardcore was incapable of matching, the new records keyed in to a prevailing mood which had overtaken the dance scene since the honeymoon period of 1988's Summer of Love. The stern, sombre angles and bruising rhythms of UR articulated the new mood perfectly.

But the diversity and experimental drive which had fuelled the group's career so far was still very much in evidence. **X-101** (1991) was an ambitious full-length offering which stretched the parameters of Techno into hitherto unexplored realms. Soon after its appearance, Mike Banks headed to Europe with his former comrades Members of the House. During his absence, Mills began experimenting alone in the group's Black Planet studio. The result was "The Punisher", a bruising workout that pinned a colossal synth riff to a tensile percussive backdrop and which offered hints of the minimal abstraction that was to become a feature of Mills' later solo career.

X-102 Discovers the Rings of Saturn (1992) erased any doubt that Underground Resistance were pioneering a whole new concept in Techno. From the record pressing itself (the tracks were etched into the vinyl to correspond with the size and relationship of Saturn's rings) to the music it carried, this was a revolutionary release. "Tethys" was the most abstract moment in Techno's development so far – synthetic pulses floating free-form in an almost tangible gravity of icy reverbs and processors. "Groundzero (The Planet)" was, perhaps, even more astonishing, locking a dense UR groove to layers of harmonised vocals that sounded like the choir from a '70s blaxploitation flick or – depending on your state of mind – the voices of angels.

Revolution for Change (1992) collected moments from releases such as the **Riot** EP, "Sonic Destroyer" and "The Punisher" to deliver an intriguing snapshot of a creative entity in the process of going supernova. But even then, just as they seemed within reach, Underground Resistance beamed back into the future with more outstanding transmissions, including **World 2 World**, "Death Star" and the extended **Acid Rain – The Storm Continues** EP.

The departure of Mills to take up a residency at Peter Gatien's Limelight club in New York saw Oldham take over as UR's official "assault" DJ for a tour of Australia. On their return, Hood left to help Mills set up the Axis label and Underground Resistance became a significant element in the development of Submerge, the Detroit-based distribution organisation which has become a crucial conduit for Detroit Techno labels such as Metroplex, KMS, 430 West and, of course, Underground Resistance. There is little doubt that, over the years since then, Submerge has been as influential in determining the forward course of Techno as any artist or label.

In recent years the UR operation has become even more covert. Even details about the group's current line-up are impossible to ascertain. Yet the restless innovation of their releases continues to push Techno in new and unexpected directions. 1995's exceptional **Electronic Warfare** double-pack harnessed tough angles and soulful warmth, 1997's "Codebreaker" fused a hard dancefloor groove with morse code sonics (cracking the code provided UR enthusiasts with a secret message) and 1998's Octave One/UR double-header "Day Star Rising/Aztlan" was constructed so that, when mixed together, both sides created a third "hidden" track that blended embrasive strings and deep minimalism.

"The Turning Point" offered a ground-breaking fusion of Techno, soul, gospel, funk and Electro. The release of **Interstellar Fugitives** (1998) seemed to suggest that Underground Resistance is now a collective effort rather than the vehicle for one producer or group of producers with artists such as André Holland ("UR On Mir"), Marc Floyd ("AfroGermanic") and the mysterious Chamaleon ("Zero Is My Country") all contributing. UR operates at the furthest remove from the mainstream's cult of celebrity – a shifting, nebulous and indeterminate entity which can only be defined by the music itself.

◉ Revolution For Change   Underground Resistance, 1992

Almost every UR release has broken new ground for Techno, but this essential collection is a fine place to start.

◉ X-102 Discovers the
Rings of Saturn   Underground Resistance, 1992

Breathtaking innovation that seemed to stretch somewhere out beyond the stars and back again. Another of Techno's giant leaps into the future.

◉ World 2 World   Underground Resistance, 1993

Better than dreams, this EP produced "Jupiter Jazz" – an anthem to rival even Rhythim Is Rhythim's seminal "Strings Of Life" and one of UR's most spine-tingling moments.

Underworld

Karl Hyde, from the West Midlands, and Rick Smith, from a tiny South Wales village, had met at college in Cardiff. Hyde had a power pop band, Smith joined, and when the band fell apart the two stayed together, trying to fuse their primary influences – dub and Kraftwerk – and eventually landing a record deal on the condition they pumped up the pop element of their sound.

They became Freur, an electro-pop act with New Romantic stylings, released two albums through CBS and achieved a certain success, especially in Italy. As Rick Smith later commented, it went straight to their heads. They regrouped under the name Underworld, toured American stadiums with The Eurythmics, were big in Australia, but claim to have never made much money. Disillusion set in. Smith and Hyde despised the pop game and what it did to them. Both were the wrong side of 30 and wanted to keep working in music. By this time, Acid House had arrived, and Smith particularly believed that somewhere in that vibrant, unstructured new form, there might be a way. Smith wanted to work with a DJ. He moved to Romford in Essex. Hyde became a session guitarist, working at Prince's Paisley Park studio in Minneapolis and touring with former Blondie frontwoman Debbie Harry.

In Romford, Smith met a young DJ called Darren Emerson, who at ten years his junior had a whole different musical background in breakdancing, hip-hop, and early Chicago House. Emerson had already remixed Gat Decor's Progressive House classic, "Passion", and he and Smith began working together as Steppin' Razor, even remixing Simply Red's "Thrill Me" into a Techno-dub oblivion.

While still with Debbie Harry's band, Karl Hyde had spent time in

New York and he too had fallen for dance culture. Inspired by sampling techniques, he began cutting up the *Village Voice* newspaper and rearranging words into lyrics. He too moved to Romford, where Underworld Mark 2 came together. The new Underworld released their first single under an alias, Lemon Interrupt. "Eclipse/Bigmouth", a double a-side of melodic House with Balearic twists, excited tastemaker DJs.

Underworld announced a unique creative agenda with their very first single in early 1993. "Mmm… Skyscraper I Love You" was an intricate, throbbing Techno record that used singer Karl Hyde's poem to a skyscraper as another noise, not just a vocal. Signed to the highly credible Junior Boys Own label, they followed with an album, **Dubnobasswithmyheadman** (1994), that startled dance music fans with its vision, mixing Jamaican dub, Detroit Techno, rock guitar and Karl Hyde's bizarre cut-up lyrics to exhilarating effect. One track, "Cowgirl", was a vocal version of a previous twisting Techno single called "Rez" that added what sounded like a Jew's harp and a chorus of "I'm visible, I'm visible" to an Acid frenzy. Released as a single, it quickly became an international club anthem.

Their music was hard, groove-based and funky, given a technicolour feel by the pop sensibilities of Smith and Hyde. By the next album, **Second Toughest in the Infants** (1996), they had widened the sound further, playing with Jungle rhythms on tracks like "Pearl's Girl" and slower, moodier numbers like "Confusion the Waitress". Underworld developed a remarkable, free-form live show that leaned towards the harder side of their dub-heavy, melodic Techno sound. Tracks would be rearranged on stage, melting into one another, and the audience never knew when Karl Hyde was going to take to the mic and start ranting his cut-up lyrics, pasted together from billboard slogans, snippets of overheard conversations, clippings from newspapers, and whatever else took his fancy.

The group became frequent headliners at radical new dance events like London's Megadog, which was pioneering live dance music to a an audience more used to indie rock. They achieved a rare crossover by appealing to Megadog's indie dance audience with live shows while continuing to stun House clubs with forceful 12"s. Their label Junior Boys Own were content for them to experiment. More importantly, they could afford to take creative risks because of another venture: their design and advertising agency, Tomato.

Underworld albums have sold considerable numbers internationally and they have performed all over the world. But in 1996, Underworld suddenly became popstars again when "Born Slippy", a powerful Techno number with a cut-up chorus that included the rant "lager! lager! lager! lager!" was included at a crucial point in the film *Trainspotting*, going on to #2 in the British charts when released as a single, and selling nearly half a million copies. This was especially ironic, as the track had actually been written as a satire on the dance genre, with its sledgehammer kick drum and euphoric breakdowns, and had already been released once, the year before.

Named after a sample recorded by Smith on a fishing trip with his American cousins in the Deep South, **Beaucoup Fish** (1999) was a mixture of vocoders, Deep House, juddering hip-hop, pianos and trademark Underworld fluttery Techno.

⊙ **Dubnobasswithmyheadman**   Junior Boys Own, 1994

Hailed as a dance classic, this stirring mix of dub, Techno, and cut-up lyrics redefined the dance album.

⊙ **Second Toughest In the Infants**   Junior Boys Own, 1996

Bigger in sound and wider in reference, this is their finest album, and toys with breakbeat, blues, and funky hard House.

Dom Phillips

Mijk van Dijk

hen Mijk van Dijk moved to Berlin in the late '80s to pursue a career in journalism, the city was on the cusp of a major trans-

formation. Berlin's vibrant club scene had already begun to align itself with House and Techno when van Dijk teamed up with a friend, Johannes Talirz, to buy a sampler. Together the pair began making House and hip-hop tracks, but by 1989 van Dijk had decided to go solo. As one of the first German journalists to interview artists such as Derrick May, 808 State and Peter "Baby" Ford, he had the advantage of a direct line to the source of the new music.

In 1990, under the name LoopZone, van Dijk released his first 12", "Hate/Les Enfants du Paradis", on Superstition. As Berlin shifted towards a harder sound, he began collaborating with Tanith who was, by this time, a well-known DJ on the local scene. Together, the pair produced the **What Is Noise?** EP for Berlin's Bash label and continued to collaborate over the next eighteen months, turning out "Robocop" (as 9-10-Boy) and, early in 1992, Tanith's **T2** EP. A deal with MFS Records provided a platform for two new solo projects –

Microglobe and Mindgear. It was as Microglobe that van Dijk scored his first major international success with the upbeat "High on Hope" becoming a dancefloor staple.

In 1993, van Dijk returned to the LoopZone project with "Home Is Where the Hartcore Is", by now running a career as a DJ alongside his production work. Another LoopZone release, the hard-edged 404 EP, followed, but a new collaboration with Marcos Lopez as Marmion delivered one of his most significant dancefloor hits. Initially, Marmion's Berlin EP was a low-key release on Hamburg's Superstition Records that slowly gathered momentum through word-of-mouth as Trance DJs picked up on the kinetic riffing of one track in particular. "Schön- berg" was reissued in its own right a year later with remixes by Marmion and Kid Paul, becoming a key release in the emergent nu energy scene.

Microglobe's **Afreuropamericasiaustralica** (1994) delivered a sound by now familiar to fans of van Dijk's rapidly proliferating pro- jects which now included Mijk's Magic Marble Box and a growing number of sometimes uncredited collaborations, including produc- tion assistance on DJ Hell's **Geteert & Gefedert** (1994). Van Dijk closed the year with an extensive tour of Japan which brought him into contact with a number of Japanese producers and provided the inspiration for 1995's Mijk's Magic Marble Box release, "Tokyo Trax".

Van Dijk's subsequent visits to Japan resulted in remixes for Denki Groove and Parts Of Console and a sneak preview of *Depth*, Sony's music-making game for the PlayStation. At his birthday party in 1996 he unveiled a live set constructed purely with the game (which was eventually released in Europe two years later as *Fluid*). Sporadic appearances since then with the PlayStation have attracted consider- able attention, though, so far at least, van Dijk is the only producer of note to have championed the game's potential as a serious artistic tool.

By the time **Glow** (1997) appeared, van Dijk was expanding his musical endeavours into film soundtracks (David Jazay's *Kiss My Blood* and the Charles Finkbeiner/Donald Kramer short *Femme*), computer games (*Ghost in the Shell* for the PlayStation), commercial soundtracks (Renault) and even theatre (collaborating with the Berliner Ensemble for a performance at that year's Love Parade – again van Dijk constructed all the music on a PlayStation).

A Japan-only release, **Multimijk** (1998), mixed by Tokyo DJ Toby Izui, provided a worthwhile best-of set, while **Mind Control Vol. 2** (1998) was van Dijk's own mix album. **Teamwork** (1999) emphasised van Dijk's taste for collaboration. A series of tracks co-written and co-produced with other artists (including Claude Young, Toby Izui, Thomas Schumacher and Humate), it garnered useful reviews though some critics complained that van Dijk's forceful, Trance-oriented production style had submerged the input of his guest collaborators underneath trademark layers of fizzing sequences and solidly four-to-the-floor grooves.

The long-promised Marmion album, **Five Years and Tomorrow** (1999), finally emerged on MFS, preceded by a commercially successful single, "Best Regards", which suggested that van Dijk's prototype blend of kinetic beats, amphetamine riffing and naggingly insistent melodics was still as popular as ever.

⊙ **Microglobe – Afreuropamericasiaustralica**   MFS, 1994

Unpronounceable, but entertaining, debut which provided the definitive blueprint of van Dijk's sound.

Paul van Dyk has become one of the key figures at the more commercial end of the Trance/Techno scene. After playing at a club called Turbine he quickly graduated to a residency at E-Werk, playing the club's Friday night Dubmission parties, where he was spotted by English ex-pat – and noted Berlin character – Mark Reeder of MFS Records.

Van Dyk's accessible, upbeat style made him a bankable DJ, though it wasn't until 1992 that Reeder managed to persuade him to embark on production work. His first releases, made with Cosmic Baby under the name Visions Of Shiva

INPHO PR

(1992's "Perfect Day" and the following year's "How Much Can You Take?"), helped blueprint the commercially successful vein of Trance. But the partnership dissolved in an acrimonious, and widely publicised, dispute after Van Dyk claimed in an interview that he, and not Cosmic Baby, was the driving creative force behind Visions Of Shiva.

Van Dyk struck up fresh production partnerships with 030's Johnny Klimek and studio engineer Voov, resulting in **45RPM** (1994). Full of grandiose string melodies, long portentous intros and a pop-sweet mix of Progressive House and Trance stylings, **45RPM** was a huge success for both MFS and Van Dyk who quickly became a fixture on the international DJ and remix circuit as a result (his remixes were eventually collected together on 1998's lavishly packaged **Vorsprung Dyk Technik** triple album).

A second album, **Seven Ways** (1997), offered no radical change from the sound that Van Dyk had outlined on his debut. The anthemic, epic feel of his productions was still evident, launching the singles "Forbidden Fruit" and "Words" into the lower reaches of the charts – though in commercial terms these were easily outstripped by the success of his remixes (in 1998, ten Top 40 entries in the UK charts included Van Dyk mixes). A subsequent re-release of **45RPM** on Deviant, spawned a chart hit of his own in the shape of "For an Angel '98".

Van Dyk began 1999 working with MFS label-mates Humate on their **Love Stimulation** album. His reputation and his records now exist securely in the nebulous, but financially rewarding, space somewhere between the Techno underground and outright mainstream acceptance.

⊙ **45RPM**   MFS/Deviant, 1994

Epic breakdowns, spiralling Acid Trance and soaring melodies that anticipated the formula later successfully exploited in the chart hits of Robert Miles.

Sven Vath

The notion of Techno as a faceless, anonymous art form became more accepted as the '90s wore on. One of the most significant figures in German Techno, however, seemed unconvinced by this strategy and spent most of the early decade experimenting with an increasingly risible wardrobe and the kind of image that even heavy metal groups might have winced at. With his distinctive Yul Brynner-as-Ghengis Khan hairdo and goatee beard, Sven Vath didn't have to tell the world that he was an extrovert. Most of us had already guessed.

It wasn't always this way. As a schoolboy, Vath had been a promising footballer, but took up an apprenticeship as a fitter instead. He had a brief flirtation with DJing, playing at Frankfurt's Dorian Gray club when he was 18 years old, before he formed the group OFF with Michael Münzig and Luca Anzilotti (later Snap). In 1987, OFF had a major European hit with "Electrica Salsa" and went on to record two albums. With the proceeds from "Electrica Salsa", Vath and Münzig set up The Omen in Frankfurt and Vath became the club's resident DJ until its eventual closure in 1998.

In 1990, Vath began collaborating as Mosaic with Stevie B-Zet (Steffen Britzke) and Matthias Hoffmann who'd been a member of OFF for a brief period during the recording of the group's second album. It was Hoffmann who was again drafted in when Vath and his manager Heinz Roth decided to set up a label. Eye Q eventually became one of Germany's best-known dance labels and its subsidiaries, Harthouse and Recycle Or Die, provided a home for a number of well-known names.

Soon after setting up the label, Vath struck up an enduring production partnership with Ralf Hildenbeutel. They recorded together as Bar-

barella, producing three well-received singles before delivering **The Art of Dance** (1992). **Accident in Paradise** (1992) was typical of Vath's output, a mildly overblown and sprawling affair which tried too hard to be grandiose and ended up sounding like the Techno equivalent of pomp rock.

"L'Esperanza" provided a chart hit and helped to propagate Vath's growing fan base. However, the cult of personality which had sprung up around him served only to inflate his pretensions and the subsequent concept album, **The Harlequin, The Robot & The Ballet Dancer** (1994), was an epic of ostentation. The legendarily bad sleeve featured a painting of Vath dressed up in a jester's outfit, and things only got worse from there. Tracks such as "Harlequin's Meditation" and "Ballet

Romance" sounded like a prog-rock group let loose in a Techno studio. Others weren't even that good.

Despite the truly magnificent awfulness of **The Harlequin, The Robot & The Ballet Dancer**, Vath continued to be one of the most revered figures on the European Techno scene. By early 1995, however, a number of factors – including an increasing shift towards so-called Goa Trance – were eroding his position. With Stevie B-Zet, Vath made **Electro Acupuncture** (1995) under the name Astral Pilot, but the release made little impact.

Vath continued to be a solid draw as a DJ and – along with B-Zet – even contributed the soundtrack to a feature film, *The Cold Finger*, but business problems at Eye Q were beginning to surface. Early in 1997, Vath split from his business partners and set up a booking agency, Cocoon. Eye Q and its sub-labels limped on for a few months, but filed for bankruptcy that summer. The catalogue was later purchased by UCMG. Despite the setbacks, Vath re-emerged in 1998, this time signed to Virgin Records. **Fusion** was an eclectic offering from the self-styled "king of Trance", but the album failed to capture the imagination of a dance scene which had separated course from Vath some years before.

⊙ **Accident In Paradise**   Eye Q, 1992

The definitive Vath album.

Cristian Vogel

" **G**ood Techno should be like good shaggin'," reckons Cristian Vogel. "Though you're essentially doing the same activity, it's different every time…"

It's been a long, strange trip since Vogel's 1993 debut with the hard-as-nails **Infra** EP on Dave Clarke's Magnetic North label. Since then he's gained a reputation for making the kind of speaker-shredding Techno that's usually described as "uncompromising" with releases like the relentlessly metallic **Intersync** EP on Frankfurt's Force Inc. or the equally bruising **Defunkt** EP on Solid.

In the beginning, Cristian Vogel was a kid with a Sinclair Spectrum computer who "messed around, just trying to make music with machines". "I don't really have that many influences," he admits, because most of the time, when he could have been listening to music, he was trying to create his own. "I got into it through the machines," he says. "I can't remember ever hearing one particular record and thinking 'this is it' - it was more a case of recognising that what I was doing and what the records I was hearing were doing seemed to overlap somehow."

Vogel's approach to music-making is based on a single, fundamental principle: "to experiment at all costs…". His first album, **Beginning to Understand** (1994) on Mille Plateaux, pulled structures and textures apart, floating weightless chords over fiercely angular, abstract backings (as on "Machine") and stretching deconstructed Motor City funk over sharply detailed production effects (as on "Alien Conversation"). The result was both enduringly faithless and endlessly purist. By creating his own, defiantly individual take on Techno, Vogel was in fact adhering rigidly to the music's central guiding tenet: innovate. And that's exactly what he's continued to do ever since.

The powerfully minimal **Absolute Time** (1995) followed on Berlin's Tresor label. Despite the often difficult surface of Vogel's records, it's possible to submerge deep inside the spaces and oblique angles of his music and find connecting themes and ideas; the tiny trademarks which link, say, the muscular bass pulse of "Absolute" to the dizzy bottom-heavy funk of "Information Power Revolution". In the prepared statement which accompanied his third album, **Body Mapping** (1996), Vogel drew parallels with other producers like DJ Rush and Alec Empire and with labels like Oval and Irdial. And then, finally, he concluded by offering a concise statement of the album's intent: "The music on this LP is loose, disorientating, and hyperactive. It keeps you on your toes, perhaps. The music on this LP is anti-trance/pro-reality. It's about feeling the dynamics of being awake and being alive…" On tracks like "Bite and Scratch" or "Mad Sex", relentless electric impulses punctured grooves which had a less sequenced, more live feel to them. Elsewhere, as on the relatively introspective "Puss", extreme modulation and non-linear percussives combine to create one of Vogel's most intriguing pieces to date.

And the experimentation is continuing with the "Demolish Serious Culture" outing on Edinburgh's Sativae label and Vogel's fourth album, **Specific Momentific** (1998), on Mille Plateaux. In 1999 he pushed the boat even further with the more mellow **Busca Invisibles** and his House-wrecking collaboration with Jamie Lidell as Super Collider, **Head On.**

⊙ **Body Mapping**   Tresor, 1996

A minimal classic that's difficult but rewarding. Vogel's unique sound on this album went on to influence a new generation of Techno producers.

Orlando Voorn

One of European Techno's most revered moments, Fix's "Flash" on KMS, was almost universally ignored when it was first released back in 1992. Since then, however, the single has gone on to become one of a handful of records without which no Techno DJ's collection is complete. Fix is just one of the many aliases of Orlando Voorn, a one-time teenage hip-hop prodigy who went on to become one of Holland's most respected Techno producers. Heavily influenced by Detroit, he's collaborated with both Juan Atkins and Blake Baxter, though his own productions – as Frequency, The Nighttripper, Basic Bastard and Baruka amongst others – have a distinctively dark European feel.

Voorn began his musical career as a drummer when he was just 13 years old. A passion for collecting American disco and hip-hop imports led to an interest in DJing and by 1983 he was competing in the DMC World Mixing Championships (he came third). But while his turntable skills were supremely impressive, he began to yearn for a more creatively fulfilling outlet and was soon experimenting with his own music. A hip-hop single, "Hurt 'Em Bad", came out in 1988 under the name Fix-O-Matic before Voorn was seduced by the attractions of House and Techno.

Voorn's early material as Frequency came out on the Lower East Side label, which brought him into initial contact with Atkins who provided a remix of "Industrial Metal" (the pair later went on to record Infiniti's classic "Game One" together for Tresor). Singles for Derrick May's Fragile ("Midi Merge" under the name Complex) and Kevin Saunderson's KMS ("Flash") made it seem as though Voorn was Detroit's European producer of choice – a suspicion which grew deeper with the appearance of his Ghetto Brothers collaboration with Blake Baxter. Yet, in common with a number of other Dutch producers – including Stefan Robbers, Max 404 and Steve Rachmad – Voorn was adept at adding his own distinctive production twists to the original Detroit template.

Voorn set up his own label, Nightvision, as a platform for his numerous aliases, debuting with **The Gate** EP under a new alter ego, The Living Room. An album, **Roomservice** (1994), was released under the same name, but, despite Voorn's solid reputation on the Techno scene, it was relatively overlooked. A collection which brought together the best of his Nightvision output with tracks such as "Flash", "Industrial Metal", "Midi Merge" and "Game One" – called simply **Nightvision** (1996) – provided a worthwhile and more commercially successful overview of Voorn's career to date. Since then Voorn has preferred to experiment with drum 'n' bass as Stalker on his own Slam Dunk label, releasing the album **The Riderman** in 1998. A hip-hop project with Guru should materialize soon.

⊙ **Nightvision** Nightvision/PIAS, 1996

With two of Techno's bona fide classics – "Flash" and "Game One" – on board, this is pretty much essential listening for initiates to the Voorn sound.

Westbam

T he number of Techno artists who have breached the charts, never mind scored a national #1, is amazingly slight considering the genre's overwhelming impact on youth culture. Germany's Westbam, however, has bucked the trend, regularly appearing in the country's charts and selling albums in numbers surpassed only by acts such as The Prodigy, Underworld and Orbital. Yet in the UK, at least, Westbam's reputation peaked in the mid-'90s and he has since struggled to recapture the esteem which he once held in the days when Sven Vath, Hardfloor and Tanith were major players on the European scene.

Maximilian Lenz began his professional career as a DJ back in 1983 at the Odeon club in Munster. The name he adopted was a contraction of Westphalia (the region of Germany he's from) and Afrika Bambaata (the DJ, above all others, whom he idolised). Within a year, he had moved to Berlin, to work at the Metropol club and, in 1985, had made his first incursion into the studio with Klaus Jankuhn to record his debut single, "17", which was loosely inspired by Paul Hardcastle's Vietnam sample epic, "19".

The independent ethos of the Acid House breakthrough led to Westbam's involvement in the founding of the Low Spirit label, one of Germany's most significant labels in terms of catapulting Techno to the kind of mainstream domestic success which has largely eluded the genre in other countries. **The Cabinet** (1989) followed a performance at the Seoul Olympics as Germany's artistic ambassador, but while claims for it as the "first DJ concept album" were exaggerated, it did produce "The Roof Is on Fire", the track which provided Westbam's breakthrough.

Techno's commercial popularity in Germany quickly ensured Westbam's elevation to star status. Singles such as "Monkey Say Monkey Do" and "No More Fucking Rock 'N Roll" sold in huge quantities, while **A Practicing Maniac at Work** (1991) became an essential addition to any German Techno fan's album collection despite being less than ground-breaking. Westbam was also involved in the conception and development of the Mayday festival, working with Klaus Jankuhm to produce custom-built anthems for each of the events. Collected together on **Members of Mayday** (1995), they provided yet another escalation of the Westbam phenomenon.

Bam Bam Bam (1994), however, marked the highpoint of Westbam's success on a Europe-wide scale. Despite the high sales of the "Celebration Generation" single, the accelerated decline of German Trance's well-worn formula signalled an inescapable reverse in the producers' fortunes outside Germany. On a national level, though, Westbam was still gaining ground. Recipient of a cultural award from one of Berlin's most prominent newspapers and preparing to release the commercially successful "Terminator" single, it seemed like he was surfing an endless winning streak.

The astonishing success of "Sonic Empire" (more than 500,000 copies sold to date), Westbam's 1997 Mayday anthem and the subsequent "Sunshine" single proved that in his home territory, he was still a force to be reckoned with. Despite this, Westbam's most recent long-player, **We'll Never Stop Living This Way** (1999), was a relatively lacklustre outing though it did finally provide the opportunity for Westbam to work with his hero, Afrika Bambaata, on the admittedly execrable "City Of Shamballa".

⊙ **Bam Bam Bam**   Low Spirit, 1994

It's not subtle, but this is a perfect introduction to Westbam's basic formula – German Trance reduced to its lowest common denominator and spiced up with occasional attempts at eclecticism.

Damon Wild

A crucial figure on New York's underground scene, Damon Wild began his musical career as a radio DJ on WTUL in his native Louisiana, playing a mix of Cabaret Voltaire, Kraftwerk and Acid House. He moved to New York City in 1990, working first with DJ Moneypenny at Brand X and Sonic Groove Records. His debut release was Chapter One's "Unleash the Groove" which was an early Strictly Rhythm success. He then hooked up with Ray Love to produce Toxic Two's "Rave Generator" which breached the UK Top 10 in 1992, just as Wild began setting up the Experimental label.

Experimental went on to become a key label in the Techno underground, providing a platform for early releases by Freddie Fresh, Tim Taylor, Cari Lekebusch and Woody McBride. Despite the label's significant creative successes, inevitably, there were tensions and Wild left to form his own Synewave label.

Synewave's first high-profile release was Morph's **Stormwatch** (1994), a collaboration between Wild and Dennis Ferrer which signalled the label's intention to occupy similar terrain to imprints such as R&S and Tresor. Tracks such as "Juggernaut" and "Morphine" drew as much from European strains of Techno as they did from Detroit and the album struck a consistent chord as the scene moved towards a harder, edgier amalgam during the latter half of 1994.

Wild continued to collaborate, notably with Tim Taylor on the hugely succesful underground hits "Bang the Acid" and "Ego Acid" which became dancefloor staples during 1995, exhibiting a tough, speed-thrill aesthetic which touched bases with Richard Bartz's Acid Scout project, Cristian Vogel and the muscular Acid Techno of Koenig Cylinders. While the label continued Experimental's drive to provide a platform for like-minded producers (Steve Stoll and Woody McBride were both early signings), Wild kept up an exhaustive studio schedule, crafting a series of uncompromising dancefloor 12"s and shaping remixes for labels in the US and Europe.

Somewhere In Time (1998) confirmed Wild's position at the forefront of a distinctively dark, adrenalised strain of dancefloor Techno. As a producer, he has proved capable of combining both his experimental instincts and the dancefloor sensibilities that were honed by the mix of industrial, hard-jack Chicago House and new wave electronica he had played on his Louisiana radio shows. Along with Kevin Saunderson, he is one of the few Techno artists to have tasted significant commercial success and retained a grass roots underground following, though it's clear that Wild's potential is nowhere near exhausted.

⊙ **Somewhere In Time**   Synewave, 1998

Hard-as-nails, dark and aimed with chilling precision, Wild's long-awaited debut is hard to find but well worth searching out.

Josh Wink

I n early '80s Philadelphia, a kid called Josh Winkelman began working for a mobile DJ company as a way of breaking into the music scene. He soon learned how to beat-mix and by 1990 Winkelman had set up his own Monday night club, Vagabond, with a group of friends playing James Brown, New Order, 808 State and a mix of hip-hop, House and Techno. Together with King Britt, another of the Vagabond crew, he made his first foray into the recording studio not

long after, emerging with E-Culture's "Tribal Confusion" which was
released by Strictly Rhythm later that year.

When King Britt left Philadelphia to tour with Digable Planets,
Winkelman shortened his name to Wink and began working on a series
of solo projects.
Two of his early sin-
gles for Sorted
defined the para-
meters between
which his sound
would oscillate.
"Don't Laugh" was
a throwaway novel-
ty record that
seemed designed
to spin out acid
trippers with a
"Laughing Police-
man" style laughter
sample (almost cer-
tainly this aspect of
the record didn't
occur to Wink – a

fastidious keep-fit fanatic who doesn't drink, smoke or take drugs),
while "How's the Music" was an atmospheric, darkly narcotic groove
that seemed designed to enhance the aeronautical possibilities of the
post-peak MDMA experience.

"How's the Music" became an underground dance classic, placing
Wink alongside a number of other producers who seemed to be charting an impeccably detailed psychedelic trajectory for the dancefloor in

the later months of '93 and '94. A single in the summer of '94 for the Glasgow label Limbo, "Thoughts of a Tranced Love", did little to dispel the image of Wink as a studio *wunderkind*. As the year drifted to a close, a Strictly Rhythm compilation, **The Deep and Slo** (1994), introduced a trippy Ambient track called "Higher State of Consciousness".

By the time Strictly got around to releasing a 12" of "Higher State…", it had been transformed from Ambient dreaminess to pure energy with a dense percussive loop and a warping 303 spun out into the ether. The few imports that leaked into Europe were hungrily snapped up, but most Wink fans had to console themselves with "Meditation Will Manifest", a variation on the theme for Belgium's R&S label which contained a similar Indian swami sample.

With "Don't Laugh" long forgotten, Josh Wink's reputation was impeccable within the underground. Tracks such as "Red Lights" (under the name Crusher for London's Kickin' Records) may not have equalled the imaginative flair of "How's the Music" or "Higher State…", but they were still capable of doing some damage on the dancefloor. But when Virgin released the grotesque handbag House of Size 9's "I Am Ready" there were few who were prepared to accept that Wink's creativity could encompass such creative highs and lows. Better indicators of his talent were to be found on his remix of Havana's "Discorder" or the "Feel the Warmth" track which he contributed to **The Deepest Shade of Techno** (1994) compilation for Nu Era's Reflective label.

United DJs of America: Josh Wink (1995) provided a worthwhile glimpse of Wink's talents as a DJ, sewing together a neat mix of spaced-out drugfloor classics. Recorded live at Philadelphia's Milk Bar it suggested that Wink's heart really lay where the Techno underground had always presumed, though the Wink track which closed the set – Firefly's "Supernatural" – was cut from the same sub-standard cloth as

"I Am Ready". As an introduction to Josh Wink's talents, the mix album proved a more convincing full-length effort than **Left Above the Clouds** (1996) which tried hard to reconcile the twin creative pulls of Wink's sound, but wasn't cohesive enough to fulfil the promise of his best work. By the time of the album's release, "Higher State…" was beginning to manifest a life of its own. "That record is selling 700 copies a week," Wink had told journalist Kodwo Eshun in 1995. "If you think it's big now that's nothing compared to what's gonna happen. It's gonna be massive." It was remarkably prescient advice.

Licensed to Mercury Records, "Higher State…" was in fact being remixed by the label as **Left Above the Clouds** was released. Wink wasn't impressed. The remix edited out all the subtleties of the original, delivering a cartoonish impression which focused solely on the increasingly manic 303 line. As the single headed towards the charts, he was disowning the track, claiming that he hadn't given permission for the remix and eventually refusing to comment on it at all.

His first for the Ovum label which he had set up with King Britt back in 1994, **Herehear** (1998), acknowledged the schizophrenic nature of Wink's talent by splitting itself into two distinct halves. **Herehear** revealed an interest in the proto-Ambient sound of Jon Hassel, Kitaro and Andreas Vollenweider and delivered at least some kind of closure for fans on opposite sides of the divide.

⊙ **United DJs of America: Josh Wink**   DMC, 1995

Tata Box Inhibitors, Dan Bell and Murk meet on this superb mix set that's probably the best introduction to Philly's finest.

Susumu Yokota

Japanese Techno producer Susumu Yokota has always charted a fairly maverick route through techno's hinterland. Yokota's first major break came after Sven Vath discovered his music thanks to a convoluted process involving one of his friends, a demo tape of his early material and a German Techno fan in Goa. Eventually, the demo found its way onto a vinyl bootleg and reached the ears of Vath who promptly signed Yokota to his Harthouse label. **Frankfurt-Tokyo Connection** (1993) made a big impact on the European dance scene with its blistering Acid Trance. Despite the considerable commercial success of his debut album, however, Yokota quickly changed direction towards the subtler, more playful, but ultimately less commercial material of **Ebi Zen** (1993).

Influenced by his new-found contacts on the German underground scene, Yokota began exploring a deeper sound which eventually emerged the following summer on **Acid Mt. Fuji** (1994). Tracks such as "Zenmai" or "Tambarin" plotted a fine line between Yokota's obvious melodic sensibilities and a surprisingly delicate take on the heavily syncopated tribal rhythms which were then sweeping through Techno. But the album's restless creative spirit also hinted that Yokota had plenty of other ideas in reserve.

Some of these surfaced a few months later on the album that some consider to be Yokota's underrated masterpiece. Released under the name Ringo, **Plantation** (1995) was an exuberant mix of ecstatic synthetics and muscular dancefloor grooves. "Sumire", released simultaneously on 12", was typical of the album's upbeat mood. Combining a dizzying array of melodies and counterpoints with a shuffling House rhythm, it touched base with the mellow jazz-Tech of Heidelberg's

David Moufang, the spiralling Acidic Techno of Richie Hawtin and the most wide-eyed of Acid House anthems.

Yokota confirmed his ability to weave heart-melting melodies into the fabric of Techno on the material he subsequently released as Prism. If there had been any doubt about the classic status of **Plantation**, then the first Prism album, **Metronome Melody** (1995), offered decisive proof of Yokota's immense talent as a producer. The album was the perfect fusion of his seductive melodic shapes with a prescient hybrid of House and Techno that drew comparison with everyone from Carl Craig to acclaimed label-mates Global

Communication. Tracks such as the exquisite "Gemini" or "Crystal Edge" provided a blueprint for the dreamier latitudes of Tech-House, while the drum 'n' bass-tinged "Prominence" traced a path that Yokota was later to fully explore on **Cat, Mouse and Me** (1996).

A second Prism album, **Fallen Angel** (1997), saw Yokota in a quieter, more reflective mood. In place of the wildly exuberant melodic shapes of its predecessor, **Fallen Angel** had an understated feel, full of shimmering rhythms and the kind of bittersweet melancholy that suggested a kinship with the most recent work of House pioneer Larry Heard. The experimental vein continued with the Japan-only release of **Magic Thread** (1998), a quasi-Ambient offering that dispensed with beats in favour of an exploration of atmosphere and texture.

The rhythm returned on **1998** (1998), a fluid jazz-Tech affair that drew its inspiration as much from hardcore funk, salsa and rare groove as it did from Detroit Techno. The album placed Yokota firmly alongside such cutting-edge producers as Max Brennan, Kirk Degiorgio and Charles Bullen with tracks like "Golden Stamen" or "Cat & Rabbit" floating a jazz feel through the dense tapestry of beats, samples and virtual acoustic programming. Despite the high-quality production, however, it was hard not to miss the distinctive melodic flair that had made **Plantation** and **Metronome Melody** so compelling. Only the swooning strings of the aptly named "Sexy Planet" indulged Yokota's considerable skill with a well-crafted tune.

⊙ **Prism – Metronome Melody**   Sublime, 1995

The Yokota album that every home should have. Loaded with irresistible tunes and captivating grooves, this was an early indicator of the coming fascination with Tech-House.

Claude Young

Maybe it was inevitable that Claude Young would end up pursuing a career in music. His mother worked for one of Detroit's biggest record distributors while his father, Claude Young Sr., is one of the city's most legendary radio DJs. As a teenager, Claude looked set to follow in his father's footsteps by holding down DJ gigs on both college and commercial radio stations.

Young was still a teenager when he began providing edits and remixes for a number of other Detroit artists (including Kevin Saunderson, Random Noise Generation and Jay Denham), but it was his long-time friendship with Dan Bell that led to a recording career in his own right. Under the name Brother From Another Planet, he released two seminal singles on Bell's Seventh City label – "Planet Earth" and "Acid Wash Conflict" – which quickly achieved classic status.

A series of equally exceptional singles followed on labels such as Dow, Utensil (1994's "One Complete Revolution" was a particular stand-out), Djax, Acacia and Frictional, but Young's profile remained relatively low thanks to a seemingly irresistible habit of shifting project names and aliases: in addition to Brother From Another Planet, he's recorded as Project 625, Dub Street Posse, Low Key, Rhythm Formation, Golem Craft and, his long-standing collaborative venture with Terrence Parker, Younger Than Park. Yet it was his blistering sets behind the turntables which helped establish his name as one of Detroit's most promising producers during the mid-'90s.

Given Young's gunslinger reputation on the decks, it was perhaps appropriate that his first long-format offering was a mix album. **DJ Kicks: Claude Young** (1996) did, however, feature a number of his own tracks including "Acid Wash Conflict" and a collaboration with Essex's

Ian O'Brien on "Joe 90" (the pair also contributed to Ferox's stunning **Adventures In Techno Soul** compilation that year).

A deal with Belgium's Elypsia Records provoked much anticipation, but the relationship wasn't particularly happy and the resulting album, **Soft Thru** (1997), didn't do Young's considerable talents justice. A second mix offering, this time for Vienna's Central Records – **Welcome to Central** (1998) – provided a more positive glimpse of Young's powers.

Currently working on his second album, reportedly for Holland's Djax, Young continues to be one of the most revered DJs on the Techno scene. As a producer he is more than capable of matching that feat, though it's likely that we'll have to wait for his next long-player since his extraordinarily busy schedule as a DJ attraction has effectively minimised the time he has available for studio projects.

⊙ **DJ Kicks**   Studio K7, 1996

Behind the decks, Claude Young is unstoppable. This set offers a worthwhile introduction to his productions as well and features the much-sought-after "Acid Wash Conflict" alongside a specially commissioned "DJ Kicks" track.